Mary Turner and the Memory of Lynching

JULIE BUCKNER ARMSTRONG

Mary Turner and the Memory of Lynching

The University of Georgia Press   *Athens and London*

Chapter 2 appeared in different form as "'The people . . . took exception to her remarks': Meta Warrick Fuller, Angelina Weld Grimké, and the Lynching of Mary Turner," in *Mississippi Quarterly* 61, no. 1–2 (2008). "dirty south moon" © 2007 Honorée Fanonne Jeffers, is reproduced by permission from *Red Clay Suite*, by Honorée Fanonne Jeffers (Carbondale: Southern Illinois University Press). Quotations from manuscript draft of "The Waitin'" in Angelina Weld Grimké papers at Moorland-Spingarn Library, Howard University, used by permission.

© 2011 by the University of Georgia Press
Athens, Georgia 30602
www.ugapress.org
Set in Berthold Baskerville by Graphic Composition, Inc.,
    Bogart, Georgia

Printed digitally in the United States of America

Library of Congress Cataloging-in-Publication Data
Armstrong, Julie Buckner.
    Mary Turner and the memory of lynching / Julie Buckner Armstrong.
        p. cm.
    Includes bibliographical references and index.
    ISBN-13: 978-0-8203-3765-4 (hardcover : alk. paper)
    ISBN-10: 0-8203-3765-X (hardcover : alk. paper)
    ISBN-13: 978-0-8203-3766-1 (pbk. : alk. paper)
    ISBN-10: 0-8203-3766-8 (pbk. : alk. paper)
1. Lynching–Georgia–History–20th century.
2. Georgia–Race relations–History–20th century.
3. Murder–Georgia–History–20th century.
4. African Americans–Georgia–Social conditions–20th century.
I. Title.
    HV6465.G4A76 2011
    364.1'34–dc22   2011012366

British Library Cataloging-in-Publication Data available

For it is better to speak

remembering

we were never meant to survive

Audre Lorde, "A Litany for Survival"

CONTENTS

ACKNOWLEDGMENTS

No writer ever makes a book alone. Even though sometimes one has to be very selfish to bring a project to completion, or one feels very lonely when working on such a difficult subject as lynching, the writer's network of support extends quite far.

I begin by acknowledging the person I know best and who helped me the most, my partner in life and work, Thomas Hallock. He was the one who told me in 1998 that I should pursue this topic because it was more than just a journal article, and he was the one who begged me in 2009 to finish up and move those lynching books out of our house. In between, he comforted me through continual existential crises, he listened to my gruesome stories, he spent vacation time on my research trips, and he edited draft after draft after draft. Anyone who knows my writing knows that I would never have a catchy title, crisp prose, or semicolons without Tom's help. Saying "thank you" seems insufficient given all that he has done.

A crucial part of the writer's support system is financial. Without funding for travel to different research libraries and other collections, this book would not have been written. A Faculty Development Grant from Valdosta State University in 2000 paid for my initial investigation of primary and secondary sources at the New York Public Library's Schomburg Center for Research in Black Culture. A New Researcher Grant from the University of South Florida in 2003 financed a trip to multiple sites: the Beinecke Rare Book and Manuscript Library at Yale University, the Moorland-Spingarn Library at Howard University, and the Library of Congress. During the 2005–2006 academic year, I had the privilege of working as Scholar-in-Residence at the University of Mississippi's William Winter Institute for Racial Reconciliation. While my primary duties there involved assembling *The Civil Rights Reader: American Literature from Jim Crow to Racial Reconciliation* (University of Georgia Press, 2009), the experience clearly informed *Mary Turner and the Memory of Lynching*. I would like to thank Susan Glisson in particular for being a model practitioner of positive dialogue and an all-around good person whose wise counsel I have sought on multiple occasions. I followed an uplifting year at the Winter Institute with a Virginia Foundation for the Humanities Summer Fellowship in Charlottesville. The quiet workspace and easy access to library facilities helped me make excellent headway on this book's first draft. Unfortunately, Anne Spencer's papers were in the process of being transferred from her home in Lynchburg to the University of Virginia for cataloging, so I could not consult them in person. Nina Salmon at Lynchburg College patiently answered my many emails, and Sharon Defibaugh at UVA's Albert and Shirley Small Special Collections Library generously photocopied manuscripts of "White Things" for me. Finally, I want to thank the University of South Florida St. Petersburg's Honors Program for two honoraria, one to help fund copyright permissions, and one that went toward a trip to Emory University's Manuscript, Archives, and Rare Book Library. Someone once told me that no research project in African American history and culture is complete until the scholar has talked to Randall Burkett. Good advice.

I would especially like to thank the multiple parties who gave me permission to reproduce images and manuscripts: Honorée Fanonne Jeffers and Southern Illinois University Press for "dirty south moon"; the Library of Congress Prints and Photographs Division for various photographs; the Museum of African American History in Boston, Massachusetts, for Meta Warrick Fuller's *In Memory of Mary Turner*; the National Association for the Advancement of Colored People for various images and Walter White's "Memorandum to Governor Dorsey"; Roderick S. Quiroz for Prentiss Taylor's *Christ in Alabama*; the Walker Art Museum in Minneapolis, Minnesota, and Sikkema, Jenkins and Company, New York, for the untitled image from Kara Walker's *Do You Like Creme in Your Coffee and Chocolate in Your Milk?*; and, last but certainly not least, David Wishner of E+D Architecture and Design, St. Petersburg, Florida, for the map. He is the world's best brother-in-law, as well as a good cartographer.

In addition to financial and research support, a book needs intellectual and spiritual backing. My apologies in advance for those whose names I have inadvertently omitted from this list. Several people from the Valdosta area past and present have helped me in ways large and small: Doug Fraser, Molly Sholtz, Anne Mayer, Leonard Finn, Ann Kasun, Gary Cooper, Pat Miller, Carol Stiles, Jeff Vasseur, Shirley Hardin, David Williams, Viki Soady, Laurel Hahlen, Ari and Pat Santas, Ronge Milledge, Corey Westbrook, John Rogers, George Rhynes, Rev. Floyd

Rose, and especially in the book's final stages, Mark George. Friends and colleagues from USFSP have helped as well: Bob Dardenne explained early-twentieth-century newspapers; Tiffany Chenneville and Mark Pezzo helped with psychology and memory; Dawn Cecil provided insights into race, gender, and crime; and James Kessenides was always a quick e-mail away for historical resources and questions. My department chair, Lisa Starks-Estes, has stood by me through lean and fat years, and for that I will always be grateful. Beyond USFSP, I have consulted experts in a variety of fields, including Jamie Downs, coastal regional medical examiner for the Georgia Bureau of Investigation; Elijah Gosier, Albert Pendleton, James Everett "Pete" Young, Donald Davis, and Betty Horton on the history of Brooks and Lowndes counties; Robert Thurston on Hugh M. Dorsey; Dora Apel on visual art; and Fitzhugh Brundage and Christopher Waldrep on lynching history. Members of the Moore's Ford Memorial Committee have been very kind on multiple occasions, especially Robert Howard, Bobbi Paul, and Rich Rusk. I owe a huge debt to those who have read this book in its many incarnations; the finished project is decidedly better as a result. Adam Gussow, Amy Wood, Susan Donaldson, Noel Polk, and Koritha Mitchell read chapter 2 in excerpt or in its entirety. Janet Badia, Natasha Barnes, and Barbara McCaskill read chapters 3 and 4 in excerpt. Members of my writing group – Anda Peterson, Russ Crumley, and Jon Wilson – violated our first *and* second rules for my introduction (No Academic Work, No Alcohol at Meetings). Libations to the coffee goddess, JoEllen Schilke, for giving us a meeting space, for letting me volunteer on her radio show while I was on sabbatical finishing this book, and for all she does to keep art alive in Tampa Bay.

Finally, I want to thank those people who have become, next to Tom, this project's most consistent cheerleaders. Christopher Metress never seemed to find it odd that I needed to sit for hours drinking coffee and talking about lynching. Honorée Fanonne Jeffers didn't tell me I was strange for thinking that something bigger than all of us compelled me to write this book. Nancy Grayson at the University of Georgia Press has encouraged me through two books now. Her enthusiasm prompts writers and staff to create the best product possible. Because of people like Nancy, editorial assistant Beth Snead, project manager John Joerschke, cover designer Erin New, and freelance copyeditor Bob Land, *Mary Turner and the Memory of Lynching* is better than when it left my hands.

Students in my classes at VSU and USFSP have faced this material with a mixture of anger, frustration, compassion, grief, and curiosity. Members of a 2008 USFSP honors seminar on Racial Violence and Racial Reconciliation – Laura Hadeed, Erin Jensen, Greg Lindberg, Evelyn Peters, Hailey Praught, Kelleigh Simpson, and Chris Thornton – helped me especially with learning how to talk about difficult subjects with the people that matter: a younger generation that represents the future.

Mary Turner and the Memory of Lynching

Introduction

In May 1918 a week of mob violence following a white farmer's murder spread over two Georgia counties, Brooks and Lowndes, and claimed at least eleven African American lives. One of the victims, Mary Turner, was eight months pregnant. After learning that Turner planned to press charges against mob members for lynching her husband, Hayes, the men captured her from the Quitman home where she was hiding and took her to a bridge overlooking the Little River. There a crowd of several hundred watched the mob hang her upside down, shoot her, set her on fire, remove her fetus, and stomp the unborn child into the ground.

Surprisingly, reactions to the incident varied. The *Savannah Morning News* reported events matter-of-factly: "the people in their indignant mood took exception to her remarks as well as her attitude and took her to the river where she was hanged." A letter to the *Augusta Chronicle* cried out, "Where are the grand juries? Where are the petit juries? Where are the sheriffs? Where is our public opinion? Is it dead? . . . God in heaven have mercy upon us!"[1] A month after the lynchings the National Association for the Advancement of Colored People (NAACP) sent its new assistant secretary, Walter White, to investigate. White submitted a copy of his report with a list of mob members' names to Georgia's governor, Hugh M. Dorsey. For the rest of the year, the NAACP struggled to have the men prosecuted. Dorsey did not cooperate, and attempts at federal intervention also failed. Iowa Senator William S. Kenyon showed some interest in forming an investigative subcommittee, but the case could not proceed without eyewitness cooperation. No one was willing to testify. Mob members and their supporters had cowed an already traumatized local community into a silence that would remain a palpable tension for almost ninety years.[2]

The story might have been forgotten had Walter White not also published a version of his report in the NAACP's magazine, the *Crisis,* in September 1918. Before White, no one had reported publicly that Mary Turner was pregnant. His article, "The Work of a Mob," initiated the process of constructing this case as a key event in African American cultural memory. The Anti-Lynching Crusaders, an NAACP affiliate, used Turner's story as a centerpiece of their fundraising efforts to support the 1922 Dyer Bill, which tried unsuccessfully to make lynching a federal crime. During the 1920s and 1930s, the Commission on Interracial Cooperation (CIC) and the Communist Party USA (CPUSA) also cited Turner's story in their antilynching pamphlets. Artists and writers responded as well, most of them drawing upon White's *Crisis* account. Meta Warrick Fuller sculpted *In Memory of Mary Turner: A Silent Protest against Mob Violence* (1919). Angelina Weld Grimké published the short story "Goldie" (1920). Carrie Williams Clifford included a poem, "Little Mother," in her collection *The Widening Light* (1922). The year 1923 saw publication of two texts that remain well known today: Anne Spencer's poem "White Things" and the "Kabnis" section of Jean Toomer's modernist classic, *Cane.* After this early peak, Turner faded from the spotlight as other lynching stories captured national attention. Her memory never completely disappeared, however. More recently, artist Frieda High Tesfagiorgis painted *Hidden Memories* (1985), and writer Honorée Fanonne Jeffers published a short story, "If You Get There Before I Do" (2005), as well as a poem, "dirty south moon" (2007), all of which reference Turner. Tributes appear regularly via Web sites, Internet discussion groups, and online videos. The National Great Blacks in Wax Museum in Baltimore, Maryland, includes a striking commemoration of Hayes and Mary Turner among its many historical figures. Outside specific responses, the incident began entering the realm of metaphor and urban legend the moment it happened. Its imagery informs scenes of violence against black women and communities in Oscar Micheaux's film *Within Our Gates* (1919), selected notebook sketches from Kara Walker's *Do You Like Creme in Your Coffee and Chocolate in Your Milk?* (1997), and annual reenactments of the 1946 lynchings at the Moore's Ford Bridge near Monroe, Georgia. Back in Brooks and Lowndes counties, a limited, mostly private oral history always existed, but local residents rarely acknowledged the story publicly until a group called the Mary Turner Project commemorated the lynchings in 2009 and put up an official historical marker in 2010.

Both the silences and the responses make this a compelling tale, one that encapsulates the complex, contradictory ways people remember and represent racial violence in America. From the moment that she dared to mention justice for her husband's death, Turner disrupted traditional lynching narratives. Her act of talking back, and the price that she paid for it, continue to resonate today. Turner is one of countless black women whose stories have received insufficient attention in a history of racial violence that for too long has been triangulated between white men, black men, and white women. As this case shows, black women played multiple roles: as victims, as loved ones left behind, and as those who fought back using grassroots, institutional, and artistic forms of resistance. Turner's story illustrates what can – and cannot – be said about lynching. The incident defies conventional ways of portraying mob violence, posing aesthetic and sometimes personal challenges for artists and writers. In the creative responses, form and language fracture, and images of silence and voice, blindness and sight prevail – demonstrating how a pregnant black woman killed for speaking out pushes the boundaries of artistic expression. Local silence about the 1918 lynchings also reveals as much as it conceals. Despite its long absence from official public memory, the legacy of racial violence in southern Georgia remains a tangible presence – one that seems obvious to many African Americans, yet one to which many whites seem oblivious. Finally, the diverse range of material about the 1918 incident, alongside the local silences, offers a valuable, yet underutilized, resource for the study of lynching. The first wave of activists, artists, and writers who memorialized Turner's death did so at a key moment: lynching violence reached a new high after World War I, but the antilynching effort gained new momentum throughout the 1920s. These early responses show the successes and failures of troops on the ground level of what James Weldon Johnson called the battle to save "black America's body and white America's soul."³ More contemporary responses mark another important shift in the way people remember and talk about lynching, with the growing movement toward racial reconciliation. As individuals, communities, and the nation consider the necessity of confronting, seeking justice for, and healing past wounds of racial violence, stories like Turner's show how difficult that process can be.

An Education in Race

I know that difficulty firsthand. I learned about the 1918 incident while teaching at Valdosta State University (VSU) in Lowndes County. While preparing to attend a 1998 National Endowment for the Humanities (NEH) Institute on Teaching the Civil Rights Movement, I read about Mary Turner in Leon Litwack's history of Jim Crow brutality, *Trouble in Mind.*⁴ Lynching history was not part of my formal education, and being white, I had not sought to learn it on my own. Litwack's book compelled me to know more. One rarely hears stories about female mob victims or women killed so brutally for speaking out, and my academic interests in women's studies and civil rights (I'm a native of Birmingham, Alabama) propelled me toward such buried histories of oppression and resistance. This one also happened close to my new home, twenty-two miles to be exact. My husband, Tom, and I had recently moved to the area from the Northeast (a lucky-to-be-employed academic couple in a tight job market), and we were eager to learn all we could about local history, culture, and environment. "No, not where the onions come from," we kept telling friends and family. "That's Vidalia." Valdosta intrigued us, with its water tower proudly proclaiming, "Southern Charm . . . Not Gone with the Wind." Both the place and the people are indeed charming. The VSU campus is architecturally consistent in a neo-Spanish mission style, with a wide sabal palm–lined avenue leading to its stucco and barrel tile–roofed main building, West Hall, where we both taught in the English Department. We found a renovated 1920s bungalow, a pale yellow house surrounded by pink azaleas, two blocks east of campus, a quaint neighborhood of long-leaf pine, magnolia, and pecan. I read Litwack's book and others for the institute while sitting on the porch swing and drinking sweet iced tea. The art teacher who lived around the corner gave a wave and a "howdy neighbor" every time he passed by. Tom and I have never had people care as much about our social and spiritual lives as the folks in Valdosta. Colleagues made sure that we had potlucks, happy hours, and dinner parties to attend each weekend, and everyone from VSU staff to neighbors to bank clerks asked if we had found a church home.

But as a native southerner, I remained skeptical. Experience has taught me the thin line between big smiles and bared teeth. Tom and I tried to dismiss what disconcerted us: the Confederate "Southern Cross" on the Georgia flag, reports from students of segregated dormitories and high-school proms, far too many subdivisions named "Plantation," and people who referred to our block (near a black neighborhood and hotels that lodged migrant workers) as "dangerous" and "the other side of the tracks." Litwack's book confirmed my worst suspicions and a gothic sensibility weaned on William Faulkner and Flannery O'Connor. Here was the quintessential small southern town with the dirty little secret. Because I perceived myself to be insulated from that secret – as an outsider, a white person, and as a reader who saw the place as "other," a literary cliché – I thought that doing some basic research would be easy. I had dipped into Litwack's nightmarish historical chronicle enough to satisfy a morbid curiosity, then backed away when the book became distasteful or threatened my emotional detachment. I assumed that I could do the same with Mary Turner's story. Naively, then, upon my return from the NEH institute, I set out to discover what happened in May 1918.

My first stop was the VSU library, where the helpful archivist turned up nothing but the fact that the *Valdosta Times* (now the *Valdosta Daily Times*) for that summer, and that summer only, was destroyed in a fire. She did not know the details. The Lowndes County Historical Museum claimed at the time to have no information on local lynchings. The director said that to his knowledge the area never had one. Shortly afterward, a VSU colleague told me that the museum had a small cache of lynching photographs. A couple of years later, a more accommodating director showed me the photos. They are too grainy to make out any details and appear to be much earlier than 1918. Their origins are unclear. The same director put me in touch with a community historian who rattled off details about every event in the county's past except for this one, which he claimed never to have heard of. The most I could coax from him were directions to a rumored "hanging tree" outside of town, where his father told him that "bizarre things" had happened, but he could not elaborate.

I hit the same brick wall at the Brooks County Historical Museum. Located in Quitman (the county seat and another charming small southern town), the museum sits across from a white Greek Revival courthouse built, a brochure told me, during the "War Between the States." I marched through the museum's doors, met the welcoming white-haired volunteer, and declared, "I'm here to find information about the pregnant woman who was lynched back in 1918." For a few seconds we stood in silence, matching each other southern-lady smile for southern-lady smile. The blue of her irises turned a deep gray as she replied that such a thing seemed impossible to imagine. She told me that the museum did not have the kind of information that I sought, and she walked me through their collection of maps, pictures of historic homes, quilts from yesteryear, and other celebratory memorabilia. Pausing in front of some faded photographs of town fathers, she told me that no lynchings had ever happened in Brooks County. One of her ancestors had been sheriff in 1918, she said, and he was a kind man who always treated blacks fairly. I was certain that she was hiding something: what her blue-to-gray eyes revealed was the moment of rupture between my question and everything she grew up believing about Brooks County, Georgia.

Her approach to historical memory was unfamiliar, almost unrecognizable to me, a child of Birmingham. During the 1960s our racial sin made the nightly news, and we've been forced to wrestle with it openly ever since. I'm used to negotiating complete strangers' misguided statements, usually made in fake southern accents, about my hometown and its history. It's the Quentin Compson effect, named from the questions Shreve asked his roommate in Faulkner's *Absalom, Absalom!*: "What's it like there. What do they do there. Why do they live there. Why do they live at all."[5] In this case, quite the opposite of Faulkner's novel, everyone refused to "Tell about the South." Even the local technology maintained a stony silence about the past: the microfilm machine at the Brooks County Public Library broke down when I tried to spool through copies of the 1918 *Quitman Free Press.* In fact, the initial research on this project made me feel like a conspiracy theorist. No book, no person, no record of official local history that I could find would yield information about the incident that Litwack described in *Trouble in Mind.* I began to think that maybe he, like so many people outside Georgia, had confused Valdosta with the place that grows the onions.

But other puzzle pieces fell into place – some by coincidence, others in unexpected ways. I stumbled upon a review of Kathy A. Perkins and Judith L. Stephens's *Strange Fruit: Plays on Lynching by American Women*, which mentioned Grimké's story and Fuller's sculpture.[6] Not long afterward, I reread *Cane* without giving up on the "Kabnis" section, which had seemed like an incomprehensible mess during previous efforts. This time, title character Ralph Kabnis's inability to process the juxtaposition between an oppressive ugliness in southern Georgia and the spiritual beauty of its people made perfect sense. At the crux of Kabnis's existential breakdown was the story of Mary Turner, referred to as Mame Lamkins in the text, a page I had never made it to or had forgotten.[7] Where there had been no information about this case on the local level, now there were several artistic responses. A colleague in VSU's History Department directed me to Walter White and the NAACP's Anti-Lynching Papers on microfilm. The catch was that, to get the resources I needed, I would have to use Interlibrary Loan or drive several hours to a different university. A passage from "Kabnis" kept echoing in my head. Tom and I had both marked it with double lines in the margins, not because it seemed key to the story, but because the words seemed key to *us* at that place and time: "Christ, how cut off from everything he is. And hours, hours north, why not say a lifetime north? Washington sleeps. Its still, peaceful streets, how desirable they are. . . . New York? Impossible. It was a fiction. He had dreamed it. An impotent nostalgia grips him. It becomes intolerable. . . . Things are so immediate in Georgia" (86). Kabnis's "impotent nostalgia" spoke to a longing for urbanity that we both had felt, four hours south of Atlanta, two hours from the nearest major airport (Jacksonville, Florida), and a lifetime away from the Philadelphia where we had married and the New York where we had gone to school.

Kabnis's sense of racial disparity, articulated during a historical moment far more brutal than we could fathom, seemed "immediate" to us, too. The same semester I was trying to learn more about Mary Turner, fall 1998, brought a police department scandal to Lowndes County: a black man named Willie James Williams died of a brain hemorrhage while in custody. White officers say that he fell, witnesses say that he was beaten, but the arrest tapes disappeared. The incident split the community along racial fault lines that we had tried not to see before. Those lines were now too visible for us to ignore further. We joined protests over the incident organized by a grassroots group, the People's Tribunal. We attended meetings of an interracial campus club, HOPE. We participated in forums designed to encourage antiracist community dialogue that were sponsored by a national initiative, Project Change. During the next couple of years, as my public life became more integrated, and I began to ask questions of community residents whom I did not think to consult originally, the local wall of silence about the 1918 incident began to show cracks. "My uncle took me to where it happened when I turned thirteen and told me to watch out for white people," one young man said to me after class. "Some folks around here have a lot of anger, and sometimes that story comes up," an activist told me at a town meeting. Indeed, Leon Litwack had gotten the place right, and so had Jean Toomer. To paraphrase Kabnis, things *can* be so immediate in Georgia.

In fairness, things can be just as immediate in Birmingham. Or Philadelphia and New York, for that matter. Like many white people, I chose to acknowledge the impact of race superficially at best. History happened all around me but did not touch me as a child. Police dogs and fire hoses, Bull Connor, Martin Luther King—I saw it all on television. My aunt served on the jury that convicted Robert Chambliss for bombing the Sixteenth Street Baptist Church in 1963, killing four girls. My mother went on a date with George Wallace (she called him "a redneck" with only one thing on his mind—and it wasn't segregation). At Robinson Elementary School I joined an integrated cheerleading squad for the black Rebels basketball team. In high school I might give a ride home to a black guy from class, then, in my own neighborhood, pull hate-group recruitment fliers from underneath my windshield wipers. The strange twists of a postsegregation Birmingham grew as familiar to me as the paths I took each day between school, work, and home. Very often, however, the most familiar thing is one least noticed. My Valdosta experience became the starting point for the kind of history lesson I never received. Certainly not from any 1970s Alabama curriculum, nor from any of the black kids I called friends. We operated under a tacit agreement not to discuss the Big White Elephant in the room, especially after interracial fights broke out in school. (Where we lived, race as Big Black Panther was not allowed anywhere near the room.) Nor was I educated in the supposedly more liberal and culturally diverse mecca of my Northeast graduate school days. Not much separated West Philadelphia and the South Bronx from North Birmingham but an invisible line named after Mason and Dixon. Nor did much separate the tensions that sparked Valdosta's Willie James Williams incident from those that erupted into the violence that left Philadelphia police officer Danny Faulkner dead and activist Mumia Abu Jamal in prison. Or those that killed Amadou Diallo and beat Rodney King, and unfortunately the list goes on. Growing up in Alabama, we used to say, "Thank God for Mississippi." Now, having lived a lot of places (including Mississippi), I know better. That metaphorical ur-space of racism is not located "down there" or "back then," but everywhere, right now. Valdosta forced me to confront what most white people look at but never really see: the hard facts of America's racial history and the responsibility we all share for the present we have inherited.

If Valdosta started educating me, then the summer of 2000 brought my first real test. I flunked. A VSU Faculty Research Grant took me to the New York Public Library's Schomburg Center for Research in Black Culture, where I completed an initial review of the NAACP's investigation, artistic responses, and secondary resources on lynching. The material on the May 1918 lynchings was a rich mine, virtually untouched. The research trip happened to coincide with the exhibition of *Without Sanctuary,* James Allen's collection of lynching photography and memorabilia, at the New-York Historical Society.[8] *Without Sanctuary* made contemporary audiences come face to face with the ruthless, physical reality of lynching: the mutilated, burned bodies; the satisfaction of mob members; and the ghoulish glee of spectators. Viewers debated the exhibit because it bore witness to a history that had remained a shameful secret of our national past and because it replicated what historian Jacquelyn Dowd Hall has referred to as the "folk pornography" of lynching – the sadistic images of tortured black bodies that earlier turn-of-the-century white audiences could not seem to get enough of and later ones were filling up galleries to see yet again.[9] It was nearly impossible to see those images without a visceral reaction. I visited the Historical Society exhibit about the same time that I was reading through the NAACP records, giving me a double dose of the horror against which I thought I was inoculated. Those who study racial violence need strong emotional immune systems – not as much for the gore as for what this knowledge does to one's faith in humanity. My protection for *Without Sanctuary* came in the form of a notebook that I clutched tightly over my chest when I was not using it for writing. I see now that I made it through the exhibit by describing the room's layout in detail and recording captions rather than looking too carefully at the photographs themselves: "5 display cases, 54 plates . . . Thomas Shipp and Abram Smith, Marion IN, photo with lock of hair, caption: 'Bo pointn to his niga' . . . . May 27, 1908, amendment to U.S. postal laws, no mailing of 'matter of a character tending to incite arson, murder, or assassination.'" Clinical note-taking beat feeling. I practiced that skill all summer.

The objectivity broke down soon enough though. Shortly after the exhibit, I read in the NAACP papers about Willie James Howard, a fifteen-year-old who was lynched near Live Oak, Florida, in 1944. Howard had sent Christmas cards to coworkers at a department store, including one to a white girl named Cynthia Goff, who was upset to see hers signed "With Love." In a note of apology, Howard wrote, "I know you don't think much of our kind of people but we don't hate you all we want to be your all friends but you want let us please don't let any body see this I hope I haven't made you made [*sic*]." The girl's father and two other men dragged Howard to the Suwannee River and drowned him, while his father was tied to a tree and forced to watch. Howard's father was sent back to work, as if nothing ever happened, and the white men were never prosecuted.[10] I read the story, went to the bathroom, threw up, turned in my materials, and left. Why did Willie James Howard's story do me in? Why not Mary Turner's? Shipp's and Smith's? Jesse Washington's? Emmett Till's? Claude Neal's? Or anyone else's? I wandered the streets of Harlem the rest of the afternoon in a daze and did not return to the Schomburg again that summer. Not too long afterward, a migraine sent me to Columbia Presbyterian Hospital, and I decided to abandon this project altogether.

Still, the Brooks-Lowndes case would not leave me alone. Back in Valdosta that fall, VSU's director of African American Studies asked me to present my research during the 2001 spring lecture series. Phrases from the past two years' interracial dialogues began to gnaw at me: "Knowledge comes with responsibility." "You can walk away only because you're white." No one had collected and studied the full range of creative and documentary response to Mary Turner. Was I going to continue letting the heroic, redemptive part of the story go untold because reading about human suffering and evil made me uncomfortable? One day, on a whim, I pulled out a photocopy of Walter White's NAACP report and a detailed map. The general site mentioned for Turner's lynching, Folsom's Bridge on the Little River, was still there. I drove fifteen miles west from my house to Quitman, then followed the road north toward Morven and Barney, past where I thought the white farmer might had lived and the violence had originated. I passed Okapilco Creek, where Hayes Turner was lynched. Along the way I saw other familiar signs – streets and businesses whose names still bore those of the mob members White recorded. A line from Nikki Giovanni's "Alabama Poem" ran through my head: "if trees could talk / wonder what they'd say."[11] When I got to the Little River, I pulled over to listen but heard nothing. To be honest, I did not want to hear anything. History was already coming alive too much for me, and I was not sure that I wanted to meet the ghosts alone. I quickly drove the twenty-two miles home, grabbed Tom, and went back. We walked down the river's embankment on either side. It was littered with cigarette butts, beer cans, and hubcaps. On the south side, a deer, struck by traffic, lay rotting, flies buzzing all around its open belly. The river smelled like death. Tom's white shirt was dotted black with mosquitoes. My own arms were covered. We ran back to the car, slapping ourselves all the way, then drove to the first bar we could find.

I spent the next several years alternating between anger and revulsion, white-hot creativity and paralysis before getting to the point where I could write this book. There was clearly an important story to be found in the tension between local forgetting and national remembering, in the creative responses that are powerful yet so often flawed or insufficiently discussed, and in the still-to-be-told history of this iconic female lynching victim. But I was not sure how to link this disparate material or what to say about it. Even harder was how to say it. The story overwhelmed me. I felt inadequate as a literature scholar to handle the historical elements. I struggled to find the right words and style. I failed abysmally in my first investigational task. (Lesson one: be more subtle; lesson two: seek alternatives to institutional histories.)

I also felt that it was not my place as a white person to address these painful aspects of black history, especially after behaving so naively about lynching at the beginning. How could I have pretended not to understand the impact of racial violence when I grew up in a city nicknamed "Bombingham"? Another part of me did not want to think any more about such a horrible topic that hurt to the soul. Living down the legacy of police dogs and fire hoses was enough without having to take on the ghost of a lynched pregnant woman, too. Conversely I was consumed by a desire to "tell all," to explode the happily smug official version of southern Georgia's race relations that contradicted what most African Americans, past and present, had to live with on a daily basis. "My city's sins got televised," I wanted to scream at that water tower, "and as God is my witness, your 'Southern Charm' will go down in flames." Every time I put pen to paper, I wrote with such rage and sarcasm that publication, at least through regular academic venues, seemed impossible. When I lived in Valdosta, the past took tangible shape and began folding into the present. Willie James Williams overlapped onto Willie James Howard, who overlapped onto Mary Turner – an origami of horrific injustice shaped like a noose. Everywhere I turned in Brooks and Lowndes, the whole landscape started talking, not just the trees. Every time I drove west to see friends in Quitman, I crossed Okapilco Creek and heard a voice in my head saying, "Hayes Turner died right here." Every trip north up Interstate 75 meant passing the exit for the Little River where Mary was killed. Every single day when I walked to work, I crossed Patterson Street knowing that the castrated, bullet-ridden body of Sidney Johnson, another 1918 victim, was dragged up it in an awful celebratory parade. That Confederate emblem on Georgia's flag, waving in front of VSU's West Hall and said to symbolize "heritage not hate" made me gut-sick for all the Marys and all the Willie Jameses. The faces of white people from the area began to merge with those of mob members from the *Without Sanctuary* photos. I began to wonder how many local blacks were descended from those who died in 1918. During my last year in Valdosta, I knew two men who actually bore mob victims' names. It was time to leave.

Distance helped a lot. In 2001 I took another job, moved to another state, and focused on other projects. My education is not yet complete. To say that I know what I need to know about race would be an articulation of pride that would surely set me up for the kind of fall I do not want to have again. But I did learn enough to write this book. Over the past few years I figured out that Mary Turner's story was not about my pain. It was not about my realization that the metaphorical Mississippi is everywhere, even inside me. It was not about my anger toward some small southern town whose dirty little secrets I could play heroine by exposing. Every liberal southern white girl has her Scout Finch fantasy, but this story refused to be my sacrificial mockingbird.

I had to renegotiate. What makes Mary Turner's story important on its own terms? Why is it worth telling to academic and general audiences alike? And why is it important to tell now? I realized that "the story" is not only about bad things that happened in 1918. One cannot separate the incident from the multiple retellings, or even not-tellings, of activists, artists, writers, and everyday people trying to comprehend the incomprehensible lynching of a pregnant woman and her fetus. One cannot separate the incident from the symbol of brutality, injustice, and trauma that it has become. I gradually came to see that my difficulty with this topic was a shared one, albeit shared very differently across racial lines. Turner's story has at points frightened away, silenced, obsessed, confounded, and overwhelmed those who have tried to represent it. Still, most have managed to transform that story into compelling documentary and creative works. Jean Toomer's "Kabnis" was, coincidentally, the catalyst that moved me from inability to write to finished product. In Toomer's story, Ralph Kabnis does not leave Georgia. He binge-drinks, has angry outbursts, feels soul-dead – all because, he says, he cannot write. Yet "Kabnis" closes with images of childbirth and resurrection. Appearing in the final section of *Cane*, a signal artistic achievement, these hopeful images offer a powerful statement about the triumph of human spirit over horrific oppression. As a writer, Toomer succeeded where Kabnis failed, and therein lay my own strategy: do what Toomer did and foreground the struggle. My experience with this story is not the same as others'; various historical, rhetorical, and aesthetic circumstances determine how one represents a story such as this one. Still, common ground might be found. Whether activists, artists, writers, local residents, or academics, most of us share a desire for healing. People tell this story seeking justice, change, and closure. They tell to bear witness, to understand, and to mourn. Sometimes people don't talk because they have a personal, institutional, or civic interest in protecting those responsible for the 1918 lynchings. I cannot account for them; they will ultimately have to account for themselves. Learning to distinguish between – and have compassion for – silence that protects pain and silence that protects injustice has been a difficult, important lesson. Sometimes people don't talk because they cannot find the right words.

A Case Study of a Story

Mary Turner and the Memory of Lynching traces Turner's story through newspaper and activist accounts, literature, visual art, popular culture, and public memorials. In doing so, the book differs from most works on

racial violence. Those that focus on particular incidents usually operate within the realm of specific facts: who, what, when, where, and why.
Those that focus on issues of representation and discourse tend to use
multiple examples from which to draw general conclusions. I look at
how a particular incident has been represented in order to draw general
conclusions about discourse. A close equivalent is Christopher Metress's
The Lynching of Emmett Till: A Documentary Narrative, which shows how
Till's iconic 1955 story was constructed and remembered by collecting diverse material related to it. *Mary Turner and the Memory of Lynching*
might be described as "case study," though the term is not entirely accurate. Works such as Patricia Bernstein's *The First Waco Horror*, Leonard
Dinnerstein's *The Leo Frank Case*, James Madison's *A Lynching in the Heartland*, James R. McGovern's *Anatomy of a Lynching*, and Stephen J. Whitfield's *A Death in the Delta* examine incidents in detail, providing valuable ways of understanding what happened within local, regional, and
national contexts. Unlike Jesse Washington, Emmett Till, Claude Neal,
and other important figures studied in these books, Mary Turner does
not have her own case study – an omission that I wanted to rectify. Such
a goal seems especially relevant given the dominance of male-centered
stories within this genre. Laura Wexler's *Fire in a Canebrake*, dealing with
the two African American couples killed in 1946 at the Moore's Ford
Bridge near Monroe, Georgia, emerges as a rare exception. Scholars
such as Philip Dray, Kenneth Robert Janken, and Christopher Meyers
have made valuable contributions toward providing historical coverage
about the 1918 lynchings.[12] Missing from their discussions, however, are
examinations of the creative and activist response. Such considerations
remain atypical of the case study more generally. Here, the notable exception may be found in Edwin T. Arnold's *"What Virtue There Is in Fire":
Cultural Memory and the Lynching of Sam Hose*. As Fitzhugh Brundage argues, some case studies (although certainly none of the excellent examples mentioned above) suffer from poverty of imagination, focusing
on facts to the exclusion of larger questions.[13] If so, the fault lies not with
the form itself, which remains open to new ways of writing and thinking.
Mary Turner and the Memory of Lynching, then, defines itself as a case study
of a story, not an event, and considers how that story might be used to
understand the broader subjects of memory and discourse.

Asking that question prompts others. First, what do I mean by "memory," a word that might be considered as either a noun or a verb? As

a noun, memory exists as a psychic phenomenon in individual or collective consciousness, a mental, physical, or even metaphorical place where past experiences get stored for recall. As a verb (defined loosely), memory exists as a process via acts of remembering and memorializing. Because I look at a range of creative and documentary works as well as collective experience across the twentieth century, I draw from different disciplinary approaches to understand the place and process of memory. A starting point is French historian Pierre Nora's concept of *lieux de mémoire*, or sites of memory, which refers to those spaces infused with historical significance for particular groups. Sites of memory can include places, such as museums, churches, historic homes, and cemeteries; practices and ideas, such as rituals and sayings; and objects, such as monuments, symbols, and texts.[14] The National Great Blacks in Wax Museum, the historical marker on Folsom's Bridge, and literary works about Mary Turner all exist as *lieux de mémoire*. Nora's ideas are useful for understanding memory as noun, as a thing weighted heavily with meaning. Sites of memory are crucial for telling people where they have been, who they are now, and where they might go. As Geneviève Fabre and Robert O'Meally explain in *History and Memory in African-American Culture*, *lieux de mémoire* that arise from the black experience in the United States often function as counternarratives, providing stories that get left out of traditional and mainstream histories. As such they help to recover, define, and empower a collective black selfhood. Even when the memories in question are traumatic, they merit recognition – not just because they validate knowledge that most African Americans are "born knowing," Fabre and O'Meally claim, but because they provide a more complete and multifaceted account of American history.[15]

Where sites of memory can fall short, however, is in showing *how* people create identity and meaning from memory, which can be unreliable, incoherent, and incomplete at best. Here is where the shift from noun to verb begins – and where the perspectives of literature and psychoanalysis become useful. In *Unclaimed Experience: Trauma, Narrative, and History*, Cathy Caruth explains that psychic traumas – wounds of the mind – are not simple and easily intelligible. Traumatic experiences communicate themselves in a language like that of art and literature, she says, one "that defies, even as it claims, our understanding." It is the incomprehensibility of the violence that troubles survivors. What happens does not fit into the usual frames of reference. Shaping traumatic experience is a necessary component of healing, however, even if the process takes a long time, as it usually does. Caruth explains that trauma paradoxically finds its most poignant expression in memory, but memory, in turn, becomes an "attempt *to claim one's own survival*" (emphasis in original).[16] What Caruth outlines has proven true time and again with Mary Turner. In talking about this material at conferences, in classrooms, or in everyday conversation, the first reaction I get is shock. How could this have happened, people want to know. What literary scholar Jaqueline Goldsby calls lynching's "cultural logic" is unfathomable to many contemporary audiences, and Turner's murder encapsulates that incomprehensibility.[17] Likewise, the creative and documentary responses struggle to make meaning, to claim survival out of traumatic violence. Even when the struggle seems more readily apparent than the meaning, as in "Kabnis," the effort itself emerges as powerful testimony of human resilience. Likewise, moving from memory to story involves acknowledging that language is an inadequate tool, but the only tool we have.

Psychoanalysis, too, can go only so far in explaining the complicated dynamics of memory as they apply to Turner responses. Language, like memory, is not static but conflicted, with meanings that shift over time. Lynching was both an individual and a collective trauma that victims, perpetrators, bystanders, and ordinary Americans experienced very differently. Their descendants likewise inherited a very different "memory of lynching." Sociologist Jeffrey C. Alexander's introductory essay for *Cultural Trauma and Collective Identity* defines memory as verb. What Alexander calls the "trauma process" involves key agents called "carrier groups" (a term he takes from Max Weber), who use specific institutional arenas as vehicles for representing a collective's painful events for a wider audience. The goals of this process include establishing responsibility for the injury, managing consequences, and reshaping the collective sense of identity away from feelings of anger and shame toward those rooted in communal healing and sacred value.[18] Alexander's trauma process reflects the memory of lynching as I describe it in this book. Between the late nineteenth and mid-twentieth centuries, lynching's meaning shifted. What was a variant of criminal justice became a national crime. Antilynching activists, artists, and writers (Alexander's carrier groups) effected this change in consciousness through a broad-based, multifaceted public relations campaign. Not all opponents agreed on how to define lynching or how to stop it, but most agreed that it contradicted basic human decency and core American values. The idea that lynching threatened all Americans, not just African Americans, played a major role in its demise. Lynching moved from community-sanctioned act to national shame, something dirty and hurtful, a topic not for polite conversation. The result, however, is contested memory – with descendants of multiple stakeholders disagreeing over why and how lynching should be remembered. This trauma process, as I have learned, has not yet reached its end. Contemporary works of art, literature, and public memorial attempt to mediate what novelist Milan Kundera calls "the struggle of memory against forgetting."[19] Mary Turner plays a role in that struggle.

Lynching gets remembered very differently across the various lines of race, geography, age, and gender. If nothing else, this book has taught me the importance of acknowledging and respecting those lines, rather than pretending they do not exist. One cannot simply presume that remaining "blind" to difference makes difference disappear. I acknowledge my own perspective as well (mostly here, in chapter 4, and in the conclusion), instead of playing a disappearing trick with it. I am somewhat surprised that more scholars have not taken similar first-person approaches to the subject of racial violence, given the personal turn that academic writing in the humanities has taken during the past decade. Then again, too many academics have learned to hide behind an objectivity that we have designed complex institutional structures to support. Most of what I learned in graduate school was like the notebook I used to detail the exhibit specs for *Without Sanctuary*. It did nothing to guide me through anger and grief to insight and faith. I believe that process, treated honestly and responsibly, can speak to others. An important line exists that one must be wary of crossing, however. In his book on Sam Hose, Edwin Arnold describes his process of negotiating that line. Originally thinking that he would write some type of memoir but discarding the "approach in distaste," he still had to remember that "the voice narrating these events is one influenced by sometimes unrecognized investments and prejudices."[20] Arnold is right. Memoir, unless done well, in cases like Timothy Tyson's *Blood Done Sign My Name*, can go egregiously awry. Conversely, one cannot remain oblivious to the shaping power of subject position in an area where the politics of spectatorship remains so heavily fraught. The case of Joel Williamson, whom other scholars chastised in an infamous *Journal of American History* roundtable for his admitted failure to confront lynching, exists as a prime example.[21] Productive dialogue about the history of racial violence cannot take place unless the people engaged in that conversation remain accountable for their perspectives. As Goldsby asserts, "What we know about lynching has settled into narrative molds that are hard to break apart so that we might ask other kinds of interpretive questions." Those questions, she explains, involve rethinking both *"what* is known about lynching" and *"how* one knows it."[22] Approaching an unconventional subject (a female lynching victim) through an unconventional form (a case study of creative and activist responses) and unconventional research methods (foregrounding my own process) helps me see what new questions and answers this complex subject can yield.

A primary question to consider is what happens when one places a black woman at the center of a lynching study. To use Goldsby's terminology, can Mary Turner's story break apart those narrative molds? As historian Crystal Feimster points out, too much current thinking in this field understands lynching as a complicated, nuanced phenomenon while still buying into relatively narrow ideas about it. The white mob/accused black rapist/white woman triangle dominates the conversation today almost as much as it did one hundred years ago. Refocusing that conversation around the women who, traditionally, received the least amount of attention provides new, much-needed insights.[23] Continuing to privilege male narratives is the equivalent of thinking that one will reach a new destination by driving the same old road. Activists, artists, and writers typically look to Turner's story to provide a new direction. During the late 1910s through the early 1930s, her death represented not only a terrible injustice but also a challenge to those who rationalized mob violence. Mary Turner was eight months pregnant, not a mythical male "Burly Black Brute" in pursuit of virginal southern ladies; her only "crime" was trying to seek justice for her husband's lynching. Mobs go after men, women, and even fetuses with equal brutality, the early responses to Turner cry out, undermining pro-lynching arguments with both logic and emotion. More contemporary reactions note how Turner continues to be mostly absent from lynching's collective memory. Granted, men fell victim to mob violence at rates substantially higher than women (an NAACP report published the year after Turner's death lists 3,224 male deaths since 1889 and 61 female).[24] Even though Turner and other women were statistical anomalies, their stories still count. To understand the value of these stories, they must be recovered and examined rather than erased. New information, in turn, provides new insights. Put more scientifically, changing the data changes the hypothesis.

Mary Turner and the Memory of Lynching joins a growing effort to examine the complexities of lynching from a woman's perspective.[25] The initial, and most basic, approach to the subject involves looking at female victimization. Elsa Barkley Brown suggests that focusing on historically marginalized women like Turner shifts the conversation toward some provocative questions. Brown wonders why millions of women suffered along a continuum of violence, but the history of racial oppression remains male centered:

> Why it is that the other experiences of violence that have so permeated the history of Black women in the United States – the rape, the sexual and other forms of physical abuse as employees in white homes, the contemporary domestic and public sexual and other physical violence – are not as vividly and importantly retained in our memory. Why it is that lynching (and the notion of it as a masculine experience) is not just remembered but is in fact central to how we understand the history of African American men, and indeed the African American experience in general. But violence against women – lynching, rape, and other forms of violence – is not.[26]

As Brown points out, women were hardly immune from racial violence, but the default image continues to be male. Writers, artists, and other activists constructed Turner's story specifically to counter that image. Their constructions have much to say about representations of black women and violence, and how those representations have shifted across the twentieth century. Turner's lynching generated a substantial outcry during the late 1910s and early 1920s, quietly disappeared as male stories captivated national attention once again, and then began to emerge during the late 1970s and early 1980s as a story central not just to female but to African American historical memory. Responses to Turner at particular points spur me to ask what ways of thinking and talking facilitated this ebb and flow? The importance of recovering women's stories of victimization becomes not only to acknowledge what has been omitted but also to consider why particular stories get valued at particular times. What do they point to beyond themselves?

A female-based approach to racial violence must include stories of resistance alongside those of victimization. Obviously, not everyone who responded to Turner was female. The NAACP investigation and prosecution attempts were male led, and one of the most well-known literary treatments is Jean Toomer's. The documentary and creative writing that Walter White, other male NAACP leaders, and Toomer produced yields important insights about lynching representations during a key historical moment. However, their work has received significant scholarly attention.[27] Most of this book's female figures have yet to be considered sufficiently. During the past decade, Angelina Weld Grimké's antilynching work has been the subject of several articles.[28] But figures such as the Anti-Lynching Crusaders' Mary Talbert, Carrie Williams Clifford, and Ann Spencer deserve more study. Such women did the difficult, day-to-day work of institutional and grassroots struggle that makes any kind of progressive social transformation possible. Recovering their stories serves a dual purpose of honoring their lives and altering our thinking. Again, changing the data changes the hypothesis. Literary critic Sandra Gunning explains that more inclusive narratives open discursive possibilities. "Thus we must reimagine the discourse on racial violence," she states, "as including not just men *and* women writing, but men and women writing in different tonalities, with different strategies, and with different concerns" (emphasis in original).[29] What did it mean for a woman – or a man – to speak out against lynching? How did gender affect what a person could or could not say? What role did gender play in one's chosen method or style of speaking out? A variety of people, not just a few high-profile men, waged the battle for "black America's body and white America's soul," and they fought on multiple fronts: as local individuals, through national organizations, and with art. The stories that emerged from these multifaceted efforts are worth hearing, for they deepen our notions of what counts as resistance and how that resistance operated along the conflicted terrain of gender.

The rich, varied response to Mary Turner provides a particularly useful way to frame how lynching has been remembered and discussed. I examine the discourse surrounding her death or, to echo Goldsby's words, both *what* is known and *how* that knowledge was produced and circulated. Such an approach is relatively new to a field that has focused more on the phenomenon and less on its representations. For many years, the only book to study the subject in depth was Trudier Harris's *Exorcising Blackness: Historical and Literary Lynching and Burning Rituals.* That situation has begun to change. Just as historians Fitzhugh Brundage and Edward L. Ayers, and sociologists Stewart E. Tolnay and E. M.

Beck, outlined a more complex reality behind the facts of racial violence, scholars from a variety of disciplines have begun to document how that reality was constructed through media, art, literature, and popular culture.[30] Christopher Waldrep traces how the meaning of the term "lynching" shifted over time. Grace Hale argues that spectacle lynchings and their easily reproducible representations were key components underlying modern, white identity. Jonathan Markovitz probes the relationship between lynching imagery, race, and gender in contemporary society. Goldsby, Gunning, and Dora Apel carry forward Harris's pioneering work by studying the ways that writers and artists struggled to create new stories, images, and meanings as forms of resistance against oppressive violence.[31] These scholars suggest, when they do not say it directly, that one cannot separate phenomenon from discourse. What anyone knows about lynching today, whether expert or layperson, comes filtered through more than a century's worth of oral history, institutional history, journalism, literature, film, visual art, photography, and more. Demonstrating how those filters shape knowledge and perceptions is essential. The range of materials on Turner allows a scholar to study the ways knowledge and perceptions emerged and changed over time. Two different sets of questions arise: not just who, what, when, where, and why, *but what historical conditions, rhetorical situations, and artistic practices* determine the portrayal of *who, what, when, where, and why.* I said before that most of what I learned in graduate school did not prepare me to write this book, but some of it did. Scholars of literature are trained in the rules that govern oral, written, and visual rhetoric. We devote much time and energy to figuring out how stories and images work, where they form patterns, and why they break down.

With this story, the breakdown is key. My own struggle to write about Turner helped me to understand better how others have dealt with the subject. It also made me realize why few scholars had written about responses to her lynching, and no one had studied them in their entirety. This material is difficult on a variety of levels. First, I had to *find* it. Constructing an archive meant visiting multiple locations over a period of years. One does not exactly pore through "The Mary Turner Papers" at one convenient, centralized location. Second, once I found the material, I had to figure out how to *interpret* it. Texts often fall apart or violate traditional criteria for aesthetic success. They span a diverse range of documentary and creative writing, visual media, digital media, public art, and more, reaching back to the late 1910s and forward into the present day. Writing successfully meant learning how to juggle many disciplinary approaches as well as my own emotional reactions. These challenges reap both academic and spiritual rewards, however, and the two are often intertwined. Over the years I learned how to honor Mary Turner and others that I write about. Sometimes the bravest action a person can take is telling the truth. Turner paid with her life. But the memory of her murder retains an uncanny defiance. Through the responses to her, Turner lives on as a narrative disruption that refuses to be contained. Her story reveals or, more appropriately, calls out patterns, shifts, and ruptures in the ways lynching gets remembered today. Because different people have worked with this material in different rhetorical situations, using different forms, during different periods, Turner's specific case shows how discourse shifts and adapts. More simply put: The ways people represent lynching depend upon when and where they live, what modes of expression are available to them at a given moment, and how they need to express themselves to accomplish particular purposes for particular audiences. Turner's story provides a focal point for looking at the ways discourse falls apart and talk breaks down or, more positively, changes direction. I struggled with this material; so did others, and some refuse to acknowledge the memory, period. The problem here is not just local and not just centered on Mary Turner. Many contemporary responses grapple with the most effective means of conveying such a troubling story for an audience that might not know about, care about, or remember lynching at all.

How we remember and talk about lynching matters. One does not have to dig very deeply into U.S. popular culture to see that the images and rhetoric supporting racial violence continue to influence American thinking about race today. The myth of the "Burly Black Brute" still plays a major role in ideas about black male criminality. Stories about abducted and assaulted white females make immediate headlines, while stories about similarly imperiled black females rarely do until those stories are thought to be hoaxes. White people are often puzzled by the way black people respond to high-profile police brutality and other criminal justice system cases. Debates over nooses, Confederate flags, and other such icons proliferate. The memory of racial violence lies at the root of these issues and many more. In *Legacies of Lynching*, Jonathan Markovitz borrows an idea from Wahneema Lubiano to describe lynching as synecdoche or code, "the shortest possible shorthand" for racism.[32] The difference lies in whether one acknowledges those roots, denies them knowing that they exist, or remains ignorant of them. Scholars and activists in this field face a twofold task: educating those who do not know or care, and then negotiating the difficult terrain of talking about race and the memory of racial violence. Grassroots groups across the country – the Rosewood Heritage Foundation, the Philadelphia Coalition, the Moore's Ford Memorial Committee, the Greensboro Truth and Reconciliation Commission, and others – are starting to have those conversations. Their success, as Sherrilyn A. Ifill explains, lies in providing new models of discourse with goals rooted in racial reconciliation, restorative justice, and healing.[33] For me, Mary Turner acts as a synecdoche of two opposing tensions. What happened to her represents racism at its worst. The ways that she has been remembered, conversely, represent the struggle over oppression at its best. Her story has the potential to open up new ways of talking about racial violence and reconciliation.

That potential is ultimately where the academic meets the spiritual, and what makes this book worth doing. If I still thought that Mary Turner's story spoke of nothing but brutality and injustice, I would not have made the effort. The questions I learned to ask were not only what makes it worth telling, but also what makes it worth telling now. I needed to think about the perspective that I had to offer, what insight I could bring as a scholar and an individual. Being able to write more perceptibly about the difficulties of representing lynching, via training and lived experience, was part of the equation. Another part relates to Ifill's ideas about new discourse models and to why Turner's story is worth talking about at this particular historical moment, when racial reconciliation dialogues seem so necessary yet complicated. During the hardest times of writing this book, the heroes and heroines who worked to change the conversation about lynching kept me going. Ida B. Wells, W. E. B. Du Bois, Walter White, James Weldon Johnson, Mary Talbert, Jessie Daniel Ames, and so many others died before fully realizing the fruits of their labor, but they did not give up. Because of them, many people today remember lynching as human evil. That was not the case a century ago, when lynching thrived mostly, but not only, in the Jim Crow South. Activists did not succeed to the extent they hoped in changing laws, but they did succeed, with the help of artists and writers, in changing hearts and minds. Their legacy lives on in those who work to memorialize and seek justice for acts of racial violence today. Mary Turner plays a small part in this larger national story. I cannot rewrite the awful history of what happened, but maybe I can help others to see how she fits into that bigger picture in important and redemptive ways. That is a debt I owe to her, to the past and present conversation changers who paved the way for me, and to the local community where I lived and worked for several years. The question that this book tries to answer is how one *should* remember lynching. Mary Turner's story provides a compass for navigating those troubled waters.

1 Birth and Nation

Mary Turner and the Discourse of Lynching

On the night of May 18, 1918, the *Augusta Chronicle* reported, Georgia residents had a final opportunity to see D. W. Griffith's *Birth of a Nation*.[1] The film played to sold-out theaters when it first ran in 1915 and made its way across the state again three years later, wowing audiences as spectacle and wooing them as romance. The plot follows two families, linked in friendship between Phil Stoneman, from the North, and Ben Cameron, from the South. Pulled apart by Civil War, the two young men reunite during Reconstruction to battle a similar threat, specifically coded as racial. A mulatto politician named Silas Lynch tries to force Phil's sister Elsie into a relationship, and Ben's sister Flora jumps off a cliff to her death rather than succumb to the advances of a black soldier named Gus. Ben joins a local Ku Klux Klan to punish the offender and wrest order from the chaos of slavery's end. The group finds and kills Gus, saves Elsie from Silas's clutches, rescues Phil from the black militia that surrounds him, and ultimately disenfranchises and disarms local blacks. The violent, bloody purging of an African American scapegoat thus enables the birth of a new nation from the union of North and South, represented by the two couples that come together at the film's close: Elsie and Ben, Margaret (another Cameron sister) and Phil.

"A simple human story of love," the *Augusta Chronicle* said, "that grips the hearts of the audience." Moviegoers had never seen filmmaking like Griffith's: large outdoor panoramas juxtaposed against intimate domestic scenes; innovative camera work with crosscutting, panning, dissolves, dramatic chase sequences, and action shots; elaborate title cards and an orchestral musical score to swell emotions; historically accurate costuming and tableaux to make simulated events look real. "It is like writing history with lightning," President Woodrow Wilson exclaimed. "And my only regret is that it is all so terribly true."[2] Wilson's statement captured what protests against *The Birth of a Nation* complained was its central problem: audiences mistook fantasy for fact.

A key issue was the glorification of racial violence. Griffith based parts of *The Birth of a Nation* on Thomas Dixon's 1905 novel, *The Clansman: An Historical Romance of the Ku Klux Klan,* and the film imbues the Klan with a quasi-religious stature. Griffith presents the group as redeemers who consecrate their actions – the eradication of enemies – through blood sacrifice. After Flora dies while fleeing Gus, Ben raises the small blood-stained Confederate flag that she carried on her belt as his symbol of revolt. At the film's end, a Christlike figure floats over the lovers Elsie and Ben to bless their union, as well as that of North and South, both made possible by the Ku Klux Klan. Such powerful imagery had real-life repercussions. Federal legislation helped stop the organization during the 1870s, but the film's 1915 Atlanta premiere led to a Klan revival that quickly spread outward. By 1918 the aforementioned *Augusta Chronicle* article accepted Klan activity as a given. The many amazing features it primed audiences to see included the "25,000 yards of white muslin" used to create "the regalia of the Ku Klux Klansmen." It was not the robes that upset the NAACP's Moorfield Storey, who refused to shake Griffith's hand when the two met in Boston about potential censorship of the film; it was the film's equation between lynching and rape.[3] Almost twenty-five years earlier, Ida B. Wells had described the notion as "a thread bare lie."[4] The statistics that the NAACP compiled in 1919 remained consistent with Wells's findings. Of the 3,224 people lynched between 1889 and 1918, 2,552 were black. Less than 30 percent of those cases resulted from accusations of rape, and many of those accusations were spurious at best.[5] Numbers on a page could not compete with figures larger than life on screen. In *The Birth of a Nation,* a lascivious Gus licks his lips as he pursues the terrified Flora through the woods; Silas rubs his hands with glee and locks Elsie in a closet as he plots to have his way with her. Small wonder that Georgia filmgoers welcomed white-robed saviors to deliver them from the black savagery they perceived around them. Griffith transformed "the thread bare lie" into a block-buster hit so convincing that the president himself found it "all so terribly true."

The president's words speak a truth themselves that contemporary audiences should not underestimate but may find hard to grasp. *The Birth of a Nation* was more than entertainment for early-twentieth-century audiences: it told a story that many filmgoers believed and wanted to see performed repeatedly, in ways that bordered on the ritualistic. Its underlying values, however, belong to another place, another time, despite the fact that D. W. Griffith pushed cinematic technique into new directions. At best, today's filmgoers find his worldview silly; at worst, offensive. It creates as much cognitive dissonance as a mouth moving with no words coming out, followed by a title card praising our national Aryan birthright. It makes as much sense as a lynching. Yet *The Birth of a Nation* sets the stage for understanding what happened in Brooks and Lowndes counties in May 1918 and, paradoxically, why current readers of this book may find such an event incomprehensible. Although the film played in Augusta's Grand Theater during the same weekend that lynchings peaked in Brooks and Lowndes, *The Birth of a Nation* did not *cause* the rampage that went on 250 miles to the southwest. It does, however, epitomize the mind-set that condoned the violence. The film's widespread popularity also explains, in part, why the Brooks-Lowndes lynchings became a sensational news story on the state and national levels. Griffith cinematically manipulated a narrative that had been popular in print media since Reconstruction.[6] Residents of Brooks and Lowndes could indulge their thirst for stories about whites coming together to purge the black threat not just by going to the movies but also by performing the story in real life. In turn, those not participating could follow what happened in daily installments – with the newspaper serving both as information and entertainment. Certainly the concept of news as infotainment, and the knowledge that violence dominates media, resonates today. But who really understands, much less condones, lynching? The worldview that Griffith spoke to is now foreign because activists, artists, and writers made it that way – by changing mainstream attitudes about lynching. This chapter uses the Brooks-Lowndes lynchings to sketch out those attitudes and to begin telling the longer story of how they shifted over the next two decades.

The location: Two counties that lie along today's Georgia-Florida border, near Interstate 75 (figure 1). The time: May 16–23, 1918. The situation: A spree of mob violence that prompted Georgia's governor Hugh M. Dorsey to declare martial law and send in Savannah's Home Guard. The specific details of what really happened will never be known. Initial news reports so diverge that most official historical versions today use as their definitive source an NAACP investigation that Assistant Secretary Walter White conducted in June.[7] Although a skilled investigator, White had his faults and biases, which anyone must take into account before considering his version as unvarnished truth. Still, the story's general outline remains consistent. Trouble started when a black laborer named Sidney Johnson killed his white employer Hampton Smith and wounded Smith's wife after a wage dispute. Johnson and a possible accomplice fled into a nearby swamp, and a posse began rounding up Johnson's friends and family members. Over the next few days, the posse's numbers, along with its number of victims, swelled dramatically. The recorded body count, including Johnson (who died in a shoot-out) was eleven; the rumored one, eighteen. State and local newspapers reported the manhunt and the lynchings in detail, with each new edition bringing exciting, if conflicting, developments in the story about the "murdered" farmer, his "attacked" wife, and the unknown accomplice, known variously as "Black Trouble" and "Black Terror."[8] By Monday, the mass lynching began making national news. The two victims to receive the most attention were Hayes and Mary Turner, the latter killed for protesting her husband's death. For a brief time the story also fed wartime paranoia. A rumor originating in Valdosta, Lowndes's county seat, had local blacks in league with Germans, plotting to overthrow southern farm operations. While whites in Brooks and Lowndes watched their backs for "skulking Huns," editorials across the country fulminated against South Georgia residents who engaged in the "Hun-like" activity of lynching a woman.[9] How could Wilson urge the nation "to make the world safe for democracy" when the nation could not make Georgia safe for women like Mary Turner? Some of the more forceful protests emerged, perhaps not surprisingly, from Augusta, fresh from *The Birth of a Nation*'s second run.

The NAACP had good reason to send its young, new investigator, Walter White, to check out the story that June. The organization saw

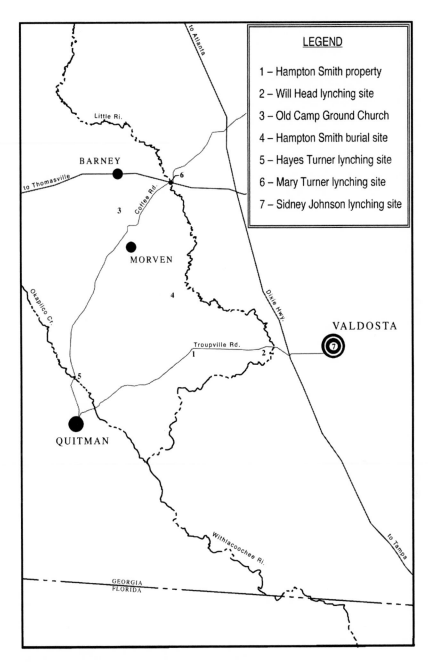

Figure 1. Locations significant to the 1918 Brooks-Lowndes lynchings. (Courtesy of David Wishner, E+D Architecture and Design.)

the Brooks-Lowndes incident as a potential counter to the kind of ideas about lynching that *Birth of a Nation* had popularized. As White's boss James Weldon Johnson explained, the majority of Americans did not condone such violence, but they did not condemn it either. Johnson blamed mass media for perpetuating the idea that lynching offered a solution to an imaginary problem, the Burly Black Brute, when the real threat to American values was lynching itself.[10] The NAACP believed that South Georgia's mass killing with its female victim could challenge the rape myth, helping to push public opinion's ambivalent majority to the right side of the ideological fence. The story of Mary Turner's lynching had powerful mainstream appeal, having already circulated quickly and widely before White's arrival on the scene. Protestors called her death an affront to humanity and God as well as democracy. White's job was to channel the energy and distill the broad-ranging rhetoric toward a tangible goal: building a case against mob members. Prosecution could prove lynching to be a legal and a moral wrong. To help serve that end, White had to investigate and create coherency from the multiple versions of the story in circulation. Then he had to reach men like Dorsey and Wilson, who had the power to punish and legislate. Beyond those in power lay Johnson's ambivalent majority, who genuinely believed the values that lay behind *The Birth of a Nation*: that black criminality threatened the larger social fabric through its threat to white women and that vigilante violence offered a justifiable solution. White's investigation into the Brooks-Lowndes lynchings yielded two documents, an initial report titled "Memorandum to Governor Dorsey," and a revised version, "The Work of a Mob," which was published in the *Crisis* and circulated as a pamphlet. White did not accomplish what the NAACP had hoped in terms of prosecution, but he achieved more than anyone had planned through his publications. Local residents reacted with "unlimited fury" to his work.[11] The case's primary informant stopped cooperating, and prosecution attempts, which had gone as far as the U.S. Senate, came to a halt. Despite this initial setback, "The Work of a Mob" saw long-term success as a foundational work of antilynching exposé. The article compelled other activists, artists, and writers to respond, forever changing the way the story would be remembered. Before Walter White, no one reported Mary Turner's pregnancy and the removal of her fetus. What had been an atypical story now took shape as collective trauma. Just because he altered the conversation, however, does not mean that prior material should be discounted. In the wake of World War I, racial violence and the campaign against it intensified. News accounts and grassroots protests of Mary Turner's death capture the direction that both sides of this debate would take as rhetoric began to shift in ways that allowed antilynching forces to gain the upper hand. The question one must consider is why White said what others did not. The answer provides an introduction to lynching discourse itself.

Early Press Coverage and the Black Terror Threat

The story of the Brooks-Lowndes lynching had a rich, varied life before Walter White that is mostly forgotten. Newspapers across Georgia followed the hunt for Sidney Johnson and the lynchings that preceded his in detail, giving daily, usually front-page coverage. Main sources included the *Valdosta Times* (now missing), the *Quitman Free Press*, the Moultrie *Daily Observer*, the *Macon News*, the *Augusta Chronicle*, the *Savannah Morning News*, and the *Atlanta Constitution*. Accounts often contradict one another and sometimes even themselves. Reports of violence carrying the dateline "Valdosta, Georgia," also circulated in papers from Washington, D.C., to Richmond, Baltimore, New York, Bridgeport, Philadelphia, Pittsburgh, Chicago, St. Louis, Memphis, Birmingham, Shreveport, Houston, Denver, and San Francisco. Most Georgia papers focused on what happened to the white farmer and his wife the night of May 16, 1918, and the fates of those who allegedly played a role in those events. Nationally the story's peculiar plot twists garnered the most attention. What occurred in Brooks and Lowndes counties began as a replay of events, real or fictional, familiar to most Americans at the time. "Hamp Smith Murdered; Young Wife Attacked By Negro Farm Hands," the headline read in Quitman (Appendix 1). A posse gave chase, lynched the accused, and the community's power centers pronounced justice served. Similar stories had been told so many times – through the deaths of Jesse Washington, Leo Frank, Sam Hose, and other victims; in speeches by "Pitchfork" Ben Tillman, Rebecca Felton, and other public figures; and, of course, most vividly on screen – that savvy newspaper readers did not need the names of Hampton Smith or Sidney Johnson to know how the plot would unfold.[12] Yet no one on the state or national level expected the sudden, disruptive appearance of two new narrative presences: a black woman and German spies. These figures catapulted an otherwise predictable, provincial story into the shifting currents of lynching discourse during World War I and its immediate aftermath. Initial press coverage of the Brooks-Lowndes case – its first official versions – reveals the potency and marketability that black male rapist imagery had for early-twentieth-century audiences. Readers on the state level especially could not get enough of this story, following its labyrinthine, sometimes nonsensical turns like an obsession, even as they could predict the outcome. National readers wanted the digest or novelty version of stories from elsewhere (reserving their own obsessions for violence that occurred nearby). For all their seeming strangeness to readers today, these accounts contain patterns that later activists successfully manipulated toward positive change.

The White Farmer's Murder and the Attack on His Wife

The first story line involved what happened the night of May 16, 1918. The *Quitman Free Press* had Hampton Smith leaving the kitchen of his farmhouse around nine o'clock that evening and crossing a small porch into the couple's bedroom. He picked up his pipe, lit it, and noticed that his Winchester rifle, normally kept in the corner, was missing. He asked his wife about it, but before she answered, someone fired four shots into the room from outside. Two hit the wall behind Smith, and then a third hit him in the shoulder and spun him around for a fourth to land in his chest. Mrs. Smith screamed and ran outside. What happened next is not clear. At some point, she was shot in the shoulder, but the timing is uncertain. A few papers, including the *Free Press*, suggested she was raped. Her husband's attackers "maltreated her terribly," tearing off parts of her clothing and leaving "evidence of a terrible struggle where the young woman fought as long as consciousness remained." Her "delicate condition," words the paper used to describe her third trimester of pregnancy, "made the matter problematical." Mrs. Smith recovered sufficiently that night to identify two attackers that her husband had recently brought over from Valdosta: Sidney Johnson and a man whose name she thought might be Julius. Moultrie and Savannah papers placed three men at the scene. Accomplices' names were reported variously across the state as Julius Jones, Julius Brown, Shorty Ford, and "Black Trouble." Some papers said that the men pilfered Mr. Smith's new suit, a gold watch, and any money they could find while his wife lay bleeding on the ground. The *Atlanta Constitution* reported that Mrs. Smith did not pass out but staunched the blood flow from her shoulder with her apron and fled while the men ransacked the house. When they realized she was gone, they gave chase but did not catch her. Most state papers gave the men several hours' head start. According to the *Quitman Free Press* and others, Mrs. Smith did not regain consciousness for some time. When she woke up, she staggered to a stream that ran behind the property, bathed her wound, and then headed across the road to some workers' cabins. Someone took her in and alerted the county sheriff, J. P. Wade.[13]

The Hunt for Black Trouble

By the time Sheriff Wade assembled a posse to find him, Johnson and any accomplices were long gone. The question was where. The *Quitman Free Press*, Moultrie's *Daily Observer*, the *Macon News*, and the *Savannah Morning News* detailed the posse's chase, but accounts vary. Some reports had hounds following Johnson's trail in the direction of Valdosta, then losing it. Others had him fleeing by car, possibly driven by the character "Black Trouble" or by a Simon Schuman of Morven (between Quitman and Barney). Still others claimed that Johnson and his accomplices tried to steal Smith's car, could not start it, and fled on foot. Someone speculated that Johnson covered his feet in turpentine-soaked rags to throw the dogs off his scent. Reports had him hiding in Mud Swamp, between Valdosta and Quitman, or in the swamps southeast of Valdosta.[14] Wherever Johnson might have been, whites were looking. The *Daily Observer*'s Friday afternoon edition noted that a large posse from Brooks and Lowndes counties was "scouring the countryside" between western Brooks and eastern Lowndes. The ominous headline, in varying fonts, was its own story: "Hampton Smith of Barney Is Assassinated: Negro Blamed. Wife of Man Killed Was Shot, Also – Recognized Sid Johnson, She Says. Big Posse Is On Trail of Negro. Lynching May Follow If the Assassin Is Captured, Reports Declare."

The newspaper arrived just in time for locals to gather at a spot on Troupville Road called "the hanging tree." A man named Will Head had been arrested near Barney for complicity in the case. The *Moultrie Observer* (a weekly paper, different from the *Daily Observer*) and the *Macon News* reported later that Head had "stoutly denied any connection with the crime at first, but later made a detailed confession before several hundred witnesses." He allegedly put himself, Sidney Johnson, and another man named Will Thompson at Smith's house near suppertime (he made no mention of Julius/Black Trouble). Mrs. Smith provided meals for some of the farmworkers, and while she was distracted fixing plates for the men, Head snuck into the bedroom and stole Smith's rifle. Later, when the men saw Smith light the lamp and then his pipe, Johnson fired the shots that killed him. After Mrs. Smith ran outside, Johnson and Thompson assaulted her, Head supposedly claimed, although he did not "violate" her as others did. After the assault, they shot her, left her for dead, ransacked the place, and came out to find her gone. The *Macon News* stated that a Valdosta man asked Head if he knew he would be lynched for such a crime, to which Head allegedly replied, "Yes, sir, but it is no use to worry about that now." According to the *Moultrie Observer*, Head asked for time to pray; a bystander yelled out that he had not given Smith the same courtesy. The two newspapers reported what followed differently. The Moultrie paper said that a mob member jerked the rope that had already been tied around Head's neck over a branch, pulling him into the tree. The Macon paper wrote that Head had been forced to climb the tree and then jump, with the quickly held coroner's inquest declaring, "The deceased came to his death by jumping from the limb of a tree with a rope around his neck." Either way, eager souvenir hunters converged upon Head immediately, carrying away pieces of his flesh, "before his body ceased swaying," according to the Moultrie paper. The crowd lingered until word spread that another man had been captured near Morven, and then rushed to the scene of the next lynching.[15]

The violence erupted with so much frequency on Friday and Saturday that newspapers could not keep straight who died where. Moultrie's papers had a man by the name of Eugene Rice captured and killed near Morven three hours after Head's death, while Savannah's papers listed Will Thompson as the mob's next victim. (The *Atlanta Constitution* reported that Eugene Rice was also known as James Isom, a name that does not appear in other documents.) By Saturday night, at least four black men and possibly seven were dead. Three more bodies were eventually pulled from the Little River; some, like Chime Riley's, were never recovered.[16] Beyond Will Head's supposed confession, which implicated himself and Thompson, no reasons were given for the deaths. At least some, but not all, of the men were Sidney Johnson's friends and family members, whom mob members picked up hoping to get information about Smith's assailants. The *Daily Observer* reported that several of Johnson's family members were being held in the Lowndes County Jail for safekeeping.[17] The lynching victims merely may have provided the bloodthirsty mob with convenient substitutes for the real murderer. Another mass lynching in 1894 established precedent in the area for indiscriminate torture and killing. That incident, occurring in Brooks County, presaged 1918 in frightening ways. A white posse looking for an accused killer randomly picked off blacks, one an elderly woman. Farm workers fled to the swamps or took refuge on the plantation of a sympathetic white man, Mitchell Brice. It took the combined efforts of Brice, who threatened to press charges against mob members for harming his workers, and the state militia, whom the governor had dispatched after local blacks, desperate for help, wired him to stop the violence. Five died in the melee.[18]

In May 1918 the hunt for "Black Trouble" paused for Hampton Smith's funeral. The *Quitman Free Press* covered services in detail. Mrs. Smith was too ill to attend, but doctors remained confident that she would recover. Local undertaker S. E. McGowan picked up her husband's body early Friday morning and took it for embalming to his offices on Screven Street, Quitman's main east-west thoroughfare. On Saturday afternoon, family, friends, and onlookers gathered at Dixon and Mary Smith's home for the funeral procession, which wound its way through the county to the Pauline Church, on the Valdosta-Morven Road, just a mile or so north of the hanging tree. The Reverend W. T. Gaulden, a family friend, conducted the services, and mourners beat back the May heat with fans that the undertaker provided.[19] Sample fans from the time (available today at the Brooks County Historical Museum) include "Daily Inspirations" from the Bible printed on one side. Among them, verses of comfort and admonition: "Walk worthily of God, who calleth you unto His kingdom and glory" (1 Thessalonians 2:12) and "For I have given you an example, that ye should do, as I have done to you" (John 13:15). The words apparently had little effect. After saying prayers, singing hymns, and watching Smith's body lowered into the ground, several mourners rejoined the mob. Later that evening, according to eyewitness reports, they lynched Hayes Turner.[20]

The *Quitman Free Press* and Moultrie's *Daily Observer* report that Saturday night Sheriff Wade, Clerk of the Court W. R. (Roland) Knight, and a county superintendent named Youngblood took Turner from jail in order to drive him to Moultrie, supposedly for safekeeping. Wade had arrested Turner earlier that day and charged him with conspiracy to kill Smith. The attack was allegedly planned at Turner's house. Just north of Quitman, forty to fifty armed and masked men surrounded the car, some of them jumping onto its running boards, and demanded the prisoner. Wade and his men complied, and the mob marched Turner down the road to the bridge over Okapilco Creek, on the Old Coffee Road. They hanged him from a tree with his hands still cuffed behind him, leaving his body, as they had Will Head's, on view until the following day (figure 2). By Sunday morning, hundreds of people – including children, the papers said – had come by to see it.[21]

Narrative Disruptions

Many viewers very likely passed Hayes Turner's body on their way to see his wife killed. Newspapers across the state usually reported the two deaths together. If mob members picked up Mary in Quitman on Sunday morning, as these accounts say, they probably drove her past Hayes's body as well. The mob would have several reasons for lynching its victim at the Little River and for taking the Old Coffee Road to get there. The route provided the shortest distance between the two points. It allowed the mob to display its trophy to multiple members of Hampton Smith's family. His father, Dixon, owned large tracts of land in eastern Brooks County that he had dispensed among his sons. A sizable population of black farmworkers also lived along Old Coffee Road, allowing the mob to make a firm statement about the extent of white power. Mob members ultimately carried Mary Turner close to an important crossroads: where the Dixie Highway (Georgia's primary north-south route) met a primary road to a tourist destination, Thomasville. Most important, the mob brought her back to Smith land: the Old Joyce Place on the Little River east of Barney. Which Smith owned that land remains unclear. White reported that Hampton Smith lived on the property. Brooks County real estate records have him owning parcels farther south, on both sides of Troupville Road east of Quitman, and his brother Thomas owning the Old Joyce Place. Local news articles provide contradictory information, referring to Hampton as both a Quitman and a Barney resident. Whether Hampton or Thomas occupied the spot, Mary

Figure 2. Walter White, photograph of the tree where Hayes Turner was lynched. (National Association for the Advancement of Colored People Records, Library of Congress; used with permission of the National Association for the Advancement of Colored People.)

Turner's lynching ultimately functioned as an elaborate performance in defense of Smith turf.[22]

A key question is why a mob went after her in the first place. The *Daily Observer* wrote that Hayes confessed and implicated his wife in Smith's murder. The "plot to kill Smith, assault his wife, and rob his home" was hatched in Hayes and Mary's cabin, the paper said. As evidence of Mary's complicity, "a gold watch belonging to the murdered man was found in her possession." The *Savannah Morning News* explained that Mary was accused of what might have been a more serious crime: talking back. She apparently was overheard saying that she would press charges against the men who had lynched Hayes. Driving her past his body would have had the added effect of making her see how she would pay for daring to consider trespassing against white power in that way. A speech act that drew state protection when a local white man, Mitchell Brice, did a similar thing in 1894 led to a black woman's public condemnation and death. The paper stated, "The people in their indignant mood took exceptions to her remarks as well as her attitude and took her to the river where she was lynched."[23] Few accounts, whether from Quitman, Moultrie, Savannah, or Atlanta, shied away from details that Mary Turner's lynching included being hung, set on fire, and shot multiple times before a crowd of five hundred to one thousand people. None, however, mentioned her "delicate condition"—words evoked for Mrs. Smith's advanced stage of pregnancy.

Turner's death and the weekend's end marked a shift in the reporting of this story, but the violence continued. On Monday, the *Daily Observer* stated, a Brooks County coroner's jury ruled the cases closed, returning verdicts that all the blacks killed over the weekend "came to their deaths at the hands of parties unknown." Christopher Meyers, in "'Killing Them by the Wholesale,'" notes that the verdict should come as no surprise, as White later identified the foreman of the coroner's jury among the mob's ringleaders. The weekend lynchings satisfied bloodlust only temporarily, and the verdicts gave whites permission to keep killing. In the same article that reported Mary Turner's death, the *Savannah Morning News* said that mob members were looking for "other negroes." White residents of Brooks and Lowndes were afraid because Sidney Johnson remained at large, along with his alleged accomplice, whom the *Daily Observer* had begun to call "Black Terror." The name alone shows that these men personified what white southerners feared most. Armed black men who apparently had no fear of whites were lurking nearby, but no one knew where. The Savannah paper kept its readers poised for more violence, assuring them that the men would be put to death—probably by burning—when they were found.[24]

By Monday morning, reports of a mass lynching with a female victim in South Georgia hit national newspapers. Most reprinted the facts as they came from Valdosta, thus duplicating the local perspective, whether intentionally or not. Very few questioned those facts or the viewpoint they implied. New York dailies carrying the dateline "Valdosta, Ga. May 19" told the same story almost word-for-word about the hangings of Hayes and Mary Turner, and the attack on Smith and his wife.[25] Reports attributed motive to the Turners, said to have quarreled previously with their former landlord, Smith. These accounts also mentioned the on-going pursuit of Sidney Johnson and the deaths of Will Head and an-other man, named as Will Thompson. Four of the farm workers (sto-ries state that Thompson's role is unclear) allegedly hatched a plot at the Turners' home to rob and kill Smith. Head stole the gun, and Johnson fired the shots. Such reports played into white readers' notions of black criminality, even if they did not use terms such as "Black Trouble" or "Black Terror." The Turners, out of revenge, enlisted others to harm the Smiths. Blacks were predators, whites prey. Conversely, the *Baltimore Daily Herald* and the *New York Post* carried the same Valdosta dateline but took a more critical perspective. Baltimore's paper told a story similar to those in New York, but its judgment upon events was clear from the headline: "Georgia Huns Lynch Negro Woman and Three Men." Such a headline put a decidedly different spin on the story from the *New York Sun*'s more generic "Mobs Lynch Four; Seek Two Others." In a detailed editorial, the *New York Post* spelled out why the *Herald* would choose a word like "Huns" to describe the mob. Lynching a colored woman, the *Post* says, was the kind of crime Americans fought against overseas. "We do not like to accuse anybody of pro-Germanism," but "every fresh lynching degrades us to the Prussian level and makes it the more difficult for Americans to hold the Germans up to scorn for their crimes against humanity."[26] The *Baltimore Herald* and the *New York Post* reversed the equation made by other stories that relied on Valdosta re-ports. Here, blacks were prey, and those who lynched them were worse than predators. They resembled the current national enemy, whose be-havior against Belgian citizens in 1914, including women and children, lent popular support for a war.

The link between events in South Georgia and events overseas would take a surprising turn when a different story broke on Tuesday morn-ing, May 21. A report from the *Valdosta Times*, now missing but quoted directly in many state papers, announced "Pro-Germans Had a Hand." A plot, revealed by some of the area's "best known negroes," spoke of German agents in the area, trying to cripple farm operations by stirring up racial tensions. Although the Valdosta paper hedged on any "direct connection with the assassination of Smith," the *Atlanta Constitution* did not mince words: "Tragedy at Barney Laid to Hun Agents."[27] The story had its roots in what is known as "the Zimmerman Note," the infamous telegram intercepted in January 1917 that led to the United States declaring war against Germany and its allies. The note was said to describe a German-Mexican alliance that was organizing blacks across Georgia's southern tier to help them seize Savannah for a base of operations. As Georgia historian Donald L. Grant explains, black leaders spent months afterward doing damage control, holding meetings in Augusta, Macon, and Thomasville to deny German influence or sympathies.[28] The rumors ultimately proved false, but they remained psychologically potent in May 1918. During the weeks before Smith's death, local headlines railed against "Hun hordes," German "dogs," and "assassins"–using terms similar to those describing Johnson and others. The biggest news story in the *Quitman Free Press* before the May lynchings was Brooks County's attempt to form a Home Guard for protection. Paranoia and demonization of Germans ran statewide. A cartoon and accompanying editorial that ran in the *Atlanta Constitution* on the day Hampton Smith died exclaimed, "The Devil Resigns Office in Favor of the Kaiser." "My Satanic soul grew sick . . . [when] I knew the pupil had become the master," the Devil said. The paper singled out the particularly heinous crimes committed against women and children: torpedoing the *Lusitania* so that babies and mothers wind up devoured by sharks, forcing men and women – even pregnant ones – into hard labor in Belgium, and the Armenian genocide, where Prussian officers stood by and watched nude women get disemboweled by "Swarthy Turks."[29] The *Constitution* missed the ironic disconnection between this cartoon and its reportage of events closer to home.

The conflation of lynching and wartime rhetoric fed national criticism and local tensions. Papers such as the *Memphis News-Scimitar* and the *Pittsburgh Courier* joined the *New York Post* and the *Baltimore Daily Herald* in seeing through the reports coming out of Valdosta. "Skulking Hun is Blamed for Racial Break in Georgia," the Memphis paper explained, while a more alliterative headline in Pittsburgh read, "Crackers Try to Foist Fiendish Work on Huns."[30] Back in South Georgia, whites kept looking for "Black Terror." Many local blacks fled the much more tangible threat facing their communities. The *Savannah Morning News* stated that nearly all the blacks living around Barney, just over the bridge from where Mary Turner was lynched, had vacated their homes at least temporarily. Even trying to escape could be dangerous. The same story reported that on Wednesday morning Dixon Smith picked up a man who was walking through the woods, concerned that he had no particular destination and thinking that he might be Johnson's elusive accomplice. The man protested his innocence, saying that he was from Adel (up the road from Valdosta) and knew nothing about events further south. Local authorities kept him in jail nevertheless.[31] If leaving was dangerous, staying could be worse. The situation had become so volatile, the *Savannah Morning News* stated on May 23, that Valdosta Circuit Judge W. E. Thomas wired Governor Hugh M. Dorsey for help. Dorsey responded promptly, declaring martial law and offering a reward of five hundred dollars for the capture of any person involved in a lynch mob. The governor then contacted Major Beirne Gordon, of Savannah's newly formed Chatham Home Guard, instructing him to prepare his troops for dispatch. The Savannah paper did its best to cast the 150 men as heroes riding to the rescue, but the hastily assembled, ragtag group used donated weapons and had few uniforms among them (they tied red cloth around their arms to distinguish themselves). Nevertheless, Home Guard members interviewed before leaving longed "for a touch of real warfare" in Valdosta.[32]

The Expected Outcome

Savannah's Home Guard missed the battle by a couple of hours. By the time they pulled into town around 1:30 Thursday morning, the *Savannah Morning News* said, they found it "quiet as the proverbial church mouse."[33] In the meantime, the spectacle lynching of Sidney Johnson had ranged the full length of Valdosta. Local news reports state that around 10:45 p.m. Wednesday, Valdosta Police Chief Calvin Dampier led his brother, a patrolman, onto the porch of a house on South and Troup streets (different from Troupville Road), where a local black resident reported Johnson to be hiding. Patrolman Dampier kicked in the front door and met a shotgun that he knocked out of the way just as it fired, wounding both the chief and himself. At the same time, the *Quitman Free Press* said, hundreds of men from surrounding counties who had been hiding out nearby began firing their rifles into the house. Miraculously, none of the bullets hit the chief or his brother, but most of them got Sidney Johnson. His coat, delivered to police headquarters later, was "shot to shreds and covered with brains," according to the *Savannah Morning News*. Several hundred other people joined the melee (forming "an orderly crowd," the paper said), and waited for the gunfire to cease. When it seemed safe to proceed, someone went inside to remove Johnson's body and tie it to the back of a car. The crowd and its trophy then paraded up Valdosta's main thoroughfare, Patterson Street, to the wooded outskirts of town. From there it took a northwest turn back to Barney and the Old Camp Ground Church, where some of the other men had met their fate. Mob members placed Johnson's remains on a fat pine stump, saturated them with oil, and then, according to the Savannah papers, "cremated" him. Chief Dampier expressed regret to reporters, claiming that he and his brother had gone to the house only to arrest Johnson, but that Johnson had fired first, and they had to defend themselves. Putting a positive spin on events, Dampier noted that the killing was not done in mob fashion.[34]

With the Black Terror threat eliminated, local whites responded with denial and deflection. News reports pointed fingers at outsiders, blacks themselves, and of course, Huns. What the *Quitman Free Press* could not rationalize in terms of brutality, it minimized in terms of numbers. Other papers reported five or more people lynched, when only four had died; what happened was led by a "comparatively small" vigilance committee made up of no more than "forty or fifty men"–not a mob. Only six of them had "examined the Head negro and obtained the detailed confession," the *Free Press* editorial continued, but those who got out of control, played games with corpses, and took home souvenirs had come in from adjoining counties. Other Georgia papers had blown the case out of proportion, the *Free Press* argued. There was no "intense feeling among white and black" in Brooks County, and in fact, "a great many negroes visited the scenes of the lynchings Saturday and Sunday."[35] The paper neglected to mention that those scenes of lynching drove right through their neighborhoods. The *Valdosta Times* responded with a similar mixture of denial and blame, claiming, "There has been no . . . lynching here, and not the slightest bit of friction between whites and blacks." But if any lynching did occur, those outside Lowndes County were responsible: both "Smith's murderer and the members of the posse hunting him all came from Brooks County." Lowndes also provided a different picture of Brooks's "serious men" who, it said, "lacked the organization and leadership that was needed to make a success of the work they had undertaken." Johnson never would have been caught if not for Valdosta's Chief Dampier, the paper explained.[36] Area papers agreed on one thing: blacks were ultimately at fault for the violence. The *Daily Observer* put matters into clear terms: "If the world wants to know how much longer the American people are to tolerate lynchings, we will answer it frankly: As long as they have to tolerate rape." Locals do not hate blacks, the editors continued, as long as they remain in their place – namely, "a good laborer, and a good servant." When blacks go beyond the boundaries set for them, they "stir quiet, peaceful citizens to violent actions." In this particular instance, they may have had outside help. Not only might Germans have encouraged blacks to disrupt farm operations, but they also might have encouraged raping and killing. The paper did recommend a solution to the race problem: a "detention camp where they [blacks] could be interned before they commit these crimes."[37]

Enclosing and putting away seemed to be the correct move for recent events, at least according to local papers. After the initial flurry of editorializing, public silence prevailed for the next ninety years. The official lynching story was over for those who had the power to construct and tell it openly, if only to justify their actions to themselves. In the Brooks-Lowndes version, a white man was murdered and his pregnant wife attacked. The blacks responsible posed a threat not only to the Smith family but also to the social order. White men eliminated that threat and sent a message about the fatal consequences of challenging power dynamics in the Jim Crow South, even through such seemingly minor actions as speaking one's mind. Such a story, as foreign to contemporary audiences as a skulking Hun, was truth to most white Georgians, and to many white Americans, in 1918. Other versions, other truths – including lynching's power to traumatize victims, bystanders, and perpetrators alike – did not fit the more compelling narrative that the daily newspapers reinforced and thus went ignored. Only an equally compelling narrative could intervene, and antilynching protesters were busy searching for one that might work.

Grassroots Protest and Appeals to American Values

Local silence corresponded with remonstration from outside, much of it originating in Augusta. White individuals and black organizations sent protests to state newspapers that circulated nationally. The first came, unexpectedly, from a former Civil War major, Georgia Bar Association president, and state legislator, Joseph B. Cumming. Cumming's May 21,

1918, letter to the editor of the white-run *Augusta Chronicle* later ran (in whole or part) in the black-run *Atlanta Independent, Savannah Tribune,* and *New York Age* (Appendix 3). The black press also ran a resolution that an Augusta group, the Colored Welfare League, sent to Governor Dorsey (Appendix 4). Signing the document were Jacob H. Dorset, president; E. A. Lyons, secretary; R. B. West, assistant secretary; and T. H. Dwelle, chairman, Committee on Resolutions. Dorsey's response to these men set off a debate about black responsibility for lynching that was widely publicized in both the black and white press. Drawing less immediate attention, but perhaps having more long-term impact for its connection to a later group, the Anti-Lynching Crusaders, was a resolution by Georgia's Colored Federated Clubs (Appendix 5). Educator and civil rights activist Lucy Craft Laney, also based in Augusta, coordinated the protest.[38] Laney's plan involved a day of fasting and prayer along with a model petition, reprinted in black newspapers across the state, that clubs forwarded to Governor Dorsey and President Wilson. Taken together, writings from Joseph B. Cumming, the Colored Welfare League, and the Colored Federated Clubs encapsulate a broad range of public outcry that appeared nationally in newspapers during the weeks following the Brooks-Lowndes incident, offering an important focal point for antilynching discourse during and after World War I. This writing did not emerge from a vacuum, nor did it enter one. The skewed ideal of nation founded upon the violent expulsion of blacks that one sees in *Birth of a Nation* blended with Woodrow Wilson's vision of a more democratic world to create a ripe environment for Augusta's protests to do their cultural work. These writings called upon a variety of rhetorical strategies popular at the time but eventually coalesced around a central theme. Lynching, especially that of a woman, contradicted the very values Americans claimed to stand for and defend abroad. From the Augustas of America, from grassroots protests occurring across the country, emerged the foundational tropes that would play a significant role in future antilynching arguments.

Appeals to Humanity

Early responses to the Brooks-Lowndes case took three forms. The first was an appeal to notions of humanity. Cumming's letter was particularly detailed and poignant in this regard. He distinguished between Turner's humanity and that of her lynchers, referring to her as a "poor abject negro woman" and them as "hot fiends from hell." He asked readers to sympathize with her plight, directing them specifically to "look at this picture." Mary Turner had little or no choice in her response to her husband's lynching but to blurt out unwise remarks. Her pain was such that she had no recourse to "silence," to "terms of Christian forgiveness," or even to phrases from "fine old pagan philosophers." Cumming argued that mob members did have choices, however. They could have exercised "calm, righteous, and judicial judgment" in the face of Turner's agony. By not doing so, they forsook their roles as men of honor to become "detestable murderers and cowards" instead. Cumming's words reversed a major assumption upon which lynching rested at the time: those who commit the act served justice and defended honor, and those acted upon were less than human and worthy of punishment. Cumming made clear that Turner's death was not justice, but murder. Those who killed her were not heroes (in contrast to the soldiers he referred to later), but cowards. These men were so afraid of a woman's words that they had to kill her. Resolutions from the Colored Welfare League and the Colored Federated Clubs used language similar to Cumming's, without focusing attention on the lynchers' lack of humanity. The men of Augusta's Welfare League juxtaposed "the horrible and barbarous act" against the "millions of bruised hearts," while club women explained that "unwarranted lawlessness" has led them to be "discouraged and crushed by a spirit of humiliation and dread." The differences in these texts may have been one of audience. The resolutions, unlike Cumming's letter to the editor of a supportive newspaper, went to Georgia's governor Hugh Dorsey and President Woodrow Wilson, men who were at best ambivalent about lynching and would not be won over through association with "hot fiends from hell."

Editorials about the Brooks-Lowndes lynching in the black press took a more radical approach to the discussion of blacks' humanity and whites' lack of it. "Sidney Johnson died a man," said the *Baltimore Daily Herald*. "He knew that he could expect neither justice nor mercy from the woman killers and turned upon them at bay determined to sell his life as dearly as he could." His attackers, the *Herald*'s editorial writers (like Cumming) pointed out in a different article, made choices that relegated them to a category different from "men."[39] "Murderers are always cowards, cowards are always liars, and mob murderers are the lowest of the species," explained an article titled "Lying Follows Lynching."[40] An article from the *Chicago Defender* similarly opposed the "gang of white heathens" to the heroic actions of Hayes and Mary Turner: Hayes for overpowering Hampton Smith in a fight, and Mary for refusing to work for Smith without being paid, a version of the story that did not appear in state and local papers. The *Defender*'s rhetoric of heroism extended to all of the local black community. After the lynchings, the article stated, black women "employed at various occupations in the community failed to show up for work," dozens of citizens had put up their property for sale, and still more were contemplating moving to other parts of the country. The article emphasized multiple forms of resistance – fighting back with labor, fists, and feet.[41] An editorial from an unnamed newspaper found in the NAACP files echoed this latter response. "Georgia's Latest Contribution to Civilization and World Democracy" explained that the best way to assert one's humanity was to join the Great Migration. What are Brooks County blacks going to do, it asked. "Are they going to remain in a county and state in which . . . they are brutalized, terrorized, and their women strung up and butchered like cattle? Every Negro in Brooks County should seek a home immediately in a state where the lynching of Negroes is not looked upon as a pastime."[42] African Americans had options for asserting their humanity under the most oppressive conditions, these articles argued, and leaving was distinctly preferable to being killed.

Appeals to State and Divine Justice

Antilynching rhetoric relied upon strategies beyond juxtapositions between human victims and fiendish, cowardly mobs. Activists appealed to ideas of right and wrong on both the state and divine levels. Cumming's letter drew passionately upon these notions. In a catalog of queries still cited in accounts of Turner's lynching today, he asked, "Where are the grand juries? Where are the petit juries? Where are the sheriffs? Where is public opinion? Is it dead?" and then cried out, "God in heaven have mercy upon us! Let the governor if he will do no more proclaim a day of deepest humiliation and most earnest prayer in which we may plead humbly and agonizingly with the All Father, who dreadful thought, has said, 'Vengeance is mine.'" Cumming's words traveled between this world and the next. He expressed frustration over the lack of legal protection against – and, by implication, over community support for – lynching. If public opinion was dead, then so was the state apparatus. Yet he found consolation with the All Father, who had more powerful tools than the governor at his disposal (mercy, vengeance). The trick lay in getting one of these authority figures to help, as both apparently must be prayed to and pleaded with. Ultimately, however, Cumming put his trust in the people, in the "us" and "we" who must do the praying and pleading, the ones he sought to persuade in the first place. Those white readers – since he directed his letter to the *Augusta Chronicle*'s main audience – were the public whose moribund opinion he attempted to resurrect. They needed to seek God's mercy rather than his vengeance if they continued to allow such lynchings as Mary Turner's. Cumming's letter took a leap of faith, convincing himself that white Georgians who controlled the sheriffs' offices, the petit juries, and the grand juries could or would do something about lynching.

The Colored Welfare League's petition to Dorsey drew upon language similar to Cumming's, asking that the governor do something specific: "Therefore, we do earnestly urge an expression from you as our Chief Executive of the state." Such a response was imperative, given "the disregard of the courts and the laws in all lynchings." The resolution's multiple points directed Dorsey toward the kind of expression that he might make: one that praised black citizenship, condemned lynching, and chastised the court and the law for disregarding their roles. Dorsey circulated his response among white-owned newspapers in the same way that the Colored Welfare League had sent its petition to the black press. Dorsey's reply, twice as long as the original resolution, chastised the Colored Welfare League for not reminding peers that "lynching is an evil which can only be effectively suppressed by removing the aggravating cause," which he later pinpointed as "personal outrages against helpless women and children." Dorsey, who did not claim to support lynching but to understand its motivations, explained to the League that as long as good citizens like them continued to tolerate "the lawless among them," then "unspeakable crimes" would continue.[43] The *Atlanta Constitution* took Dorsey's words as gospel, recommending that they "be framed as the golden text in every lodge room frequented by the negro organizations whose purpose is the protection and advancement of their race."[44] No record exists of the League's reply to Dorsey (if one was made), but the response from the black press was uniform outrage. The *New York Age* reprinted samples of indignation from across the country, and closed in contempt: "So much, then, for this crime against the State of Georgia, against society, against humanity, and against God." Even though the *Atlanta Independent* disagreed with Dorsey, the paper encouraged optimism. An article titled "Might Against Right" argued that readers must keep faith in state and divine authority, despite the "great orgies that took place in Brooks and Lowndes." "We must not dash hope," author J. W. Davison wrote. "We must still look forward to the future."[45]

Back in Augusta, leaders of the Colored Federated Clubs kept faith in specific powers: God, the president, and black women's organizing abilities. A multifaceted effort called upon women "to unite in service of humiliation and prayer as a protest against the awful lynchings that recently disgraced our state, especially that of Mary Turner." Club women did not just fall to their knees; they also circulated the resolution that each forwarded to Governor Dorsey and President Woodrow Wilson. At least two, Savannah's Toussaint L'Ouverture Branch of the American Red Cross and the Colored Women of Macon, advertised their participation in the newspaper. Like Cumming and the Colored Welfare League, the club women appealed to state authority. They praised the many services black citizens performed for the state and nation (laboring in field and swamp, giving lives in defense of the country), recalled "principles held sacred by every true American," and closed with a heartfelt appeal for the leader to use his power to make a difference: "We therefore are asking that you use all the power of your great office to prevent similar occurrences and punish the perpetrators of this foul deed and urge that sure and swift justice be meted out to them." The women's words received less publicity than those of their male counterparts with Augusta's Colored Welfare League. Governor Dorsey issued no public response. President Wilson replied through his secretary J. P. Tumulty that he would bring the matter to the attorney general's attention, but nothing came of it.[46] The petition may or may not have influenced Wilson's public condemnation of mob violence later that summer. One thing is clear, however; their organizing strategies laid important groundwork for future women's activism. The resolution made its way to the National Association of Club Women Conference that June in Denver, where the larger body made antilynching legislation part of its organizational mission.[47] Many NACW members would revisit Turner's story in 1922 when, as Anti-Lynching Crusaders, they made her the centerpiece of fundraising efforts for the Dyer Bill to make lynching a federal crime.[48]

Appeals to Patriotism

The push to cast lynching as a national issue, worthy of federal intervention, began well before 1922. Activists quickly capitalized on the irony of U.S. presence overseas, fighting "to make the world safe for democracy," while African Americans were not safe in their own homes. Each of these Turner protests – like others during and immediately after World War I – made directly patriotic appeals. Such arguments, rooted in core American ideals and values, became the most popular to emerge from early responses. Huns massacre women and children, editorials pointed out again and again; Americans do not. The petitions to Dorsey made sure to include blacks within their constructions of citizenship. The club women stated that "our sons and husbands are giving their lives in defense of the country we all love so dearly," and that in every instance "the Negro" has come forward to defend "the principles held sacred by every true American." Again, the next paragraph made an important contrast, playing off other rhetorical tensions that give these petitions their power. Lynching, an "iniquitous institution," presumably did not count among those sacred principles. The Colored Welfare League noted that patriotic duty included more than fighting. African Americans, it explained, "are faithfully and cheerfully doing our part on the battle front, in the training camps, in the purchasing of thrift stamps and liberty bonds, in Red Cross membership, in food production and conservation and in all other ways of good citizenship." The League argued that Dorsey should be doing something about the barbarous acts committed against such good citizens. Dorsey's later response to them turned that argument on its head, pointing toward these documents' need for other significant appeals in addition to patriotism. Dorsey, of course, was a politician, keeping his job as governor of the state leading the nation in the number of lynchings at the time. He could not be expected to respond differently. The retired – and white – Major Cumming, conversely, could say to other white people what Dorsey and the petitioners could not. His letter closed with a plea that sounded a lot like a warning. His appeal to the "All Father" was not for help, but for mercy, to ward off any vengeance that might be deflected from Turner's actual lynchers to "our dear boys, who with negro comrades in arms, have gone to fight for the betterment of the world."

The editorials that responded to the Brooks-Lowndes lynching often emphasized its impact upon the war. Troop morale was especially important. "Georgia's Latest Contribution to Civilization and World Democracy" posed a question about Mary Turner: "Perhaps that woman has a son or brother in the trenches in France or in preparation to go to fight for the freedom of white races. What will be his feelings and the feelings of his comrades and friends when they learn of the freedom granted her?"[49] Another issue was not morale, for black troops were proving themselves quite capable soldiers, but the sheer impudence of a nation that would ask them to fight abroad for principles left undefended at home. An article from the *Houston Observer*, "'Over Here' and 'Over There,'" contrasted two stories, one about the Brooks-Lowndes lynchings and another about two black soldiers in France who fought off twenty Germans to save their regiment. The article provided an extended examination of conditions "here" and "there." To establish the general outline, it claims, "'Over here' democracy is a theoretical preachment, while 'over there' democracy is a practicality." More specifically, the article explains, "'Over here' white Americans (?) are lynching, maltreating, jimcrowing, segregating, disfranchising and treating with contempt and contumely black Americans of both sexes; while 'over there' black Americans are pouring out their life's blood for the protection and safety of their white and black brothers and sisters" (punctuation in original).[50] Other editorials went beyond troop morale. Lynching affected labor and industry. A *New York Post* editorial argued that mob violence undermined the war effort by dislocating black farm workers who fled from volatile areas like Brooks and Lowndes: "Few people realize how critical is the labor situation in the South, or how it is going to affect certain crops if the supply is not conserved." Furthermore, the *Post* continued, lynching "degrades us to the Prussian level and makes it the more difficult for Americans to hold the Germans up to scorn for their crimes against humanity."[51] The Memphis *Commercial Appeal* expressed similar sentiments. Lynching hurts the allied cause by damaging our international reputation, the paper stated, and more pointedly, it's "bad business."[52]

One of the most compelling patriotic appeals cast lynching during a time of war as treason. A group called the Tennessee Law and Order

League, spearheaded by a Memphis attorney named Bolton Smith, broadened that line of argument with the NAACP well before the 1918 lynchings and redoubled its efforts afterward.[53] Shortly after the incident, another state organization, the Tennessee Conference of Charities and Corrections, petitioned President Wilson and Congress to declare acts of mob violence "crimes against the nation." An editorial from the *Advocate* reprinted the petition in full, agreeing with its two central assumptions. First, "such occurrences are incompatible with the principles of justice and democracy for which we are fighting." And, second, lynching increased racial tensions and struck "at the very root of our national solidarity and efficiency."[54] In an editorial titled "The Georgia Horrors," the *New York Sun* suggested that Wilson make Georgia safe for democracy. If the United States felt compelled to intervene abroad, the *Sun* asked, after seeing the atrocities in Brooks and Lowndes counties, why not intervene there? The *Houston Observer* made a similar observation. Desperate times call for desperate measures, the paper said, and times of war allow a president more leeway. Georgia led the way "when it comes to acts and deeds more brutal and heinous than the German atrocities," and President Wilson had the power to put a stop to the violence. "Will he perform such a patriotic and democratic act? God grant that he will and that at once!" the *Observer* demanded.[55] If Wilson was not willing to help, other parties were. Later that summer, stockholders of the *San Antonio Express* established a fund of one hundred thousand dollars that would go toward investigating and prosecuting lynching. Raised after "the lynching orgy in South Georgia," the money would "bring to justice such offenders against the peace, dignity, and morality of the Nation, States, and communities."[56] If the proper authorities had the right information, the logic went, then surely their basic sense of human compassion and justice would compel them to act. After all, this was America.

Walter White's Investigation and Its Aftermath

Enter Walter White. His main reason for going to South Georgia in late June might not have been to check out the story of a mass lynching with a female victim. He might have been looking for Huns. Before Sidney Johnson was killed, the NAACP wrote Governor Dorsey to protest the previous weekend's violence and urge him to prevent further problems in the area. The May 20 telegram, copied to the Chamber of Commerce in Atlanta, the Board of Trade in Savannah, and national papers as a press release, replicated both the appeals to state power and patriotism of other protest efforts. "The eyes of the nation are now fixed upon Georgia to see whether your state will vindicate her laws and insist upon legal punishment of those who have defied her courts and flaunted their disregard for due process," NAACP Secretary John Shillady said to Dorsey. By not upholding U.S. law during a time of war, Shillady said, echoing the current newspaper rhetoric, Georgia was guilty of treason.[57] The NAACP changed tactics a few days later after reports of German spies emerged from Valdosta. Blacks themselves might be guilty of treason, a potential public relations disaster. On May 24, 1918, White wrote to a former colleague, John Salmon, at Atlanta's Standard Life Insurance Company to ask if the rumors might be true. White asked Salmon, whose sales territory included Brooks and Lowndes counties, for specifics: names, dates, and activities of anyone who might be sympathizing with Germans.[58] Salmon's response to White does not survive, but the words of a man that White names among the mob's ringleaders do. According to S. E. McGowan, the Germans had nothing to do with what happened: "If [they] were as thick as the grass in the courthouse yard the same thing would be done again."[59] Salmon seems to be the most likely source for the list of the African American contacts White had when he drove into Brooks County. While there, he met with Samuel S. Broadnax, a Quitman minister; Maurice Cobb, a Quitman doctor; and Athens N. Grant, a Thomasville doctor. These men put him in touch with a key informant, George Spratling. Spratling worked for McGowan, a local white undertaker, and operated independently as an undertaker in the area's black communities.[60] He apparently witnessed several deaths, including Hayes and Mary Turner's, after mob members coerced him to drive. Spratling named the mob's leaders, and White talked with at least two of them, McGowan and local merchant William A. Whipple. Whipple's account of the story left White stunned.[61] Spratling gave him details, but he did not render them gleefully, as Whipple did. The investigator left town shortly afterward, ready to report on what he learned. After White visited Quitman, rumors about Huns ceased to matter. His version of events ultimately became the story's dominant narrative, superseding previous news and protest accounts. Although White changed the way Turner's death was remembered, he and the NAACP did not single-handedly change antilynching discourse with this case. The significance of his accomplishment lies in the refocusing of grassroots rhetoric for a broader audience through the skillful manipulation of facts not previously reported.

White had been working the NAACP's antilynching beat about six months when the Brooks-Lowndes story broke. National Field Secretary James Weldon Johnson recruited him out of Atlanta. White had cofounded an NAACP branch office there in 1917 with his boss at Standard Life, Harry Pace, and other employees. Johnson reportedly heard White give a speech and was so impressed that he offered the twenty-four-year-old, on the spot, one hundred dollars a month to work for the national organization in New York. White accepted, even though it meant taking a pay cut, and moved north in January 1918.[62] One of his first assignments was investigating the lynching of Jim McIlherron in Estill Springs, Tennessee. Oswald Garrison Villard, founding member and treasurer of the NAACP, provided White with press credentials from his paper, the *New York Evening Post*, so that he could impersonate a reporter. Walter White's fair coloring helped the investigator pass for Caucasian, and his southern accent made him seem less of an outsider. In his memoir, *A Man Called White*, and an article for H. L. Mencken's *American Mercury*, "I Investigate Lynchings," White described a modus operandi developed in Estill Springs and perfected later that year in South Georgia.[63] He would enter the town on some pretext or another; spend time chatting with the locals at barbershops, stores, or places where men gathered; and gradually bring the subject around to the recent lynchings. He found locals eager to brag about what they had done. As he stated in the *American Mercury* piece, "Like most boastful people who practice direct action when it involves no personal risk, they just can't help talk about their deeds to any person who manifests even the slightest interest in them."[64] Once he gained the locals' confidence, he met with mob members, visited sites, and learned details that had gone unreported. The NAACP, in turn, publicized facts hoping to prosecute mob members, change public opinion about lynching, and fundraise for further antilynching efforts.

Along with Ida B. Wells, whose truth-telling strategies White borrowed if he did not always credit, the NAACP man was one of the best. He had one clear advantage over Wells: he could pass as Caucasian. Her advantage was an actual, not an imaginary, weapon like White describes in his *American Mercury* article.[65] The story started out in Whipple's general store. White explained how he chatted for a few minutes, then brought up recent events. Whipple offered his guest a Coca-Cola, pulled up a box for him to sit on, and started mouthing off about states' rights, disenfranchisement, and lynching bees. White joined in the tirade with his own question about "the niggers." Eventually Whipple told the whole story. He expressed pride in his role, calling Mary Turner's lynching "the best show, Mister, I ever did see," and exclaiming, "You ought to have heard the wench howl when we strung her up." White choked back the nausea while he listened to Whipple recount what happened. He had no choice: his life at that moment and other lives in the future depended on it. White stuck around a few more days, talking to locals and visiting specific sites. By the third day of his visit, residents grew suspicious about all his snooping around. Whipple confronted him: "You're a government man, ain't you?" White neither affirmed nor denied the accusation. Later that evening, a black man approached him to say that he had overheard some whites saying "something would happen" to him if he stayed in town overnight. Believing the man was sent to scare him, White tried a bluff, saying he had a "damned good automatic" and knew how to use it. Despite his bold façade, White was terrified, as he explained later. He stayed in town for two more days, his every movement watched, and went to bed without taking off his clothes.[66]

White did not rest easily for a couple of weeks. On July 9 he sent a letter to John Shillady on Standard Life letterhead. White said that he arrived in Atlanta safely after traveling through Macon, Albany, and Athens to raise money for the Anti-Lynching Fund. He told Shillady that he enjoyed his trip "with some exceptions, the latter named at Quitman, Georgia."[67] His visit to the area was successful, however, yielding more information than previous press reports revealed. White was preparing a description of the incident for delivery to Georgia's governor Hugh M. Dorsey the following day. White made good on the promise. The next day he used Villard's press passes again, this time without permission, to ease his way into Dorsey's office with a detailed report, "Memorandum for Governor Dorsey from Walter F. White," in hand. Villard was furious, but other organization members admired White's chutzpah.[68] After all, the whole point of his visit was to enlist the help of people like Dorsey. The former prosecutor in the 1915 Leo Frank case remained publicly ambivalent about lynching. During the heat of violence, he declared martial law and offered a five-hundred-dollar reward for anyone who could identify mob members. A week later he told Augusta's Colored Welfare League that lynching would stop when blacks took responsibility for "the unspeakable outrages apparently committed by members of your own race." For the NAACP, here was the lynching debate in microcosm. Getting a high-profile fence-sitter like Dorsey to change his mind would be a significant coup. In addition, providing a list of ringleaders' names to a man who had posted a bounty on mob members might lead to prosecution in this case and legal precedent for others. All Walter White thought he needed to do was give Dorsey a full account of what really happened in Brooks and Lowndes in May. Maybe then the governor would reconsider his opinions about unspeakable outrages committed by members of one's own race.

White's "Memorandum" focuses on significant details that earlier accounts had missed, gotten wrong, or omitted, and set in motion a months-long, highly public attempt to initiate a state or federal investigation (Appendix 6). White brackets the report with lists of victims and perpetrators. He identifies eleven victims, more than previous news stories but fewer than some estimates: Will Head, Will Thompson, Hayes Turner, Mary Turner, Eugene Rice, Chime Riley, Sidney Johnson, Simon Schuman, and three unidentified bodies. Rumors that eighteen people died in the melee may have stemmed from a local urban legend that mob members planned to kill that many because one white man's life equaled those of eighteen blacks. Who actually died remains confusing because of earlier news accounts. Christopher Meyers, in "'Killing Them By the Wholesale,'" lists Julius Jones – who may have been the infamous "Black Trouble"– among the men killed during the weekend, but newspapers never actually report his death. A man named Julius Brown (who may have been Jones and whose aliases were also listed as Shorty Ford and Edmund Pipkin) was picked up in July and brought back to Quitman, never to be heard from again. White adds Simon Schuman to his list because he, too, was picked up and never heard from again. The alleged confession given by Jones/Brown/Ford/Pipkin accused Schuman of driving Sidney Johnson's getaway car.[69]

In addition to naming victims, White gives what information he has about mob members:

S. E. McGowan, Undertaker, Quitman
W. A. Whipple, Cotton Broker and Merchandise Dealer, Quitman
Ordley Yates, Post Office Clerk

Frank Purvis, Griffin Furniture Company

Fulton DeVane, Agent, Standard Oil Company

Richard DeVane, Farmer, Quitman

Ross DeVane, Farmer, Quitman

Lee Sherrill, Farmer, Near Quitman

Brown Sherrill, Employed by W. A. Whipple

Jim Dickson, Farmer, Quitman

—— Chalmers, Farmer, Quitman

—— Van, Barker, Quitman

Dixon Smith, Brother of Hampton Smith

Will Smith, Brother of Hampton Smith

Two other brothers of Hampton Smith

White gets a few details wrong. Dixon Smith is actually Hampton's father. According to Brooks County probate records, the murder victim had four brothers: Will, Thomas, Walter, and Robert. The man that White identifies as "Ordley" Yates was most likely Quitman resident Audley Yates. Despite such minor mistakes, the list points to identifiable, traceable figures with established homes and businesses in Brooks County. Additionally, White situates his list as authoritative, explaining to Dorsey that he received these names from one of the men on it. The picture he paints of his informant is very different from the *American Mercury* piece he would write later, where his source spoke with braggadocio: "These names were given to me in confidence by a man . . . on the condition that I would not divulge his name, as to do so would cause him a great deal of embarrassment, and probably death." The memorandum's tone points to violent conspiracy, not cracker "show," as Whipple had put it.

Playing off of, and often contradicting, earlier news accounts, the "Memorandum" devotes considerable elaboration to the Smiths and their fate. White does not deny that Sidney Johnson murdered Hampton Smith, but the latter was no innocent victim. His reputation for beating and cheating his employees kept him short of good labor. Johnson was one of the workers he often secured by paying their court fines and keeping them on the plantation until they paid off the debt, a pervasive problem in the area at the time.[70] Johnson refused to work one day, Smith whipped him, and Johnson retaliated. According to White, multiple sources confirmed that Johnson claimed to have worked alone. No one else lynched knew anything about the crime until after he committed it. A primary focus of White's report is Mrs. Smith. She gets as much space

as Sidney Johnson and twice as much as her husband. White takes great
pains, through tortured syntax, to refute any claim that she was raped.
Two simple, declarative sentences begin and end her section, however:
"Her wounds are not serious," and "Mrs. Smith gave birth to her child."
In between, White works his way circuitously around bullet trajectories,
months until delivery, and physicians' opinions about whether a gun-
shot to the chest, rough treatment, and rape could lead to miscarriage. "I
have been infromed [*sic*] by the same physicians," White explains, "that
the shot alone would not necessarily cause a miscarriage, but that raping
or even rough handling would have caused such a condition." The gist:
Mrs. Smith delivered her baby, so she was not raped. Without saying so
directly, White builds a case that undermines Dorsey's argument against
the Colored Welfare League. Innocent black people died because a labor
dispute between a black man and a white man got out of hand, not because black criminals in Brooks and Lowndes counties ran amok.

After countering his opponent's claims with logic, as a good prosecutor like Dorsey would, White launches a powerful emotional attack.
The "Memorandum"'s next section moves from the Smiths' fate to the
Turners'. White describes how the mob captured Hayes as he was on
the way to Moultrie "for safe-keeping" and then hanged him "with his
hands hand-cuffed behind him." This portrayal of Turner as passive victim, innocent of the crime for which he was accused, mirrors in reverse
the portrayal of Smith as cruel landowner, culpable in the attack upon
his family. White's most significant parallel operates between Mrs. Smith
and Mary Turner. Both women were pregnant, due near the same time.
Mrs. Smith was not raped, as news reports insinuated. Mrs. Turner, as
news reports never mentioned, was brutally tortured and mutilated. If
White's prose is convoluted in his section on Mrs. Smith, his description
of Turner's lynching is clear and graphic:

> At the time she was lynched, Mary Turner was in her eight [*sic*] month
> of pregnancy. Her ankles were tied together and she was hung to the tree
> head down. Gasoline was taken from the cars and poured on her clothing
> which was then fired. When her clothes had burned off, a sharp instrument
> was taken and she was cut open in the middle, her stomach being entirely
> opened. Her unborn child fell from her womb, gave two cries, and was then
> crushed by the heel of a member of the mob. Her body was then riddled
> with bullets from high-powered rifles until it was no longer possible to recog-
> nize it as the body of a human being.

When one gets beyond the immediate, visceral horror of this account, White's use of passive verbs seems conspicuous. Turner's body forms most of these sentences' subjects, what happens to her constituting the terrible verbs: tied, hung, burned, cut, riddled. White uses only one active verb — fell — to direct readers' attention to the fetus's short journey from life outside the womb to death. Only once does he point, syntactically, to those responsible, when a mob member crushes the child under his heel. Conscious rhetorical decision or not, these actions stand out. And so does the information White provides next: the list of mob members' names that closes the document. Like his use of passive voice in describing Turner's lynching, White's "Memorandum for Governor Dorsey" works through indirection, yet powerfully. Dorsey should punish these men.

The NAACP did not stop with Governor Dorsey, however. Multiple groups — including, most recently, the Augusta contingent protesting the Brooks-Lowndes lynchings — had been lobbying President Woodrow Wilson for some time to speak out against racial violence. The organization took advantage of press reports that the president might actually do so to send him the information that White had gathered in Tennessee and Georgia.[71] On July 26, President Wilson issued a public condemnation. Mob activity, he said, had no place in a nation fighting a war for democracy. A recent increase in lynchings "has been a blow at the heart of ordered law and humane justice," and no one who truly loved America could in good conscience flout the law by engaging in extralegal killings. Furthermore, the president continued, lynching gave the nation's enemies fodder for propaganda. How can we argue for democracy when we do not protect our own citizens, he asked. Wilson expressed a clear, strong opinion: "I say plainly that every American who takes part in the action of a mob or gives it any sort of countenance is no true son of this great democracy, but its betrayer, and does more to discredit her by that single disloyalty to her standards of law and of right than the words of her statesmen or the sacrifices of her heroic boys in the trenches can do to make suffering peoples believe her to be their savior."[72]

Wilson stopped short of using the word "treason," as the Tennessee Law and Order League had urged, but his words served multiple purposes. Presidential backing of the antilynching cause was significant itself. Support from someone who previously had praised *The Birth of a Nation*'s truth offered an even more dramatic conversion than would a man like Dorsey's. The NAACP made sure to issue a press release designed to goad Dorsey into action. "The Association was gratified beyond measure at the recent magnificent pronouncement of President Wilson in condemnation of the mob spirit and lynching," the statement said. The three-page release continued by summarizing what happened in Brooks and Lowndes during May, specifically highlighting Mary Turner's death and reminding reporters that White had submitted the names of mob members to Governor Dorsey. The piece closed with a challenge to the state of Georgia to "measure up to President Wilson's great appeal" by putting a stop to lynching and prosecuting those responsible for the May events.[73]

Governor Dorsey, however, could not be persuaded. The material that White presented to him appeared for a while to soften the position that he had taken earlier, that lynchings would stop when black men stopped raping white women. In mid-August, Dorsey sent a telegram to the NAACP assuring them that he was doing everything in his power to bring the guilty parties to justice. But just one week later, he sent a second reply stating that there had been no results. His message – a terse, pro forma note with a stamped signature – gave the impression that he intended to have nothing further to do with the case.[74] Dorsey indeed made no future commentary specifically about the Brooks and Lowndes lynchings, despite continued pressure from the organization. One telegram referred to Wilson's statement against mob violence, stating, "Every mob murder is a direct body-blow at President Wilson, America, and democracy. Is Georgia with our President and America in fighting mob violence?" A letter referred to a *New York Times* report that the German press had been highlighting stories of American lynchings and pleaded with Dorsey to do something, if for nothing else, to help the war effort. "We cannot believe that the good people of Georgia are conscious of the irreparable injury which their neglect to stamp out lynching is inflicting upon the Nation's cause. The President of the United States must constantly be embarrassed by these lynchings which are occurring with too great frequency," John Shillady explained.[75] Dorsey's failure to respond led to near despair at NAACP offices. In early September the organization issued a press release stating that Wilson's proclamation obviously had no effect in places like Georgia, where mob violence continued unabated.[76] Still the fight against it continued. The NAACP never knew when hope might spring up in other places or a man like Dorsey might change his mind.

White and "The Work of a Mob"

Even if Dorsey did not come around, the NAACP knew that White's memorandum had other uses. A precedent existed. In July 1916 the organization had published a report of Jesse Washington's lynching as an eight-page *Crisis* supplement. Editor W. E. B. Du Bois shaped "The Waco Horror" from Elisabeth Freeman's investigative materials, along with photographer Fred Gildersleeve's images of the charred and mutilated body, to launch the NAACP's Anti-Lynching Campaign. The article's details meant to shock. The seventeen-year-old, mentally retarded Washington was tortured and burned beyond recognition before a crowd of ten thousand after being found guilty of raping and murdering his employer's wife. The accusations were probably false, Washington's defense was incompetent, and the violence was chilling. The distinction between mob and spectator was unclear. Onlookers beat and stabbed the boy on the way from the courthouse to the site of his lynching, and by the time he died, his body had been picked clean. After describing events in Waco in detail, Du Bois panned out for a larger perspective: "This is an account of one lynching . . . matched in horror by scores of others in the last thirty years." Du Bois's statistics totaled well beyond scores—2,843 men lynched to date. "What are we going to do about this record?" he asked, proposing the NAACP's Anti-Lynching Fund in response. "The civilization of America is at stake," Du Bois warned.[77] The NAACP put money behind his words. Thirty-eight thousand copies of "The Waco Horror" went out to *Crisis* subscribers, and another twelve thousand went to anyone who might provide funding, publicity, or legislative power. Afterward, Elisabeth Freeman went on a speaking tour to help fill the coffers. The organization was hoping for ten thousand dollars; they netted almost twelve thousand dollars. At the year's end, Chairman of the Board Joel Spingarn pronounced the Anti-Lynching Campaign a success: "By far the most striking achievement by the NAACP during 1916 has been to inject lynching into the public mind as something like a national problem."[78] Perhaps the Brooks-Lowndes incident might keep that equation fresh in public consciousness, especially after Wilson's public statements on the subject. For the September 1918 *Crisis*, White revised his report to Dorsey into "The Work of a Mob," which the NAACP made available as a pamphlet for general distribution.[79]

In the latter version, White had time to craft—to check spelling, tighten sentence structure, and sharpen the emotional appeal. His success lies in the crystallization of antilynching rhetoric, storytelling, detailed language, and grounding in multiple levels of authority. The "Memorandum" was bracketed with lists of victims' and perpetrators' names, but White frames the article with references to federal and state power. He starts out by saying that President Wilson's recent condemnation of mob violence surely resulted from the Brooks-Lowndes incident. He closes by saying that a list of mob members' names has been given to Governor Dorsey, and that the governor has promised to take action. The piece actually ends on Dorsey's words, in a speech given to the state legislature on July 3, 1918: "Mob violence should be suppressed, and by State authorities. If this is not done, it is very probable that Federal intervention will not be long delayed" (223). The irony is that by the time "The Work of a Mob" went to press, Dorsey had backed away from prosecutorial attempts. In retrospect, White's voice reads as if he is trying to will something into action. At the time of publication, however, the Brooks-Lowndes case carries the weight of state and national importance. This story matters as a representative, not an isolated, incident. Another significant authoritative element is the investigator himself. White notes on several occasions that his firsthand sources lie beyond question. In the paragraph describing Will Head's and Will Thompson's deaths, White explains, "The investigator learned from a man who admitted being in the mob, but who stated that he had no part in the lynching, the names of the two leaders of the Friday night mob and of fifteen other members" (221–22). White not only had insider information but also corroboration. Later on in the piece, he notes that "each detail given is not the statement of a single person" but the result of investigation and confirmation by multiple parties (223).

Establishing himself as an authority allows White to separate the facts he presents, which can seem unbelievable, from news reports that he claims to be untrue or misleading. He took a similar tack with Dorsey; here, however, the stakes involve a broad national audience. White announces near the beginning that press dispatches underestimated the number of people killed by half. He then debunks various conspiracy rumors. Sidney Johnson said multiple times while hiding out in Valdosta — not lurking in the swamps with some mythical monster named "Black Trouble" — that he acted alone. "Absolutely no evidence was found," White further states, of a German plot to foment rebellion among black farm workers in South Georgia (223). Such statements cut to the heart of lynching justifications in Brooks and Lowndes. Everyone killed, even Mary Turner, had allegedly played some role in the plot to kill Hampton Smith. White recasts them as innocent victims. But the most important myth of all to dispel was that Smith's wife had been raped. White distills his previously convoluted argument into a single paragraph to make the point stand out: "There seems to be no evidence that Mrs. Smith was raped in addition to being shot" (221). White reiterates that her wound is not serious and a recovery is expected. He does omit Mrs. Smith's pregnancy, a fact of which he was well aware, most likely because of its ability to detract attention from this story's core, Mary Turner's pregnancy. Unlike the "Memorandum," the goal is not to make all the facts known but to manipulate the right ones. The real brutes here are not black but white: Hampton Smith and the mob members who avenged his death. The most important fact that the papers left out, but White makes sure to include, was Smith's reputation as a landowner so cruel that few would work for him. He had once even whipped Mary Turner, White notes. Right before Johnson murdered him, Smith had refused him wages owed and beaten him, leading to Smith's own death.

White creates a powerful piece of journalism not only by establishing himself as a credible investigator. The information that he gleaned from his visit gives readers themselves a sense of being on the scene. White carefully selects what to describe in detail. Descriptions grow more explicit as the story moves forward, creating a sense of mounting tension. White also gauges parts of the narrative as more significant than others. Local newspapers had covered Will Head's lynching as a large spectacle affair, quoting his alleged "confession" and responses from mob members and giving the particulars of his death. "The Work of a Mob" lumps in Head's lynching with Will Thompson's as one of the first in the article, noting only that over seven hundred bullets were fired into the two men's bodies. Hayes Turner, next in the story, although not necessarily in the actual chronology, gets a full paragraph of over twenty lines. His lynching provides a context for Mary Turner's and therefore merits more detail. Sidney Johnson's story, which culminates the article, doubles the space of Hayes's. Because Johnson, as Hampton Smith's killer, was central to the case, White needs to elaborate on what national newspaper reports offered only in outline. Johnson's death provides the kinds of hard facts that readers should know. Sidney Johnson did not just die in a shootout with authorities. His body was castrated, "the amputated parts thrown into the streets," and he was dragged by car more than twenty miles down a main thoroughfare, and then set on fire (223). White also tells painful stories of men omitted entirely from mainstream newspaper reports. Chime Riley, said to have left town, was drowned. His hands and feet were tied together, and "turpentine cups, made of clay and used to catch the gum from the pine trees when 'chipped,' thus becoming very heavy, were tied to his body, [and] he was thrown into the Little River" (222–23). White's informant takes him to the spot where he thought Riley's body might wash up, but it never did. The informant showed him one of the cups that he found instead and kept as a souvenir.

The section to garner the most attention by far was Mary Turner's. White organizes the article specifically to do so. Mary Turner's lynching takes up more space than anyone else's, three paragraphs and more than fifty lines, occupying both the physical and narrative center of the piece. Other elements of the article build up to and lead away from this one. White illustrates Smith's cruelty as a landowner through Mary Turner. Hayes's lynching sets up Mary's response: "if she knew the names of the persons that lynched her husband, she would have warrants sworn out against them and have them punished in the courts." The men, in turn, decide to "teach her a lesson" (222). The article ends on a note of hope that Mary's wish will be granted: these men will receive due punishment through state or federal authorities. Before describing what happened, White prepares readers by warning them that what they will read is "revolting" and "horrible." He also notes that multiple witnesses have corroborated the details of this nearly unbelievable story. The physical description sets the stage: "a lonely and secluded spot, down a narrow road over which the trees touch the tops . . . with thick undergrowth on either side" (222). It was, in White's words, "a gloomy and appropriate spot for a lynching." His tone when describing her death mixes sentimentality, horror, and irony wrapped around outrage. Turner is a "grief-stricken and terrified woman," but her pregnant condition had "no effect on the tender feelings of the mob." After she is set on fire, she "writhed in agony" and the men "howled in glee." The article's emotional nadir soon follows. With Turner still alive, one mob member brings out a knife used for splitting hogs and cuts open her abdomen, and the baby inside falls to the ground: "The infant, prematurely born, gave two feeble cries and then its head was crushed by a member of the mob with its heel." The mob celebrates by firing a volley of bullets into Turner, "now mercifully dead," White states, "and the work was over" (222). His carefully chosen wording here – "work" – links readers to the article's title, "The Work of a Mob," and also to the labor issues that underlie these acts of mob violence. Everyone lynched in Brooks and Lowndes counties, including Mary Turner and her baby, died because of an argument over wages. Not a rape.

The parallels are significant. At all key points of this article – from the title, to its beginning and end, to its key middle scene and more – White creates links between lynching, economics, and power, especially state and federal power. The mob's work was over when it pumped hundreds of bullets into Mary Turner. Now Governor Dorsey has a job to do, White insists. If he does not succeed, then the federal government needs to step in. White uses Dorsey's own words in the exposé's closing quotation to argue that they should and to hope that they would. White also implies through his careful use of both graphic and sentimental details – the infant giving two feeble cries before a mob member crushes its head under his boot – that readers also have work to do. How could any thinking, feeling citizen read "The Work of a Mob" and not take action? Many did.

The Immediate and Enduring Results

The short-term effects of White's piece are relatively easy to chart by measuring what happened in the nation's centers of power against what happened in South Georgia's. For a brief time, unfortunately, Brooks and Lowndes proved stronger. Right after "The Work of a Mob" came out, the NAACP received a letter from Washington, D.C., lawyer C. P. Dam, who said that he had heard about the lynchings from his maid (whom he called an "upstanding colored woman"), and he wanted to help out with prosecution efforts. Dam later made contact with Senator William S. Kenyon from Iowa, who said that he would be willing to hold a congressional hearing into the events if the NAACP's witness would substantiate the story in person.[80] The NAACP had been working on the black undertaker George Spratling since White's visit, offering him protection and financial help in relocating if he would come forward with what he knew. James Weldon Johnson, White's immediate supervisor, recalls in his autobiography coming down to interview Spratling that fall. Johnson met Spratling at a restaurant that his mother owned, where he told Johnson that he would not testify and leave the woman at the mercy of the lynchers. During their conversation, Johnson recalls that a car full of white men pulled up, ordered Spratling outside, and asked him what his visitor was doing in town. The cover, as arranged by Dr. Grant, was to say that Johnson was taking subscriptions for a colored newspaper. The men told Spratling to keep his "damned mouth shut," which is clearly what he did. Without getting any further details from the witness, Johnson left Quitman that afternoon, stating in his autobiography that he did not feel safe until he was in Florida.[81]

The next time someone needed to go to Quitman to talk to Spratling, the horrified Johnson sent White. In the company of Rev. Broadnax and Dr. Grant, Spratling told White again what he knew, but he refused to go north and leave his family behind, despite repeated NAACP assurances that everyone would be protected physically and financially. Efforts continued until at least November, when White returned, undercover, to meet with Spratling again. The two men spoke for about an hour, with Spratling under a doctor's care for influenza. He declined to help the NAACP further, stating that he was responsible for the care of five children, his wife having died in July, and he feared for the life of his children if he left. He also noted that since the events of May, people other than Simon Schuman had disappeared after being called from their homes by the mob. Spratling also claimed financial hardship: it would be impossible for him to dispose of his property at that time without great strain. Spratling's claims had merit. Real estate records reveal that he owned several lots in south Quitman, with each of them mortgaged through financial help from his boss, S. E. McGowan, whom he had identified as a mob member.[82] Spratling suffered more immediate forms of duress. By that November, word had circulated locally about "The Work of a Mob." A memo to C. P. Dam from the NAACP states that Spratling had been threatened by a white man, an ex–police officer, who told him that it was a shame for such lies to have been published. After that, Spratling never budged. White even tried to bully him emotionally, telling him that he would release the names of mob members and put his life in danger anyway, so he might as well talk. Spratling still refused. Broadnax called him a "hard case," and a letter from Grant in December reiterated that he would provide no further information. Spratling was not the only one. Other letters mention different eyewitnesses who also refused to come forward because they feared retribution against themselves and their families.[83] Without local cooperation, prosecution efforts barely stood a chance.

The NAACP's case against mob members unraveled on the national level as well. A series of miscommunications between C. P. Dam, Senator Kenyon, and John Shillady left the parties with a degree of mutual mistrust. The situation grew so confused that someone prepared for the NAACP files a timeline of correspondence trying to sort out who said what to whom. Dam had mistakenly told Shillady that Kenyon would help with protection and financial provisions for the witness; Kenyon later sent Shillady a letter adamantly stating that this was untrue. "I feel outraged as a citizen by this lynching and I would like to get to the bottom of it," he said, "but the evidence will have to be furnished me without my going to any expense."[84] Shillady apologized, assuring Kenyon that "we had no intention of asking you to do more than [get to the bottom of the matter], which is a good deal. All expenditures will cheerfully be borne from our Anti-Lynching Fund subscribed by public spirited citizens for the purpose of combating this monster disloyalty to America."[85] Still, little else happened in the way of Senate support, and Dam's earlier eagerness cooled, too. The problem with the senator led to problems between the attorney and the NAACP. In November Dam wrote to Shillady to insist that his feelings were not hurt because the organization had contacted Kenyon directly rather than using him as an intermediary. He reiterated that he was "not working for notoriety" and was "prompted solely by motives of humanity," but he also reminded Shillady that he either needed to have their support or "give up now." He was getting results from talking to other senators, he said. By Christmas, however, those results seemed far less tangible, and Dam's assistance seemed over. His last correspondence to the organization stated that nothing could be done about the Georgia lynchings until after the New Year, when the senators got the revenue bill off their hands. Kenneth Robert Janken attributes Dam's withdrawal from the case to race: he did not believe that African Americans should lead the fight against lynching. Indeed, his letter of November 16 states, "This is a matter that must be settled by the *White people*" (emphasis in original).[86]

With respect to the Brooks-Lowndes lynchings, the activist's struggle between hope and despair ended on a low point as the holidays approached. C. P. Dam admired his upstanding colored maid, but he did not stick around to defend a lynched colored woman when the case got too hard. In prosecuting mob members, "The Work of a Mob" did not "work." The long-term effects of White's exposé are harder to gauge, yet ultimately more powerful. Before him, no one had published details of Mary Turner's pregnancy. Any future depiction of Turner specifically as lynched pregnant woman therefore owes a debt, direct or indirect, to Walter White. Many creative responses trace their origin to White's *Crisis* article. Even though Anne Spencer's "White Things" does not reference Turner, she told her biographer that reading the piece moved her to write.[87] Angelina Weld Grimké, Meta Warrick Fuller, and Carrie Williams Clifford drew upon White to show that lynching harmed women as well as men. The NAACP and its affiliate organization, the Anti-Lynching Crusaders, came back to White's writing multiple times in efforts to make racial violence a national priority. Even White returned to this work for the influential 1929 study *Rope and Faggot: A Biography of Judge Lynch.* Governor Dorsey eventually had a change of heart, too. In 1919 he signed the NAACP's call for a strategy-defining National Conference on Lynching. Before he left office, he launched an independent investigation into Georgia's race relations and wound up condemning them publicly at a 1921 conference in Atlanta and in a pamphlet titled "The Negro in Georgia." Dorsey might have had several good reasons for not acting on White's original report, startling though some of its information might have been. Dorsey's wife was raised in Valdosta. She or other personal and professional connections there might have prevented him from intervening. He might have believed what he said to the Colored Welfare League, that what happened in South Georgia was ultimately the fault of unruly blacks, not unruly whites. He simply might have found listening to the NAACP too risky politically at that stage in his career. Whatever the reason may be, Dorsey scholar Robert Thurston directly relates the governor's later shift from lynching defender to lynching opponent to personal connections in Valdosta.[88]

Would Dorsey ever have learned about Mary Turner's pregnancy from those personal connections? Would anyone, if not for Walter White? To return to an earlier question, why did White say what others did not? His biographer notes a pattern of exaggeration in his work.[89] So did

White invent details about Turner's opened womb, the crushed fetus, and its two feeble cries? Or was he so eager to stop lynching that he believed the exaggeration of someone else? Memory could have taken strange shapes for a man like Spratling, coerced into helping the mob, or even for a man like Whipple, a mob member himself. The experience no doubt traumatized both men, albeit differently: Spratling clammed up, Whipple babbled. White's scenario, in fact, checks out physiologically. According to the Georgia Bureau of Investigation, a late-term fetus could have lived through such torture to the mother, be cut from the uterus, fall to the ground, and still have enough oxygen left to cry.[90] Several hundred eyewitnesses from multiple counties were present, and no one ever went on record to question details from White's account. Many of them later read or heard about White's "Work of a Mob." Locals' "unlimited fury" stemmed from the fact that he took the story national, not that he made it up. Had he invented Turner's pregnancy or the specifics of her lynching, state and local papers would have reacted strongly against his account. Yet their potential reaction against White raises another question. With so many eyewitnesses on hand, why was Turner's pregnancy not reported, or protested, earlier? Certainly rumors about it travelled from NAACP sources that helped White investigate to the men of the Colored Welfare League to the women of Georgia's Colored Federated Clubs to the indomitable Lucy Craft Laney. The problem was that women like Laney and men like Major Cumming either did not have the language to describe what happened or could not use it in their publication venues. The mob murder of a woman and her fetus lay too far outside the usual representative norms. This was no *Birth of a Nation*.

When "delicate condition" sufficed for "pregnancy" and "attack" was code for "rape," what words existed to discuss publicly what happened to Mary Turner before Walter White broke this story's representational rules? Appeals to humanity, justice, and patriotism could speak to the lynching of a woman, but they could not speak to the lynching of a pregnant woman and the removal of her fetus. For that, White needed to weave in Waco's language of horror. Elisabeth Freeman's investigation material and Fred Gildersleeve's photographs, as W. E. B. Du Bois shaped them for the *Crisis*, offered a proven commodity. If sensational accounts of violence could sell newspapers by titillating audiences, then graphic, visceral accounts could further the antilynching cause by shocking audiences. "The Waco Horror" helped situate lynching as a national problem rather than a national solution because it exposed the brutality behind the justification. World War I's discourse of democracy made that problem more visible. Oddly enough, so did D. W. Griffith. His film spelled out the rape myth – with its tangible enemy, the Burly Black Brute – as a story about the consolidation of white power. By making lynching's master narrative come to life so forcefully, Griffith set up conditions for counternarratives to emerge. Every Goliath eventually meets his David. The NAACP initially thought that protests could work as a metaphorical slingshot against the filmmaker's giant. When that failed, the organization tried its own cinematic response, the nearly unwatchable *Birth of a Race*.[91] By 1918 Secretary James Weldon Johnson knew a different strategy was needed. His cocky new recruit turned twenty-five on the road July 1, travelling from Quitman to Atlanta, happy to be living after pretending to be armed in order to save his skin. The weapons he packed as he pulled into the Standard Life Insurance were words: tied, hung, burned, cut, fell, crushed, riddled. These alone would not bring down the giant, but they would help to alter the plan of attack.

2 Silence, Voice, and Motherhood

Constructing Lynching as a Black Woman's Issue

On July 28, 1917, between eight thousand and ten thousand African Americans marched down New York's Fifth Avenue, from Fifty-ninth Street to Madison Square (at Twenty-third Street), to protest lynching. This was no ordinary parade. No one spoke a word. A muffled drum kept time. Banners did the talking:

> Mr. President, why not make America safe for democracy?
>
> Thou shalt not kill
>
> Mother, do lynchers go to Heaven?
>
> Give us a chance to live.

Three hundred children led the march. Next up, nearly five thousand women. After them came the men. Some wore military uniforms and carried signs to underscore the irony of black soldiers putting their lives on the line for a nation that turned a blind eye to racial violence: "We were first in France." Women and children wore a different uniform, suffragette white. Borrowing from the "silent sentinel" protest method that female voting rights activists had effectively employed earlier that year, women and children of the Silent Protest Parade used their physical presence rather than their voices to speak out. Walking alongside the marchers were black Boy Scouts passing out leaflets that explained the parade's significance. Most likely written by James Weldon Johnson, "Why Do We March?" linked the Silent Protest Parade to multiple civil rights violations: "Segregation, Discrimination, Disenfranchisement," and, in upper-case letters, "LYNCHING." Johnson cited three events still fresh in the minds of onlookers: the mob murders of Jesse Washington in Waco, Texas, and Elle Persons in Memphis, Tennessee, and riots in East St. Louis, Illinois. The latter, which happened less than a month prior to the Silent Protest Parade, claimed the lives of nearly forty African Americans and displaced thousands more. "We march," the pamphlet stated, "because we want to make impossible a repetition of Waco, Memphis, and East St. Louis by arousing the conscience of the country, and to bring the murderers of our brothers, sisters, and innocent children to justice. We march because we deem it a crime to be silent in the face of such barbaric acts."[1] By all accounts, the 1917 Silent Protest Parade succeeded. It called attention to lynching violence in ways that no demonstration ever had and served as an organizational model for future nonviolent direct actions.

Particularly significant was the Protest Parade's showcasing of two elements about to play a more prominent role in antilynching discourse: silence and domestic space. With respect to silence the parade contrasted that which condones and that which censures. To make a statement, thousands walked without speaking down one of New York's busiest thoroughfares – censuring with their actions anyone who had implicitly condoned lynching through not speaking out before. The muffled drumbeat drove the marchers' point home. Such silence was a crime equal to the barbaric act itself. The "brothers" were familiar victims of these crimes, with "Waco" and "Memphis" code for barbaric acts upon men. "East St. Louis" featured additional victims: "sisters and innocent children." By leading off with women and children (and by drawing attention to them in its publicity material), the Silent Protest Parade entered the vanguard of antilynching protest. Few had dealt openly with racial violence's impact upon black domestic space in 1917. One exception, Angelina Weld Grimké's play *Rachel*, centering on a young woman who mourns the loss of her father and brother to lynching, had been performed in Washington, D.C., in 1916. *Rachel* confronts a third form of silence that the Protest Parade's public face did not, that borne of trauma and oppression.[2] Such an omission is expected. The march itself served as antidote to despair. Protesters believed they could and should effect change, that their actions would make a difference. Despair was not complicity, but it was a moral problem if the lives of brothers, sisters, and innocent children remained at stake. In the Protest Parade, women and children walked first to bear witness to violence in direct and powerful ways. When black women began to grapple with themes of silence and domestic spaces in creative and activist works, those themes began to appear more frequently and they grew more complex. Traumatic violence complicates the relationship between censuring and condoning. As Grimké first showed with *Rachel*, and other female artists and writers returned to repeatedly, sometimes people fall silent, speak incoherently, or struggle for words because they are searching for language to articulate experience that they cannot or believe they should not describe.

At the time of the Silent Protest Parade, the subject of female lynching had yet to be broached in national public discourse. After Mary Turner's death in 1918, the first women to tackle the subject found it inextricably bound up with issues of silence and voice. Those who used their art and activism to speak out found themselves caught in multiple language traps: negotiating rhetorical minefields and unfamiliar representational territory at the same time. Meta Warrick Fuller's sculpture *In Memory of Mary Turner: A Silence Protest Against Mob Violence* (1919), Angelina Weld Grimké's short story "Goldie" (1920), Carrie Williams Clifford's poem "Little Mother" (1922), and pamphlets from the Anti-Lynching Crusaders (1922) broke the silence that mobs lynched women. In doing so these women had to depict a topic that lay outside familiar models for representing lynching and beyond the boundaries of polite conversation. On one end of the spectrum, violence against women was radically new subject matter; at another, it was taboo. Hovering between was the most paradoxical point of all. These women's acts of speaking out, prompting others toward similar action, articulated the silencing despair that lynching occasioned. Fuller, Grimké, Clifford, and the Crusaders crossed various lines when they portrayed the mob murder of a woman and her fetus. They were blazing a new trail without a map; all previous signposts were created with males in mind. Another problem involved convincing others, as the Protest Parade tried to do, to leave complicit silence behind for positive action. Fuller, Grimké, Clifford, and the Crusaders reached their target audiences, mostly middle-class women –

sometimes white, sometimes black – through the common ground of domesticity. Racial violence not only affected men, but also women, children, homes, and communities. Demonstrating just how deeply lynching violated domestic spaces meant taking a significant risk. These women needed to convey emotions that, as middle-class women, they were encouraged not to express publicly and – for those traumatized by racial violence – lay beyond expression itself. Marching silently through the streets to the beat of a muffled drum was one thing. Trying to discourage the silence of complicity by depicting the silence of shock and despair was quite another. The latter often led to a more complicated silence, where texts cannot say what they really need to say.

What choices did a black female artist or activist have for responding to Mary Turner's lynching? Fuller, Grimké, Clifford, and the Crusaders focused on Turner as mother. In creative works, motherhood takes on religious implications. Fuller, Grimké, and Clifford link Turner to the biblical Mary, the holy Mother with Child, and her killers with mortal sin. Although the Anti-Lynching Crusaders cast their own work in religious terms, they depict Turner using secular language, hoping to gain support from a diverse group of women for a specific cause: raising money and awareness for the 1922 Dyer Bill that proposed to make lynching a federal crime. In each case, artists and activists use Turner's story to show how threats against the domestic space act as common ground for women and a common problem for all Americans. Fuller, Grimké, Clifford, and the Crusaders participated in a larger effort by black women during the late 1910s through the 1920s to shift the lynching debate's focus away from issues of black male criminality. In a range of works, many of them antilynching dramas that Grimké helped pioneer with *Rachel*, the central image of the lynched male body gave way to the black woman as microcosm of home, family, and community under siege.[3] Responses to the Turner case stand out as the first to center on a female victim. Working without precedent opened up a new range of opportunities, and a new set of problems. Maternal imagery seemed a natural choice from which to draw for its iconic power. A mother with child was guilty of no rape, and equal in sentimental value to the white lady whose honor lynching purportedly defended. For Fuller, Grimké, and Clifford, religious rhetoric and biblical imagery contributed a second powerful layer, infusing the basic family unit with sacred meaning and calling down divine wrath upon its destruction. By agitating for federal legislation, the Crusaders hoped to put lynching supporters on the wrong side of human law as well.

Hence one tension that maternal imagery had difficulty negotiating. Turner died for seeking justice in her husband's lynching. Casting her as mother gave these women trouble with balancing historical reality against rhetorical possibility, forcing them to elide parts of the story they sought to depict. Mothers, of course, have a long representational history in art and literature, and the mother-with-child image involved drawing upon a constellation of associations, not all of them right for the rhetorical or aesthetic situation at hand. As Christ's birth mother, Mary embodies both ultimate innocence (a virgin mother, she remains untainted by sexuality) and ultimate motherhood (an ideal mother, her nurturing remains unbounded).[4] The Virgin Mary did not press charges. She merely adored her child in the manger. She did not take an active role in human lives, as Blessed Virgin to whom one prays for intervention, until she moved on to the heavenly realm. Works by Fuller, Grimké, and Clifford that portray Turner as sacred mother make no reference to her attempts to seek justice for her husband Hayes's lynching. Even those that portray her in secular terms displace female agency onto church or state. All wrestle with questions of justice. If no human laws existed to deal with the lynching problem, would justice then be perpetually deferred – perhaps to the hereafter? The 1922 defeat of the Dyer antilynching bill dealt the Crusaders a crushing blow with respect to this question. It plagues the work of Fuller, Grimké, and Clifford as well, where texts seem poised conceptually on the brink of faith and doubt. For Fuller and Grimké, the conceptual tension led to real artistic struggle. Fuller never completed her sculpture; it remains uncast in painted plaster. Grimké worked on multiple versions of the story that she eventually published as "Goldie," the question of justice vexing her to the end. Quite literally, "Goldie" closes with syntactical slippage that has readers wondering about faith in any kind of law if mobs can get away with lynching mothers and babies.

Grimké's trouble with ending her story returns to matters of silence, voice, and representation. Fuller, Grimké, Clifford, and the Crusaders constituted the first generation to depict female lynching victims. With the exception of Grimké, these women's contributions to antilynching art and activism remain understudied and not widely available. Recovering and examining these documents as valuable sites of memory marks an essential step in the process of reconstructing the roles black women played in the history of lynching. Each uses a black female figure to access and reshape a discourse that had marginalized women's experiences and voices. This pathbreaking work, by its very nature, maps the possibilities and limits of what black women could say about a complex topic. The subject they chose, Mary Turner, disrupted traditional narratives of lynching. Her story did not fit the conventional plotline where white men punished black men for raping white women. Models to represent female victims of mob violence did not exist. The most readily available way to depict Turner, as mother, lent itself to idealized, silent images. The Virgin Mary did not talk back. Lynching protests, however, use the maternal icon to speak out. The black press and activist groups reacted to Turner's death as an unprecedented violation, so horrific that only the *Crisis* dared to print what happened. Black women responding to Turner's death could not miss the brutal historical reality that she was killed for asserting her voice against white patriarchal authority. Such tensions become palpable in works by Fuller, Grimké, and Clifford. Each of these women was at the top of her form as an artist, each protested one of the most controversial issues of the time, and each created strangely silent figures. These tensions extend to the creators themselves. Fuller and Grimké in particular struggled artistically with their responses. Fuller subtitled hers a "Silent Protest," partially in tribute to the parade, but the phrase took on added meaning for a piece that she could not finish. Grimké wrote and rewrote, going through multiple versions of three different stories trying to figure out what to say about a woman killed for speaking out. Even the Anti-Lynching Crusaders, who set out to raise money and awareness, had to negotiate carefully the proper public sphere for outspoken women. Religious rhetoric and maternal imagery were effective tools in the fight against lynching, especially against the rape myth. But they were not the only options. They played instead to stereotypical expectations about the appropriate ground from which women's activism should emerge: religious and domestic spaces. Black women's responses to Mary Turner's lynching ultimately raise questions about the modes of expression available for representing such traumatic violence, and how broader historical or cultural forces determine those modes of expression. The 1917 Protest Parade's statement about silence was fairly straightforward; black women's public responses to a black woman's lynching could not be.

Meta Warrick Fuller's Silenced Protest

Meta Warrick Fuller was a rising star when she began working on her small Mary Turner sculpture. The Philadelphia native had gained a reputation in Paris as "the delicate sculptor of horrors" for such works as *The Secret Sorrow* (1901, also known as *Man Eating His Heart Out*) and *The Wretched* (1902).[5] Back in the United States, she made a different name, as the sculptor of racial uplift, with commissions for a series of historical tableaux at the 1907 Jamestown Exposition and a 1913 work, *The Spirit of Emancipation*, which celebrated the Emancipation Proclamation's fiftieth anniversary.[6] Fuller started her Mary Turner response after reading Walter White's article in the *Crisis*, and, at some point in 1919, she stopped. Records indicate that she might have worked on it again for a Harmon Foundation exhibition in 1931, but she never had the piece cast (figure 3). Even though Fuller left *In Memory of Mary Turner* unfinished, the little statue remained dear to her. When her health was failing in the early 1960s, she outlined instructions for its care, and she was able to recall White's description of Turner's death in almost perfect detail.[7] Clearly the incident made an impact. Her response, had she finished it, could have made waves. Art historian Phyllis Jackson notes that *In Memory of Mary Turner* "stands as the earliest sculptural statement by an African American to specifically address the savagery of lynch mobs."[8] Fuller's piece – aside from political cartoons – may even be the earliest work of visual art to depict a lynching. (A more famous lithograph, George Wesley Bellows's *The Law Is Too Slow*, did not appear until 1923.)[9] The unrealized potential of Fuller's Mary Turner sculpture prompts a question. Why did she stop working on it? Fuller was at her artistic peak, on the verge of producing her signature work, *Ethiopia Awakening* (1921). She had not shied away from human suffering or political topics before. As she remarked in a letter to her longtime friend Angelina Weld Grimké, "It is not impossible to preach a sermon in a block of granite or a cauldron of bronze."[10] Mary Turner's lynching offered Fuller a perfect pulpit for speaking out against mob violence. However, as the work's title suggests, the powerful protest ultimately fell silent.

The painted plaster tribute to Turner stands fifteen inches high, twenty including a base that includes the title inscription, *In Memory of Mary Turner: A Silent Protest Against Mob Violence* (figure 4). Atop the base stands a woman looking down toward her right and cradling a baby in a sling

Figure 3. Meta Warrick Fuller working on *In Memory of Mary Turner.* (Harmon Foundation Collection, Library of Congress, PR 13 CN 1971: 154.)

draped around her left shoulder. The woman focuses on a group of men, who are surrounded by flames and reaching toward her with clawlike hands. Her body turns away from the men and shields the baby from their grasp. The piece's angles and lines work together to form a curling motion – as if the mother and child rise up like smoke from the flames below them – with the folds of her skirt mirroring the tongues of flames. This mirroring effect operates in other parts of the piece, too. One mob member's face parallels the woman's. His, like the other men's, resembles the mask of tragedy with its open mouth and hollow eyes. Hers bears little expression, but her baby is swaddled into a teardrop shape. That teardrop runs alongside a mob member's arm, which curves around into a fist. Like many works of antilynching art and literature, this one reverses the rhetorical grounding of pro-lynching arguments, portraying whites as evil savages that prey upon innocent blacks. Fuller's formal structure reflects that theme, clearly establishing a dichotomy of good and evil through the use of overlapping planes. The piece evokes bittersweet emotions. Triumph offsets the anger and sadness called forth by its violence and strategically placed teardrop. The mother and child rise beyond the mob's grasp, and she moves from flame to smoke in a kind of apotheosis. Fuller's Mary Turner alludes to Christ's ascension to heaven after the resurrection and signifies as well upon her subject

Figure 4. Meta Warrick Fuller, *In Memory of Mary Turner: A Silent Protest Against Mob Violence.* (Courtesy of the Museum of African American History, Boston, MA, USA.)

matter's name. Christ's mother Mary had her own ascension, entering into heaven in body and soul after her death.

Some conflicts within this piece seem intrinsic to the work itself or to its relationship with other Fuller sculptures. Other tensions resonate personally for the artist. Taken together, they begin to suggest her reasons for setting her "silent protest" aside. Fuller had contemplated a lynching-related work as early as 1917, the year of the NAACP's Silent Protest Parade. *In Memory of Mary Turner*'s subtitle alludes to the event, which Fuller knew about but did not attend.[11] Directly confrontational work seems out of character for the artist, in and out of the studio. As a student in Paris, her treatments of human suffering tended to be more symbolic than representational. Additionally, as an artist of racial uplift, Fuller tended to celebrate progress and agency rather than speak out against oppression and violence. *In Memory of Mary Turner* tries to do it all. Its aims are rhetorical, to revise lynching's conventional iconography with a reminder that women and children could be lynched, and allegorical, to transform an image of violent death into one of spiritual transcendence and salvation.[12] These goals work at cross-purposes. The problem lies in Fuller's pioneering religious iconography. Her Mary of the Assumption is triumphant, but only through death, not through her act of resistance—suggesting that black victims of white mobs have no redress in this world and instead must wait for justice in the next. Assumed bodily into heaven, Mary remains condemned to silence on earth.

Both internal and external pressures may have forced Fuller to stay her hand. After drafting *In Memory of Mary Turner* in plaster, she stopped short of casting it in bronze. In 1964 she told Sylvia Dannett, working on a biographical sketch of her at the time, that the piece was "too inflammatory for the North, where most of the sympathy exists," and it "would never be received in the South where it should be a lesson."[13] Another biographer, Judith Kerr, suggests that Fuller's husband, Solomon, may also have influenced his wife's decision not to work on the piece. After Meta had completed a World War I–themed work called *Peace Halting the Ruthlessness of War*, Kerr states that Solomon discouraged her from creating sculpture that might be psychologically harmful to their children. *In Memory of Mary Turner* fit the bill. From reading Kerr, one senses that Meta's art in general, not just this specific piece, created tension in the Fuller household. Solomon often complained throughout their marriage that she spent too much time on her sculpture; Meta, in turn, often complained about him. One diary entry offers a diatribe against men and housework: "Why did God in his wisdom give us work to do to keep us out of mischief and then Man come along . . . and invent *other* work to do that would cause us to neglect God's work?"[14] Like thematic conflicts in the Turner piece, Fuller's personal conflicts were rooted in a religious viewpoint. She saw both her artistic calling and her domestic role as God's work but had trouble finding time to do both. In a May 25, 1917, letter to Grimké, she describes childbearing in spiritual terms: "many times I have looked at him [Perry, her youngest] and whispered that motherhood was God – in me." A week later she complained about being kept from her studio: "the obstacles are not however the dear little children – I would not have any one think I held them as anything but a joy despite their mischief. I mean poor facilities and being unable to find a competent person to look after *housework*."[15] In the years prior to writing this letter, Fuller's struggles to balance art and family reached a head. She married Solomon in 1909, and over the next seven years gave birth to three children. She did not sculpt at all, as domestic drudgery compounded a depression that began when a 1910 warehouse fire destroyed many of her tools and early work. At the time of Turner's lynching, Fuller had been sculpting again sporadically for a few years, and she was on the verge of doing the best work of her career. The story of a pregnant woman killed for transgressing race and gender boundaries might have proven too much for an artist who was breaking new ground personally and professionally, and whose feelings about motherhood were potent and vexed.

Fuller's next major work placed her on more familiar terrain. James Weldon Johnson commissioned her to create a piece for the 1921 Making of America Exposition, for which he chaired the "Colored Section." She responded with her most memorable sculpture, *Ethiopia Awakening* (1921).[16] The statue depicts an Egyptian-styled black woman emerging from a mummy's shroud that is wrapped around her lower body. Like her *Spirit of Emancipation* and the Jamestown tableaux, *Ethiopia Awakening* deals with more uplifting topics. Like her Paris works, the sculpture is more symbolic than representational in terms of historic events. Yet the piece builds thematically upon *In Memory of Mary Turner*, and traces of the old can be read in the new. Some kind of force constrains each figure in the sculpture's lower plane; in the upper plane each breaks free. Turner rises like smoke from the flaming mob's grasp; Ethiopia becomes a fully alive woman rather than a mummified one. Turner faces the mob, her arms cradling the baby forming parallel lines that mirror a mob member's face. Ethiopia looks outward and upward, the hand over her heart forming a perpendicular line to the one pulling the shroud away from her hip. Turner looks respectable. Ethiopia looks proud. With *Ethiopia Awakening*, Fuller found the artistic voice that she silenced with *In Memory of Mary Turner*. The later work remains a landmark achievement in African American art more generally. As Renee Ater observes, "In 1921, Fuller's statue proclaimed that African Americans were awakening to their power and testified to the transformation of a people liberated by the dawn of a new century."[17] Despite earning her youthful reputation for being the "delicate sculptor of horrors," Fuller did not use her mature art to contend with the violence that stood in the way of progress. Given the circumstances of her background and training, her own familial circumstances and personal psychology, as well as the historical moment in which she worked, Fuller's decision to memorialize Turner as a perfect mother transcending oppressive forces that attempt to pull her down makes sense. So does her difficulty completing the piece and moving on to *Ethiopia Awakening*'s more symbolic expression of powerful black womanhood.

Angelina Weld Grimké's Conflicted Resistance

Angelina Weld Grimké faced a different problem. She could not stop working on her response to Turner's lynching. For a two-year period starting some time during 1918, Grimké wrote obsessively, composing multiple drafts of three different short stories that eventually saw publication as "Goldie" in 1920. The first, called "The Waitin'," sticks closely to historical events, focusing on a husband and wife, Mary and Luke Green; the serpentlike intruder into their Edenic marriage, Mr. Smith; and the lynching hell that leaves a family dead. The second, "Blackness," offers a very different plot and perspective. Grimké invents a new protagonist, an unnamed man who successfully avenges a black woman's death. "Goldie," the final version, takes elements of both into a new direction entirely. The fiendish Lafe Coleman destroys Goldie's domestic paradise; her brother Victor Forrest avenges her death, but Victor in turn pays with his life. Like Fuller's Turner sculpture, Grimké's story ultimately raises issues of justice and voice. This time, however, the central question is just the opposite. If art historians wonder why Fuller stopped working, literary critics wonder why Grimké kept going. What was the author trying to articulate? These stories attempt to sort through the dynamics of justice and revenge, a departure from other Grimké works on lynching where victims turn their emotions inward. As with Fuller's *In Memory of Mary Turner*, one question is whether justice remains possible in this world or must be deferred to the next. Another key tension, between silence and speaking out, already a prominent feature of Grimké's writing, dominates her Turner stories. Ironically, as the stories grow more polished in terms of craft, the main female character loses her raw vocal energy. Where Mary Green is powerful, Goldie is puerile. It seems that the mother with child, a figure just as compelling for Grimké as it was for Fuller, was equally limiting in terms of what she could express.

Angelina Weld Grimké was pushing artistic boundaries at the same time as her friend Fuller. Since her birth in 1880 Grimké appeared destined for a life of political activism.[18] Her family members included the famous abolitionist sisters, Sarah and Angelina Grimké (the latter was the poet's namesake); activists and writers Francis and Charlotte Forten Grimké; and Archibald Grimké (the poet's father), a diplomat, lawyer, and president of the Washington, D.C., branch of the NAACP. Angelina had been writing since she was quite young and would go on to publish in some of the most important African American literary anthologies of the twentieth century. She was known for the natural imagery found in her occasional pieces, philosophical speculations, and love lyrics, but during the late 1910s and early 1920s she produced a number of works very different from that poetry in genre and theme, and much closer in line with her activist heritage. Grimké's drama and fiction from these years focused primarily on the topic of lynching. In 1916 she distinguished herself with the production of *Rachel*, described in its playbill as "the first attempt to use the stage for race propaganda in order to enlighten the American people relative to the lamentable condition of millions of colored citizens in this free Republic."[19] The play was both an early contribution to an African American theater of protest and – produced by Carrie Williams Clifford, Anna Julia Cooper, and Alain Locke – a focused effort involving members of the black political elite of Washington, D.C. *Rachel* also marked a new direction for antilynching literature. It dealt specifically with the effects of mob violence on black families, a perspective unusual for the time but one that writers such as Mary Powell Burrill, Alice Dunbar-Nelson, and Georgia Douglas Johnson would turn to with increasing frequency in the late 1910s and 1920s.[20] Grimké pursued this topic in several different works, including "Goldie," the short story "The Closing Door" (1919), as well as unpublished fiction and drama.

The lynching work immediately came under fire for its views of motherhood. Like Fuller, Grimké had strong, though different, feelings about domesticity. In her early twenties she renounced childbearing, marriage, and love entirely, for reasons that remain ambiguous. Her decision may have several roots, beginning with her vexed relationship to her own parents. A racially mixed couple, they divorced shortly after her birth, and she never saw her mother, who suffered from mental illness, after her childhood. Grimké's overbearing father likely prevented her from establishing any relationships outside the family unit. He intervened in at least one that may have been homosexual, with painful results. Grimké apparently struggled throughout her life with a desire for women that she could not express publicly.[21] Her character Rachel also chooses never to have children, but for very clear reasons. After learning that her father and brother had been lynched, Rachel refuses to provide more fodder for the mob. The character's decision to forgo marriage and children led some of Grimké's contemporaries to charge her with advocating racial suicide. This viewpoint was reinforced by her subsequent publication of "The Closing Door" in the Margaret Sanger–backed journal, *Birth Control Review*. In "The Closing Door," the protagonist, Agnes, goes one tragic step further than Rachel, smothering her newborn baby after hearing about her brother's lynching down South. Grimké countered these accusations in an article published in the *Competitor*, explaining that her intention was quite different from what others perceived. Her audience, she said, consisted of white women, not black ones, and her goal was to encourage them to join the fight against lynching. Grimké states, "If anything can make all women sisters under their skins, it is motherhood. If, then, all the white women of this country could see, feel, understand just what effect their prejudice and the prejudice of their fathers, brothers, husbands, sons were having on the souls of colored mothers everywhere, and upon the mothers that are to be, a great power to affect public opinion would be set free and the battle would be half won."[22] To achieve her goal, Grimké refocused the traditional lynching narrative away from black male savages who rape innocent white ladies toward the families – drawn from what she called in the article "the best type of colored people"– left behind when their male loved ones are unjustly accused of rape and then killed.[23]

"Goldie," also published in the *Birth Control Review*, refocused Grimké's own narrative away from potential race suicide onto lynching as genocide. "Goldie" approaches the topic differently from Grimké's other lynching stories in several ways. Like Rachel and Agnes, Goldie eagerly looks forward to having children. Rather than forgo motherhood because someone she loves is lynched, Goldie falls victim to lynching herself, along with her husband and her nearly full-term fetus. This story also considers the impact of racist violence upon a whole community, not just within one family. Goldie's death takes place against a climate of fear following another lynching in a nearby county. As her brother Victor travels to Goldie's house, having received her urgent letter asking for help, he recalls an earlier letter describing the small southern settlement's mood. The mob, Goldie wrote, had "threatened, terrorized, cowed all the colored people in the locality." Victor knows how easy it is to keep a population submissive. "There was absolutely no law, as he knew, to protect a colored man," he says, which is why he had left his home for the North years earlier.[24] Goldie's lynching transforms these silences into action – a departure not only for the characters but also for the story's author. Grimké's earlier work on the subject deals with characters that internalize anger after encounters with violence. The last scene of *Rachel* finds its formerly vivacious heroine babbling and sobbing from emotional paralysis. Agnes, from "The Closing Door," retreats into a "stony stillness" that culminates in the killing of her own child (278). In "Goldie," resistance takes place on multiple levels. Goldie and her family die because her husband, Cy, defends her from the amorous advances of a local white man named Lafe Coleman. After Victor discovers the massacred family, he literally takes justice into his own hands by strangling Lafe. Victor learns Lafe's whereabouts from a woman named Aunt Phoebe, who speaks up when other black townspeople will not. Aunt Phoebe, a former slave whose husband and children were sold away from her, bears "the unforgetting heart," and with the lynching of Goldie and the girl's family, she has finally had enough (304).

As with Fuller's *In Memory of Mary Turner*, however, Grimké's portrayal of resistance is problematic. The story succeeds in its reversal of lynching's rhetorical foundations. "Goldie" inverts the lynching narrative to remind readers that black women more often find themselves beset by white men than black men menace white women. Goldie and her family, too, are among the "best type of colored people" – simple, honest, hardworking country folk – not the stereotypical "savages" that mob violence supposedly punished. Mob members are this story's real savages, led by Lafe Coleman, whose stringy colorless hair, fishy gray eyes, disagreeable smell, and rotting tooth stumps code him as a trashy fiend. And Victor's act of revenge, while not legal, is certainly an understandable form of justice. What reasonable person would not be similarly motivated by "mutilated swinging bodies," and "a tiny unborn child, its head crushed in by a deliberate heel" (302). Victor pays for his actions, dying "as the other two had died, upon another tree" (305). Yet his response remains in keeping with the sentiments expressed in other antilynching literature of the time. Claude McKay's celebrated sonnet of defiance, "If We Must Die" (1919), sums up reactions of men like him in its final couplet: "Like men we'll face the murderous, cowardly pack / Pressed to the wall, dying, but fighting back!" (lines 13–14).[25]

Grimké's similarly radical response gets caught up in semantic confusion. Her story closes with a coda describing a mysterious road that runs through a "Creaking Forest," so named because each of its trees has at one time "borne upon its boughs a creaking victim." A "strange spell" holds the forest's violence in abeyance, but the spell threatens to break at any time – and the sea of trees "will move, rush, hurl itself heaving and swiftly together from the two sides of the road, engulfing, grinding, crushing and blotting out all in its way" (306). Grimké's allusion to the Red Sea, parted so Moses and the Israelites could cross safely out of bondage and then closed to drown the pursuing Egyptians, seems to indicate that God, like Aunt Phoebe, will put up with racist violence for only so long before reaching a breaking point. The problem is that Grimké's trees do not pulse with the anger of "the unforgetting heart"; instead, they are "made up of all the evil in all the hearts of all the mobs that have done to death their creaking victims" (305). They form a "sea of evil," not a sea of justice, with Grimké's language indicating that they could just as easily crush more Goldies and Victors as they could Lafe Colemans. It is unclear whether this story's ending signals defiance or hopelessness in the face of continued lynchings. Like Fuller, whose rhetorical and allegorical strategies work at odds with one another, Grimké tries to do something difficult – if not impossible. "Goldie" struggles to articulate the traumatizing silence that oppressive violence can engender. Perhaps that kind of agony might reach women "under their skins," and "the battle would be half won."

The history of "Goldie"'s composition explains the complications. For almost two years Grimké took her Turner material through several very different versions – "The Waitin'," "Blackness," and finally "Goldie" – each with multiple drafts, leading some critics to describe her work as obsessive. Claudia Tate explains that the Turner lynching "so severely affected Grimké that not only did she rewrite that story over and over again, but the activity of rewriting it seems to have been more important to her than her desire to see it in print or performed."[26] Tate is partially right. Grimké was strangely fixated on her Turner stories, but she also tried to publish at least some of her work. Letters to editors included with her submissions portray her as someone determined to see that Turner's story was told. Attached to a copy of "Blackness" that she sent to the *Atlantic Monthly* was an undated note describing the lynching in detail and chastising the magazine for writing, in an article titled "Can These Things Be?" about brutality in other countries without condemning equivalent horrors at home. Grimké observes that the "lynching upon which I based my story happened in the civilized U.S.A. in the 20th Century. Was this woman, I wonder, lynched for the 'usual crime?' 'Can These Things Be?' Even the Turks have been astounded at the brutality and the ruthlessness of the lynching in this country. Where are these lynchings leading the U.S.A.? In what will they end?"[27] The letters that Grimké wrote to *Birth Control Review* in conjunction with "Goldie" do not survive, but a response from editor Mary Knoblauch acknowledges that she does indeed "know the horrible story of Mary Turner. Of all the crimes with which our history is blackened, it is the most. I don't see how, as a nation, we can ever live it down." In another letter, Knoblauch tells Grimké that the *Review*'s staff found "Goldie" to be so "gripping" and "powerful" that they rebuilt their November and December issues around it, running the story in two parts.[28] In finding a powerful voice for Mary Turner, however, Grimké had also taken that voice away. As she moved from "The Waitin'," through "Blackness," and then to "Goldie," Grimké whittled her female character down from one who was not only gripping but also exceptional for the fiction of her day.

"The Waitin'," the ur-text of "Goldie," focuses on Mary Green, a mother-to-be who begins the story as a Virgin Mary figure but becomes more like Yahweh after her husband Luke is lynched.[29] The story begins as Luke goes off to work and Mary goes about her domestic chores, which Grimké describes in ritualistic, sacred terms. Mary keeps her soon-to-arrive baby's clothes in a chest, referred to as a shrine, that she approaches only after donning a clean white apron. Prayerfully removing and caressing each garment, she reaches a place of transcendence: "A stillness wonderful and white came to her there, touched her, enclosed her, folded her about. Perhaps she talked with God. Who knows? The annunciation comes to dark mothers-to-be as well as light" (14). Luke is lynched later that day for striking his white employer Mr. Smith, who had insulted Mary's honor, causing this "virgin" mother to change. Unlike Rachel and Agnes, who turn their anger inward, Mary clearly directs hers outward at the appropriate target, Mr. Smith. And unlike the Mary of this story's first part, this one is no passive recipient of annunciation; she becomes an agent of divine wrath. Mary confronts Mr. Smith with his crime, fixing him with menacing eyes and a pointed finger, and commanding him to listen to all she has to say. The language of rebellion and religion intersect in Grimké's telling: "There was a dignity upon her, a power that was no gainsaying, a beauty that was terrifying. She had stepped, as it were, out of her despised, downtrodden race, cowed into a seeming submission by years upon years of agonizing fears, terrible sufferings, revolting horrifying atrocities. She had stepped out of herself as well, out of the little, insignificant, unprotected Mary Green. All was sloughed off. The shining of the Old Testament God was on her. She was the flaming sword—justice incarnate, terrible, and implacable. And Mr. Smith knew it" (37).

The new Mary Green, transformed into "the flaming sword" of justice, cuts down Mr. Smith with both her words and her hands. First she enumerates his crimes, then curses him, and finally gives him a taste of his fate. For the rest of his days, no matter what he does, Mary says, he will hear the continuous "creakin', creakin', creakin' ob a rope" (38). Just when Mr. Smith thinks she is through speaking and moves as if to attack her, Mary springs upon him and strangles him, forcing him backward through her house, to the front of the cabin, and shaking him violently before throwing him down the steps. When you hear it, now you can feel it too, she tells him after he gets his bearings.

Grimké keeps to her source material in having Mary brutally lynched for threatening a representative of her town's white male power structure, but not before the author had created a black female character who was cutting-edge for the fiction of her day. In several stories that began appearing around the turn of the century, other female characters do fight back, but in indirect ways. Adeline F. Ries's "Mammy: A Story" (1917) concerns a woman who kills her white master's grandchild after her own child is sold and dies. Ruth D. Todd's "The Octoroon's Revenge" (1902) has as its stated theme the old cliché, "Hell hath no fury like a woman scorned." By contrast, Victoria Earle Matthews's "Aunt Lindy: A Story Founded on Real Life" (1893) stops short of outright vengeance. Aunt Lindy's spirit is willing, but she calls upon God to stay her hand. Grimké's Mary Green goes a step beyond these Mammy revenge tales by taking action, even if she pays a price. In doing so, she operates as an unpublished though important link between earlier and later fiction. Zora Neale Hurston's female characters, created nearly a decade after Grimké's, are famously defiant. In *Their Eyes Were Watching God* (1937), Janie reverses the power dynamics between her and Jody by jokingly calling him out in front of his friends. In "Sweat" (1926), Delia tells her abusive husband Sykes to leave her home, then listens, but does not intervene, as he dies from a rattlesnake bite. Still, Hurston's women stop short of direct verbal or physical violence. These characters differ from what Joanne M. Braxton calls the "outraged mother" who speaks through the narrator to "bear witness," but they may have similar roots. The outraged mother, whom Braxton describes as strong (almost superhuman) enough to save herself but more often others, is "the ancestral figure most common to the work of contemporary black women writers." Examples include Grandy Nanny, a figure from Jamaican Maroon folklore, Great Gram in Gayl Jones's *Corregidora* (1975), Pilate in *Song of Solomon* (1977), and Sophia in *The Color Purple* (1982).[30] With Mary Green, Grimké created a radical literary presence whether she meant to do so or not.

Rather than continue along this vein, however, Grimké shelved the draft and moved on to another, taking a major step back from her powerful act of speaking out. The character that eventually emerges in "Goldie" is not just different from Mary Green; she is innocent and sweet to the point of being silly. Where Mary's domesticity is portrayed as a religious calling, Goldie's is the dream of a romantic, slightly foolish girl. Victor recalls his sister's desire for a "cunning . . . little home" in the "prezact" middle of a clearing, filled with "kittens and puppies and little fluffy chickens and ducks and little birds in [her] trees" (288–90). The diminutive "little," which Goldie uses to describe most everything she loves in life, poses a stark comparison to the physically striking Mary Green. This attenuation is carried even further by Victor's memory of Goldie as more puppy than sister. She is the "little, loyal, big-hearted Goldie" whose hands are described more than once as "little gold paws" (284–87). Although this characterization seems calculated to create a sentimental tone that makes her lynching seem even more striking and tragic, by the time the maternal figure travels from the initial draft of "The Waitin'" to the published story, "Goldie," she has lost most of her sense of voice. Mary forces Mr. Smith to listen while she documents his guilt step by step, but Goldie speaks only through the memory of her older brother and never for herself. When she is later lynched, it is not for protesting her husband's death, but alongside him after he defends her from Lafe Coleman's advances. Goldie at least marks an advance over the female victim of "Blackness" (the second of Grimké's three completed attempts at the Turner material). That character never speaks, even through memory. But in terms of male protagonists, "Goldie" again retreats from a more powerful start. In "Blackness," Grimké develops a new character that becomes the prototype for Victor. Unlike Victor, however, the unnamed hero of "Blackness" murders the man responsible for lynching a woman he loves, escapes successfully, and is never heard from again.

Grimké's advances and retreats in these stories were typical of her work, although no critical consensus exists for viewing them. David A. Hedrich Hirsch and Erika Miller find "Blackness" and "Goldie" to be in keeping with an outspoken antilynching agenda that Grimké began to articulate in *Rachel.* According to Hirsch, "'Blackness' seeks to substantiate and give voice to African Americans silenced by the historical narratives of a dominant discourse," and Miller finds "Goldie" to be "even bolder in its revolutionary assertions by portending a black uprising against lynching."[31] Both Gloria Hull and Carolivia Herron, conversely, fit "Blackness" and "Goldie" into a larger trajectory of self-censorship that they find in Grimké's work. Hull's defining study of Grimké reveals an author who never could say what she really wanted to say. In particular, Grimké masked her feelings for women in her published poems, while her drafts and unpublished pieces remain much more open about the objects of her desire. Herron finds a pattern in the author's poetry, where her more radical thoughts were tamed for publication. In one example, she compares an unpublished draft of a poem that makes a definitive statement – "Beware When He Awakes" – to the version that appeared in print, which moves to the suppositional, and strangely ungrammatical, "Beware Lest He Awakes" (a line that is not a typographical error, for it is repeated several times). Here, as in "Goldie," Grimké falls into tortured syntax when speaking openly of resistance. When she was not editing her language, she was toning down her characters. Herron argues that the author transformed the successfully vengeful protagonist of "Blackness" into Victor, who gets revenge but is hardly victorious, because the largely white readership of journals such as *Birth Control Review* would find the latter character more palatable.[32] Editors who might wax sentimental over the deaths of innocent black people were not quite ready to cheer on an active, even deadly, black defiance.

As with Fuller, Grimké continued to explore themes from her Mary Turner depictions in her later, more frequently anthologized work. Like Fuller, Grimké also chose the safer ground of symbol when more direct treatments proved too much. Even then, Grimké found the space of resistance to be highly conflicted. In "Tenebris" (1927), the author describes a tree that bears, like Aunt Phoebe and the Creaking Forest, an unforgetting heart. Sitting next to a white man's house, the tree appears each night to become a huge black hand picking away at the bricks: "Against the white man's house, / In the little wind, / The black hand plucks and plucks / At the bricks. / The bricks are the color of blood and very small. / Is it a black hand, / Or is it a shadow?"[33] One reading suggests that the black hand threatens to undermine the white man's entire structure and, by implication, his society, through revealing its bloody foundation. Here Grimké draws upon her strength as creator of spare natural images and upon her family legacy of social activism to craft a provocative statement about the nature of resistance. Change does not happen overnight but gradually, over time. Another reading suggests that change may not happen at all. The black hand may indeed be "a shadow" and its act of resistance an illusion. The poem is typical for an author who puts forth her most powerful statements, then takes them away. "Tenebris" appeared in Countee Cullen's 1927 *Caroling Dusk: An Anthology of Verse by Negro Poets*. It would be one of Grimke's last published works. She lived another three decades.

Carrie Williams Clifford's Tiny Tendrils of Revolution

Unsung heroine Carrie Williams Clifford may have operated behind the scenes, but she seemed to be behind most every important scene in turn-of-the-century black America.[34] She helped found and served as president of the Ohio Federation of Colored Women's Clubs, one of the earliest umbrella organizations for the black women's club movement, and she remained active throughout her life in the National Association of Colored Women (NACW). She was involved in the Niagara Movement, an early incarnation of the NAACP, and after moving to Washington, D.C., she helped establish the organization's branch there. She worked for women's suffrage and published a piece in 1915 called "Votes for Children," arguing that the women's vote protected the interests of families and children.[35] Unlike Fuller's and Grimké's, Clifford's relationship to art, activism, and motherhood did not seem fraught but inseparable facets of her personality. Clifford embodied what Allison Berg calls "the race mother," who saw motherhood as a both a personal joy and vehicle for advancing civil rights issues.[36] Many of Clifford's efforts to make the world a better place for her children focused on education and the arts, including two books of poetry, *Race Rhymes* (1911) and *The Widening Light* (1922). In addition to her own creative work, Clifford supported the development and circulation of others' literary efforts. In 1913 she chaired a national NAACP committee, "The *Crisis* Thousand Dollar Fund," that raised money to support the magazine's "artistic lines, as well as in the more practical service of fighting race prejudice."[37] She also served on the Washington, D.C., branch committee that produced Grimké's play *Rachel* in 1916.[38] As Hazel Carby says of early black women novelists, women like Clifford believed that literature had the power to change society and used their works to help influence the world around them. Clifford's preface to *Race Rhymes* says it best, hoping that her poems will "change some evil heart, right some wrong, and raise some strong arm to deliver."[39] Despite Clifford's normally forthright stance, her poetry also reveals anxieties about a black woman's expressions of resistance.

As with Fuller and Grimké, those anxieties show up in her depiction of Mary Turner.

During 1921 and 1922 much of Clifford's political and literary effort focused on mob violence. As a member of the Anti-Lynching Crusaders, she worked to support the Dyer Bill's attempt to make lynching a federal crime, and several of the poems that she produced for *The Widening Light* address the topic. Beginning with "Race-Hate," based upon the East St. Louis riot that killed dozens of African Americans, the poems continue with examinations of the NAACP's Silent Protest Parade, the plight of soldiers who risked their lives fighting for democracy in World War I only to face lynch mobs upon their return ("Deceived" and "The Black Draftee from Dixie"), and "Little Mother," written as Clifford notes, "Upon the lynching of Mary Turner" (Appendix 7). When Clifford actually wrote the poem is not clear, but she had known about the Brooks-Lowndes lynchings for several years before publishing *The Widening Light.* She attended the July 1918 NACW convention in Denver, Colorado, where, in the wake of the incident, the organization passed a resolution condemning lynching and calling for federal legislation.[40] As a *Crisis* supporter, she likely read Walter White's "The Work of a Mob" in September of that year. Given the number of responses to Turner to emerge from the D.C. area – including Clifford's, Grimké's, and Jean Toomer's – the lynching had probably been the subject of more than one conversation at the literary salons that Clifford attended and hosted.[41] Turner's story, as horrible as it was, spoke to Clifford's primary concerns: a black woman's need to speak up, the sanctity of motherhood, and literature's power to change hearts and minds.

The poem focuses on the unnamed "little mother," who waits at home for a husband who does not return. Both sentimental and shocking, the poem draws its readers in to the emotions of a mother-to-be who fears the worst for her beloved husband, then provokes outrage at the evil committed against their family. The speaker addresses the little mother directly – putting the reader into her place and intensifying the emotional effect. Clifford sets up her poem visually by juxtaposing what happens inside the home (with stanzas written flush to the left margin) against what happens outside (with stanzas indented). The tension between the two moves the poem's plot along to its horrific denouement. The first lines of the alternating left, inside-the-home, verses caution the mother to "tremble" for the fates of her husband and unborn child, both named

Gabriel. While she waits inside, quiet and "helpless," the poem says, she hears outside "hideous sounds and cries": first, from her husband, whom a mob is dragging "at a stout rope's end" and, second, from the mob itself, saying that, "'She is bound to tell.'" For her possible act of speaking out against their actions, the mob threatens to "'Give her the same.'" In the poem's penultimate stanza, the little mother faces the reality of her own death. As the mob beats down the door, she realizes that she will "never feel the father's kiss, / Or the stir of the baby more." The final lines shift the scene to the following morning, which opens on two bodies, *"and an unborn babe"* (emphasis in original) lying on the ground. Clifford's poem posits the lynching as a horrific injustice. No reason is given for the husband's death – the reader knows only that he is out too late – and the excuse for the mother's – that she might reveal what the mob did under the cover of night – lies beyond reason itself. Even worse, the mob has claimed not two, but three victims, with its final one – the "unborn child" – embodying innocence itself. Set off against the purity of the child is the mob's hellishness. Clifford describes them as "pale-faced demons" who speak "dreadful" words, "human beasts" who are "ruthless" in their actions. At the poem's end, the savagery outside overtakes the sanctity inside, leaving the reader with a "ghastly" revelation. Just as the little mother faces her own death, the reader glimpses into the abyss of hell.

Religious iconography in the form of names makes Clifford's tale of innocence beset by evil even more resonant. Although the poem's text does not identify the little mother, its subtitle, "Upon the lynching of Mary Turner," operates similarly to Fuller's and Grimké's work to establish deeper connections. "Mary" evokes the sine qua non of maternal holiness, the mother of Jesus. The biblical Mary's purity, through the Virgin Birth, or her sacrificial love for her son and by implication all humankind, cannot be questioned. The mob's murder of her namesake, therefore, evokes both personal tragedy and cosmic evil. Even worse, they kill the child, connecting Clifford's poem to a larger constellation of works that draw analogies between lynching and Christ's crucifixion. Here, however, the focus remains on the mother, particularly on her emotions, even though she does not speak. The poem directs readers to empathize with her pain, not just because her son will be sacrificed but because she too will die.

In keeping with the poem's religious implications, Clifford changes the name of the 1918 incident's father (and in the poem, the son) from

Hayes to Gabriel. On the one hand, the name provides a convenient way for Clifford to maintain the poem's rather simplified schematics ("Gabe" rhymes with "babe"); on the other, someone as well schooled in Christianity as Clifford could not miss the name's connotations. In biblical tradition, the archangel Gabriel is God's messenger. In the Christian Gospels, he announces to Mary that she will give birth to the Christ, and he is also said to be the one who will blow the trumpet to announce Judgment Day. In the book of Daniel, Gabriel tells the prophet that his vision portends the fall of Babylon and the end of Jewish exile. Gabriel therefore signals truth in the form of God's revelation, birth in the form of God's son, and death in the form of God's vengeance against those who oppress his chosen people.[42] In this case, Gabriel of the poem dies, and the wife/mother remains helpless, capable only of trembling, and the revelation in the poem's final lines sounds an alarm about the evils of lynching. The poem itself sounds a Gabriel call: speaking a truth that does not "bring glad tidings of great joy" but instead bears witness to the death of the innocents. However, Clifford's outspoken cry for justice here is just as vexed as Fuller's and Grimké's. The poem's tone and trajectory seek the reader's emotional engagement and, ultimately, action. Clifford points to human suffering that demands a humane response. Conversely, the poem channels responsibility for action away from its primary readers, black women – left silent and passive through their representative, the maternal figure – and onto God. Justice is again deferred from the here and now to a future Judgment Day.

In some aspects, Clifford seemed more comfortable than Fuller and Grimké with taking an activist stance in her art. Many of her poems, in both *Race Rhymes* and *The Widening Light*, demonstrate a Gabriel-like ability to speak the truth about racial oppression and to sound the call for judgment. Like "Little Mother," Clifford's works often take a sentimental approach and employ an uncomplicated poetics, but most end up packing an unexpected punch that is biblical in tone and proportion. Leading off *Race Rhymes* is the poem "America," which directly addresses the treatment that black citizens receive at the hands of whites, warning the latter that slavery and, later, Jim Crow justice are crimes against humanity and God. "Christians," the poem's speaker states, "I come / To plead with burning eloquence of truth / A brother's cause." But the poem does not just plead, it "demand(s)" the "manhood rights of which he is denied." Refusing to grant those rights, the speaker explains, is to "despise" the "handiwork of God." Clifford's invective ends by reminding white Americans about the consequences of their actions: "He will you all repay, be thou assured! / Not here alone ere time shall cease to be, / But likewise There, through all eternity" (9–10). Clifford's words are reminiscent of Phillis Wheatley's 1773 "On Being Brought from Africa to America," where the slave-poet reminds readers that all are equal in God's eyes: "Remember, Christians, Negroes black as Cain, / May be refin'd and join th' angelic train."[43] Clifford admired Wheatley's work, publishing a tribute poem to her in *The Widening Light*. Unlike her eighteenth-century counterpart, however, Clifford explains to her nominally Christian readers that their flouting of God's laws in favor of Jim Crow justice may lead them to spend the afterlife in a "There" quite different from Wheatley's "angelic train."

If the opening poem of *Race Rhymes* damns white racists to hell, its closing poem threatens to send them there more quickly than expected. "We'll Die for Liberty," the poem's title states, with its verses explaining that the "children of oppression" are willing to fight on multiple fronts (28). The poem echoes sentiments that Claude McKay expresses in "If We Must Die" and that Victor Forrest puts into action in "Goldie." Each of these works gives voice to a growing spirit of resistance among African Americans during the New Negro Renaissance, even in the face of the extreme white-on-black violence characteristic of the late nineteenth and early twentieth centuries. However, a key difference exists between Clifford and other more radical antilynching activists such as Ida B. Wells, who encouraged her readers to keep a Winchester rifle prominently displayed in their homes.[44] Clifford did not necessarily support violent resistance. She seemed content, in her published poetry at least, to leave the more explosive justice to God and limit humans to more non-violent forms of direct action. The poem immediately preceding "Little Mother" in *The Widening Light* celebrates the NAACP's Silent Protest Parade. Such events, Clifford suggests in a sonnet series called "Appeal," "Demand," and "Warning," achieve their purpose incrementally and slowly. Even a "tiny tendril" can, over time, grow to "burst apart a granite block," she says in "Warning" (32). Clifford does not advocate battle with white America or even democracy, but with the oppression and injustice that damage black Americans and, thus, an entire democratic system. The image is telling, for the borders of each page of *Race Rhymes*, reprinted in its entirety along with *The Widening Light*, are lined with tiny tendrils of vines and flowers. Contained within those flowery borders are Clifford's words, marching incrementally through the readers' minds, doing the slow and steady consciousness-raising work of racial progress. If "Little Mother" is a call for justice, then other poems serve as reminders that no matter how bad things get, justice will be served – if not here on earth, then in the hereafter. The poem is caught between the Little Mother's silent trembling and Gabriel's cry for redemption.

For all Clifford's faith in the powers of art and divine justice, the heroine of "Little Mother" is surprisingly powerless. On one hand the poem effectively upsets the racial hierarchies that made lynching possible by casting its title character as an innocent victim of a hellish mob. On the other hand the poet's need to portray her as an innocent victim prevents her from any kind of action that might cause her to be labeled otherwise. In the face of lynching, all must keep silent, trusting in incremental resistance and justice deferred. Clifford's figure is quite different from the real-life Mary (Turner), who was lynched for threatening to press charges against the men who killed her husband. In her poem the little mother does not even have to talk back in reality – the very possibility that she might talk is enough to get her killed. The wages of the sin of asserting one's voice against white supremacist power structures are quite clear in Turner's story and in Clifford's poem as well. Still, keeping the little mother quiet and passive remains an interesting choice for Clifford, who devoted her life and her art to political action. But one must also remember that speaking out was permissible only within a certain sphere for women like Clifford, Fuller, and Grimké. As useful as maternal imagery was for recasting the terms of lynching, it also circumscribed their rhetorical and artistic limits. Their mothers remain silent victims. What other possibilities would a black woman artist be able to conceive or be willing to circulate at this time?

The Anti-Lynching Crusaders Balance Accounts

The Anti-Lynching Crusaders provide a useful point of comparison to Fuller, Grimké, and Clifford because the approach to representing lynching differed, somewhat, for those working strictly as activists. The lines between art and activism were not clearly drawn, however. Clifford believed that poetry could change the world and was an Anti-

Lynching Crusader herself. The Crusaders' publicity committee, which helped compose the pamphlet featuring Mary Turner's story, consisted mostly of women with ties to the arts: Alice Dunbar-Nelson, poet and author of an antilynching play; Jessie Fauset, literary editor of the *Crisis*; and Grace Nail Johnson, James Weldon Johnson's wife.[45] Whether artist, activist, or both, black women struggled similarly to re-gender the lynching narrative. In creative responses, the problem was metaphorical. Depicting Turner as mother forced her into silence, eliding traces of resistance and raising questions about possibilities for justice. In activist responses, the problem was rhetorical. The Anti-Lynching Crusaders highlighted unspeakable acts of violence to raise awareness, money, and membership. How they presented their female victims and, moreover, how they presented themselves publicly was of utmost importance. Like Fuller, Grimké, and Clifford, the Crusaders looked out on new territory for black women's speech, one fraught with opportunity and danger. The Crusaders took a different path from the creative responses, even while focusing on Turner as mother with child. Although they described their own work as sacred calling, they avoided religious rhetoric in their descriptions of Turner's lynching. They framed lynching as a domestic issue, affecting both the home and the nation. In doing so, they employed much more brutal descriptions than Fuller, Grimké, and Clifford. Taking an alternative route led to mixed results. The Crusaders did not succeed in their mission to change the law. But they did help to open up an unexpected avenue toward changing the conversation.

The Anti-Lynching Crusaders organized in July 1922 with specific, if ambitious, goals: before the year's end, unite one million women to raise a dollar each to fight lynching. A speech from Congressman Leonidas Dyer at an earlier NAACP gathering inspired the initial group of Crusaders. Dyer, whose proposal to make lynching a federal crime had passed the U.S. House in January of that year and would soon come before the Senate, told NAACP members that mob violence and other racial problems could be solved by changing enough minds.[46] Get one million colored people and white people together who will decide to change and change will come, Dyer reportedly said. Sixteen women took those words to heart. On July 8 they met to elect as their national director the formidable Mary Talbert, president of the National Association of Colored Women from 1916 to 1920. Under Talbert's guidance, the Crusaders offered a well-organized attack plan using strategies derived from

World War I's Liberty Loan and Red Cross drives. Her initial letters to potential state directors set aside August for planning, September for instruction, and October for intensive work. Each director would be tasked with identifying a key woman from every city or town in her state.[47] The key women would, in turn, recruit fellow Crusaders to a specific regimen: pray daily, sacrifice nonessentials during the first week of each month so that resources could be put aside for the Crusaders' efforts, and fundraise by selling buttons. The buttons, going for ten cents each, carried versions of the group's motto, "A Million Women United to Suppress Lynching." (The women of Georgia's Federated Clubs had followed a similar model to raise awareness in the wake of Turner's lynching, minus the buttons.)[48] As an NAACP affiliate, the Crusaders had a written agreement defining their term of existence, July 15–December 31, 1922, and spelling out the two organizations' financial relationship. The NAACP would provide a $500 start-up loan, give advice on publicity matters, and pay for ten thousand pamphlets and five hundred instruction leaflets. If the Crusaders met their million-dollar goal, they would pay back the loan and put the rest of the money into the NAACP's antilynching fund: an estimated $25,000 would go toward lobbying the Senate, an estimated $100,000 toward lobbying state legislatures, a minimum of $250,000 toward investigative efforts, a minimum of $250,000 toward prosecution efforts, and $100,000 toward an idea that no one had tried before, newspaper advertisements. The full-page ads would be modeled after the Red Cross and Child Welfare campaigns of World War I and run in major dailies on multiple occasions.[49]

Who had the idea for the advertising campaign or worked specifically on which pieces of the Crusaders' public relations material is unclear. Talbert was based out of Buffalo, New York, miles away from her impressive publicity committee of Johnson, Dunbar-Nelson, and Fauset, who remained more closely connected to NAACP offices in Manhattan. The women did correspond frequently with one another and exchange ideas with Walter White, James Weldon Johnson, and W. E. B. Du Bois. The Anti-Lynching Crusaders' publicity material borrowed heavily from NAACP resources. The main item for distribution was an eight-page pamphlet directed primarily at women.[50] "A Million Women United to Suppress Lynching" (titled the same as the buttons) does not mention federal antilynching legislation but does highlight the need to raise money and awareness. Women must come together soon ("on or before January 1, 1923"), because women are being lynched at an alarming rate: eighty-three since 1889. The Crusaders position Mary Turner as their lead story. This version leaves out all other victims except for Hayes, tying the lynching to a landowner-tenant dispute and Mary's threat to have mob members arrested. The pamphlet describes her death in understated but powerful prose:

> She was in the eighth month of her pregnancy, but the mob of several hundred took her to a small stream, tied her ankles together and hung her on a tree head downwards. Gasoline was thrown on her clothes and she was set on fire. One of the members of the mob took a knife and split her abdomen open so that the unborn child fell from her womb to the ground and the child's head was crushed under the heel of another member of the mob; Mary Turner's body was finally riddled with bullets.

This account borrows White's use of passive versus active verbs in "The Work of a Mob" in order to draw attention to crucial violence. Turner exists as a tabula rasa for the mob's horrific actions – "took," "tied," "hung," "split" – and the unborn child's only experience of life: "fell." However, the passage differs markedly in tone from White, where Turner "writhed in agony," the mob "howled in glee," and the infant "gave two feeble cries." When women speak directly to women, what happened to Turner needs no further embellishment. Here any sentimental view of mother and child is literally and figuratively turned upside down, with the child forcibly aborted and the mother killed by knife, pyre, and gun. Turner's is by far the most graphic of the six cases that the Crusaders list. The pamphlet continues with others that include the Shubuta, Mississippi, lynching of Alma Howze (also pregnant) and the Okemah, Oklahoma, killing of Laura Nelson, who was raped before she was hanged.

Rape spoke directly to the Crusaders' audience. After gaining readers' attention with stories of lynched women, the pamphlet directly confronts the myth. "Most people assume that rape or attempted rape is practically the sole cause of lynching. This is not true," explains the lead paragraph in the section titled "The Causes of Lynching." The material updates facts gleaned from the NAACP's 1919 book, *Thirty Years of Lynching in the United States*, to point out that murder is actually a more common charge. But the most staggering statistics are how many people have been killed for "miscellaneous and petty offenses" (454 of 3,465), crimes against persons (368) that include "talking back to a white man" and "refusing to turn out of road to let white boy pass," or worse, "no offense" at all (163). One must remember two important facts with respect to rape, the Crusaders remind readers. The local area itself, often in sympathy with the mob, determines what caused a lynching. In addition, a mob is much more likely to gain sympathy when alleging rape than something else. The pamphlet closes with a list of all known lynchings of women, both black and white. Their point: lynching is a women's issue, not because women get raped or because they know men who get lynched. Lynching is a women's issue because women get lynched.

The Crusaders' other publicity material ties their work to matters religious and patriotic. If the pamphlet did not mention pending legislation, material that accompanied it did. A press release sent to the foreign news service describes the organization's founding and its hopes to secure the Dyer Bill's passage. The Crusaders justify their activism under the twin pillars of the state and the church, both of which (like the female victims of the pamphlet) have "stood helpless" before mob violence. Now, however, the tables appear to be turning, as the Crusaders come with "a faith to overcome all obstacles and with prayer to a God of compassion," ready to work – to save themselves from the horrors of lynching and to save the nation's reputation. The Anti-Lynching Crusaders' most notable feature, the press release says, is how black women have come together "not only to enforce justice for their race, but to remove one of the ugliest stains that has been put upon the United States by its own people. For this service, all the citizens of the democracy should be grateful to its Negro women."[51] The release, announcing the Crusaders' formation, provides an admirable display of verbal confidence that differs markedly from a letter that they sent to white women asking for their help (and their money). The letter, the eight-page pamphlet, and a sample noon prayer went to women who had previously backed NACW causes. Here, Talbert pled directly with her readers as Christians, patriots, and progressive sisters. "This is the first time in the history of the colored women that they have turned to their sister white organizations and asked for moral and financial support," she reminds them with a not-so-gentle nudge, "and as we have never failed you in any cause that has come to US, we do not believe that YOU will fail us now." The Crusaders' cause is a holy one, emphasized by the letterhead's footer motto, "To Your Knees and Don't Stop Praying," as well as the connections between black and white women that Talbert establishes: "We believe that every Christian woman in America stands against lynching and mob violence." Talbert also finds common cause within victimhood. Eighty-three women, black and white, have been lynched, according to the pamphlet where she directs readers' attention. Most important, she seeks to identify with her readers in terms of patriotic duty. Helping to pass the Dyer Bill will make "for a better country with a fuller and truer meaning of democracy for which black as well as white boys died during the world war."[52]

Like the soldiers she cites in this letter, Mary Talbert eventually sacrificed her life to create "a fuller and truer meaning of democracy" through her work on the Anti-Lynching Crusaders. The Dyer Bill failed to pass the Senate under the threat of filibuster in January 1923. Talbert's heart started failing a few months later, and she died in November. Her closest associates generally agreed that working too hard played a major role. William Talbert wrote to the NAACP's chairman of the board, Mary White Ovington, on November 8, 1923, to say that his wife died "from a very serious attack of heart disease from which she had been suffering since June 10." Ovington replied on November 16, saying, "She literally gave [her life] to the cause of humanity, and especially to the colored people suffering from danger and persecution." The NACW devoted an issue of *National Notes* to Talbert's passing and included testimonials from president Hallie Q. Brown, Mary McLeod Bethune, Daisy Lampkins, and Alice Dunbar-Nelson, each agreeing that none so clearly embodied the organization's mission, "Lifting as we climb." But the memorials have an edge to them as well. A stronger, uncredited editorial, "The Cost of Leadership," states, "Mary B. Talbert died from overwork!" The piece concludes with a religious parable whose message has serious implications for women like Talbert: "In those days, they took their leaders out on the hillsides and stoned them to death. In these days, we work them to death."[53]

The Crusaders' efforts, at the time, may have given some members cause for despair. However, the organization did make a difference. If Talbert did not know it herself, some colleagues were kind enough to remind her before she died. James Weldon Johnson held the Crusaders responsible for "the greatest single stroke of propaganda ever struck in behalf of justice for the Negro." Ovington told Talbert that the organization's work ultimately helped cut the number of lynchings in half.[54] Yet the daily life of an Anti-Lynching Crusader was a struggle from the beginning. Talbert exchanged letters frequently with the NAACP offices asking for more money and chafing under the long hours. Her final report records fourteen-hour days; 22,000 letters sent out to black women, 1,850 to white women; 35,000 pamphlets; 25,000 prayers; 78,000 buttons; and 75,200 releases to the foreign and domestic press. The group fell well short of its financial goal, netting roughly thirteen thousand dollars. White women ignored them. Black "key women" mismanaged books and misplaced buttons.[55] The Crusaders met substantial resistance in the black press, with Ida B. Wells among their worst critics. Wells called them a "scheme" for the NAACP, and an editorial in the *Pittsburgh Courier* agreed, saying their fundraising campaign sounded "like an attempt to bribe."[56] Through it all, Talbert encouraged her troops even as she groused privately to Walter White about staying in the office until 11:00 at night. "We are bound to startle 'America' – Ha Ha," she wrote to Grace Nail Johnson.[57] Working in tandem with the NAACP, startling America is eventually how the Crusaders found the success that it did.

The Crusaders' money returned to the organization's antilynching fund and went specifically, as promised in the original agreement, toward costs incurred in the "Shame of America" advertising campaign. The full-page ad, which ran in major dailies across the nation on November 22–23, 1922, raised awareness about the Dyer Bill[58] (figure 5). If Johnson and Ovington exaggerated the advertisement's immediate effectiveness, they did not underestimate its long-term value. In two days, the NAACP reached larger audiences than it had with any *Crisis* investigative article. Its message was direct and simple, playing to the same patriotic consciousness that the Crusaders piqued in their press release. "THE SHAME OF AMERICA," the advertisement announced in large bold face letters:

> Do you know that the *United States* is
> the *Only Land on Earth* where human
> beings are *BURNED AT THE STAKE?*

The advertisement gives more statistics than details. Twenty-eight people publicly burned by American mobs between 1918 and 1921; 3,436 people lynched between 1889 and 1921, 83 of them women. "Is Rape the 'Cause' of Lynching?" the ad asks. "Do lynchers maintain that [these women] were lynched for 'the usual crime'? The Dyer Bill is offered as "REMEDY" for this American shame, and readers are encouraged to

THE SHAME OF AMERICA

Do you know that the United States is
the Only Land on Earth where human
beings are BURNED AT THE STAKE?

In Four Years 1918-1921, Twenty-Eight People were publicly
BURNED BY AMERICAN MOBS

3436 People Lynched, 1889-1921

For What Crimes Have Mobs Nullified Government and Inflicted the Death Penalty?

The Alleged Crimes	The Victims	Why Some Mob Victims Died:
Murder	2280	Not turning out of road for white boy in auto
Rape	571	Being a relative of a person who was lynched
Crimes against the Person	685	Jumping a labor contract
Crimes against Property	333	Being a member of the Non-Partisan League
Miscellaneous Crimes	453	"Talking back" to a white man
Absence of Crime	114	"Insulting" white men
	3436	

Is Rape the "Cause" of Lynching?

Of 3,436 people murdered by mobs in our country, only 571, or less than 17 per cent, were even accused of the crime of rape.

83 WOMEN HAVE BEEN LYNCHED IN THE UNITED STATES

Do lynchers maintain that they were lynched for "the usual crime?"

AND THE LYNCHERS GO UNPUNISHED

THE REMEDY

The Dyer Anti-Lynching Bill Is Now Before the United States Senate

The Dyer Anti-Lynching Bill was passed on January 26, 1922, by a vote of 230 to 119 in the House of Representatives

The Dyer Anti-Lynching Bill Provides:

That culpable State officers and mobbists shall be tried in Federal Courts on failure of State courts to act, and that a county in which a lynching occurs shall be fined $10,000, recoverable in a Federal Court.

The Principal Question Raised Against the Bill is upon the Ground of Constitutionality.

The Constitutionality of the Dyer Bill Has Been Affirmed by

The Judiciary Committee of the House of Representatives
The Judiciary Committee of the Senate
The United States Attorney General, legal adviser of Congress
Judge Guy D. Goff, of the Department of Justice

The Senate has been petitioned to pass the Dyer Bill by

29 Lawyers and Jurists including two former Attorneys General of the United States
19 State Supreme Court Justices
24 State Governors
3 Archbishops, 85 bishops and prominent churchmen
39 Mayors of large cities, north and south

The American Bar Association at its meeting in San Francisco, August 9, 1922, adopted a resolution asking for further legislation by Congress to punish and prevent lynching and mob violence.

Fifteen State Conventions of 1922 (5 of them Democratic) have inserted in their party platforms a demand for national action to stamp out lynchings.

The Dyer Anti-Lynching Bill is not intended to protect the guilty, but to ensure to every person accused of crime trial by due process of law

THE DYER ANTI-LYNCHING BILL IS NOW BEFORE THE SENATE

TELEGRAPH YOUR SENATORS TODAY YOU WANT IT ENACTED

If you want to help the organization which has brought to light the facts about lynching, the organization which is fighting for 100 per cent Americanism, not for some of the people some of the time, but for all of the people, white or black, all of the time

Send your check to J. E. SPINGARN, Treasurer of the

NATIONAL ASSOCIATION FOR THE ADVANCEMENT OF COLORED PEOPLE

70 FIFTH AVENUE, NEW YORK CITY

THIS ADVERTISEMENT IS PAID FOR IN PART BY THE ANTI-LYNCHING CRUSADERS.

Figure 5. The NAACP and the Anti-Lynching Crusaders, "The Shame of America."
(National Association for the Advancement of Colored People Records, Library of
Congress; used with permission of the National Association for the Advancement of
Colored People.)

telegraph their senators to ensure its passage. Readers' telegraphs still would not have been any match for the hostile takeover of the Senate floor that led to the Dyer Bill's failure. When the bill was introduced, a bloc of southern senators, led by Minority Leader Oscar W. Underwood of Alabama and Byron P. Harrison of Mississippi, seized control, demanding to read and edit the "Journal of the Proceedings of the Senate" until everyone else gave up. Even though the bill had passed the House by a vote of 231 to 119, its supporters quickly backed away under this filibuster threat.[59] America's shame was apparently not yet the legislature's. However, the bill's defeat led to the articulation of a message, one "PAID FOR IN PART BY THE ANTI-LYNCHING CRUSADERS," according to the fine print. The NAACP, of course, took full billing and larger font. The most important part, however, was the message. How that message – lynching as national shame – went on to become a more effective remedy than any piece of federal legislation is the subject of the following chapter.

The "Shame of America" advertisement did not mention Mary Turner or any other woman specifically. But black women's stories did play a role in its conception, and the Anti-Lynching Crusaders ensured that women were included in its account. The Crusaders' work more generally ensured black women a central place in the history of lynching, not just as victims but also as activists. Historian Crystal Feimster explains that although they did not meet the lofty goal they set out for themselves, they established new standards, and new strategies, for clubwomen's activism.[60] The Crusaders' story also sheds light on forms of black women's resistance. When viewed alongside Fuller, Grimké, and Clifford, that story illustrates who could say what to whom under what circumstances. When protesting injustice, work as a group. Individuals are targets, and the internal pressures can make a woman crack. When speaking about controversial or difficult topics, use straightforward prose or redirect emotions. Appropriate channels for the expression of pain, anger, or other forms of resistance – especially when speaking to men and white women – include the spiritual and the patriotic. Men's laws can see to justice, and in their absence, God will provide – some day. A woman's place is on her knees praying. (At least that is what she pretends, even if she spends most of the day on her feet selling buttons for a dime apiece, with the Drama Committee rehearsing an antilynching play, or in her studio casting sermons from cauldrons of bronze.) A woman's place is subordinate, by the man's side at best. "Paid for in part by the Anti-Lynching Crusaders," the ad campaign read even when they paid for it all. Mary Talbert paid with her life.

Respectability and Representation

Mary Turner's lynching exposed the fault lines of conflicts that women felt as activists and artists, and their struggles were symptomatic of the larger cultural milieu. Historians and cultural critics have repeatedly demonstrated that the familiar struggle between silence and voice was a defining characteristic for the women of this generation. Like men who operated under the shadow of what James Weldon Johnson called the "Burly Black Brute," whose invocation was a ready invitation to form a lynch mob, black women faced pervasive stereotypes about their aggressive sexuality that white men believed gave license for rape and abuse.[61] As a weapon against physical and sexual violence, black women developed what Darlene Clark Hine calls a "culture of dissemblance," which allowed them to give "the appearance of openness and disclosure but actually shielded the truth of their inner lives and selves from their oppressors."[62] Simply put, black women hid their true emotions in order to make their persons invisible. Plantation archetypes like Scarlett O'Hara's Mammy, who sugarcoated their emotions with a happy-go-lucky smile, could operate with relative social freedom. Women like Turner paid a deadly price when they did not. Unlike Mammy and Turner, a farm laborer, women of Fuller, Grimké, Clifford, and the Crusaders' economic and social status had the values of middle-class respectability at their disposal. Building upon Hine's work, Evelyn Brooks Higginbotham has explored the ways in which the "politics of respectability" offered "an oppositional space in which to protest vigorously social injustice." Women worked within that space when casting their responses to Turner's lynching. Grimké situated Goldie, as she did similar characters, among "the best type of colored people," in order to show just how far mob law actually reached. She and the Crusaders relied upon positive images to create what Higginbotham calls a "bridge discourse," via the politics of respectability, to mediate "relations between black and white reformers."[63] Fuller was no different. Her Mary Turner is no "she bear" (as one newspaper described her) flying into a rage and uttering vile curses, but a carefully coiffed, modestly dressed, very tender mother.[64] Clifford's "Little Mother" likewise waits passively within her assigned domestic space, trembling rather than fighting actively against her fate. The politics of respectability gave black women license to speak around a taboo subject – horrific violence – without having to go too far.

The oppositional space of respectability could also imprison. Literary critic Linda Grasso, describing the tools that nineteenth-century writers used to speak out against injustice (and, coincidentally, drawing several examples from the work of Grimké's great-aunts, Sarah and Angelina), explains that neither black nor white women could rely upon the same rhetoric of righteous anger as white men did, because women's anger was perceived as a social threat. As "the custodians of peace, love, and family harmony," women had to assume a less aggressive stance: writing in genteel, female-gendered styles, and "figuring themselves as instruments of divine justice, human enforcers of God's righteousness."[65] While conditions for women had begun to improve by the 1920s, Fuller, Grimké, Clifford, and the Crusaders faced a set of issues not too far removed from those of their foremothers. Hazel Carby describes how writers of the woman's era increasingly saw their work as inseparable from the act of speaking truth to power. However, as Carby also notes, one does not have to look much further than Ida B. Wells to see how a woman "who refused to adopt the 'ladylike' attitudes of compromise and silence" could be marginalized.[66] Defiance deflected through righteousness is a primary strategy for Fuller, Grimké, Clifford, and the Crusaders. Fuller portrayed Turner's confrontation with the mob as a battle between good and evil, with the mother and child rising to heaven and mob members cast into the fiery pits of hell. In Grimké's stories, both Mary Green and Aunt Phoebe are angry, but their anger also manifests itself as something divinely inspired. Mary Green sloughs off her former self to become "the flaming sword" of "justice incarnate," and Aunt Phoebe, too, is described as a vehicle for God's revenge. Goldie refers to the cataracts on Phoebe's eyes as "blue crowns," placed there as a sign that "she is of God's elect," which motivates her as much as the "unforgetting heart" (304). Clifford cast her poems as God's messengers, speaking revelation and revolution, but only at a gradual pace. Talbert wrote privately to Grace Nail Johnson about shocking America, but organization letterhead portrayed the Crusaders on their knees constantly praying.

Each of these women's "righteous discontent," to borrow a term from Higginbotham, was effective on one level. Lynching defenders considered themselves agents of the people, but antilynching activists and artists upped the price by casting themselves as agents of God and mob victims as his sacrificial lambs. On another level, however, righteous discontent may have been the only permissible substitute for more overt expressions of human anger. Creative responses could tell Mary Turner's story only by taking her voice away, eliding her defiance in favor of her potential use as sentimental icon. Artists and writers would have had a difficult time gaining sympathy for their subject if they portrayed her as a poor, angry black woman, threatening to press charges against men. Because the Anti-Lynching Crusaders took a straightforward approach to documenting Turner's story, they could explain why the mob went after her. Still, they too had to distance themselves from Turner's anger, her poverty, and their own emotional response. They were, after all, out to raise money and gain support among black and white women alike.

The experiences of these women raise two very important issues. The first involves conventional wisdom on black women's antilynching activism, which suggests that women had more leeway for speaking out than men. That statement is true only to a certain extent. Fitzhugh Brundage, in "The Roar on the Other Side of Silence," says that while black women often paid a price for speaking out, whites were more willing to tolerate "blatant protests by black women that would have drawn very severe penalties had they been made by black men."[67] Drawing upon the work of Brundage and others, Adam Gussow shows how blues women could express their anger more directly than blues men could. Specifically citing Mamie Smith's "Crazy Blues," Gussow states, "Sentiments that might have struck contemporary white listeners as insurrectionary if recorded by a black man could be dismissed as allowable hysteria coming from a black woman," especially one whose brain is addled, as it is in this song, by drugs.[68] While black women did not face the same kinds of threats as men, their protests could be more complex than many contemporary scholars acknowledge. As Sandra Gunning argues, and as the work of Fuller, Grimké, Clifford, and the Crusaders confirms, black women's public responses to violence were highly mediated by issues of race, class, and gender.[69] Mamie Smith, because of her gender and perceived lower-class status, could be passed off as hysterical and thus be allowed to express anger and pain in ways that a man or an elite woman would not. Conversely Turner's story shows that a woman's outrage posed a threat to white patriarchal order that could be contained in very violent ways. Such outrage may even have posed a threat to middle-class black women themselves, conditioned from girlhood to dissemble such emotions. How, then, were women like Fuller, Grimké, Clifford, and the Crusaders to depict a woman like Turner, not of their class at all, for an audience of women much like themselves? How should they give voice to unspeakable emotions? Responding to Turner and the lynching trauma more generally became a rhetorical tightrope where one missed step had broader significance for one's self and one's sisters.

Black women activists and artists walked that rope without much of a net. Beyond the perceived leeway for speaking out, another issue to consider involves the narratives and tropes available for framing stories like Turner's in the late 1910s and early 1920s. Trudier Harris, in her foundational study of literature and lynching, contends that black women writers have been "less concerned with graphic depictions" and "more willing to let some portions of their history be."[70] Other factors may also have been at stake. Relying upon the image of the mother and child did not allow much room for expressions of anger and pain, especially when that image was filtered through a lens of religious rhetoric. Madonna figures typically are silent, and that silence does not make the same kind of statement as the NAACP's 1917 Protest Parade. Women like Fuller, Grimké, Clifford, and the Crusaders were already doing something new by focusing on the lynching of women. What models did black women have to choose from in creating images of female victims? How were their choices empowered or restricted as modernism shifted forms of expression during the late 1910s and early 1920s? And how, in turn, did prevailing notions of race, class, and gender determine appropriate modes of expression? The ambivalence about speaking out that one sees in Turner responses marks Fuller, Grimké, Clifford, and the Crusaders as transitional figures caught up in changing ideas about gender, where women had access to more avenues of expression, but still faced old proscriptions about doing so. They were similarly caught between changing ideas of representation, with one foot caught in older, more genteel, traditions, and another pointing toward a new era, where taboo subject matter and experimental aesthetics prevailed. The term that Alice Walker, drawing upon Virginia Woolf, uses to describe the female artist caught in a similar dilemma is "contrary instincts." Having something to say that does not fit the tools to say it, Walker and Woolf explain, can drive a woman to madness.[71]

Fuller, Grimké, Clifford, and the Crusaders were not mad, only vexed. Breaking new ground is hard work. An ironic coda to their prescience may be found in Langston Hughes's and Prentiss Taylor's collaboration, "Christ in Alabama" (figure 6). Hughes's poem and Taylor's lithograph, both of the same title, responded to the infamous 1931 Scottsboro, Alabama, incident where nine black youths were falsely accused and jailed for raping two white women. Hughes and Taylor employ the Black Christ imagery that Clifford's poem alludes to, which was common among antilynching art and literature of the time. First appearing in literary works such as Countee Cullen's "The Black Christ" (1922) and "Christ Recrucified" (1929), and later in artworks such as Julius Bloch's *The Lynching* (1932) and E. Simms Campbell's *I Passed Along This Way* (1935), the image serves two basic functions, very similar to those of the lynched mother: to humanize black victims and to undermine the rhetoric of lynching justifications. Taylor's "Christ in Alabama," for instance, revises the familiar picture of a man's hanging, mangled body into a more redemptive crucifixion scene. Hughes's poem, of the same title, similarly links lynching to ideas of sin and sacrifice, while exposing ties between miscegenation and power. Like the lynched mother, the Black Christ image is a complicated one. As recent scholars point out, the figure allowed artists and writers to telegraph complex messages to broad audiences. The Black Christ spoke of white hypocrisy, black dignity in the face of suffering, and black subjectivity. In retrospect, however, the larger cause for which he died does not offer the same level of spiritual comfort. Christ's willing sacrifice upon the cross to redeem humankind from sin does not equate to an African American's unwilling lynching in a ritualistic show of white power.[72]

Taylor's and Hughes's pieces stand out among the many Black Christ works because they add the mother who bears witness to her son's lynching/crucifixion. Taylor's lithograph depicts a black man hanging on a white cross, framed on one side by cotton bolls and the other by a woman wearing a kerchief on her head, reminiscent of the stereotypical Mammy figure found in popular literature, film, music, and pancake mixes. Here the Black Christ lifts his hands heavenward in supplication, with his open mouth seeming to ask the same question that Jesus put to his divine Father, "My God, why hast Thou forsaken me?" The

Figure 6. Prentiss Taylor, *Christ in Alabama,* 1932, lithograph. (Prints and Photographs Division, Library of Congress, LC-USZ62-106910.)

Mammy, in turn, looks downward with crossed arms, suggesting that she has resigned herself to her son's fate and rejects heavenly intervention, that she covers her heart to protect herself from further pain, or both. In Hughes's poem, the speaker warns the "Mammy of the South" to "Silence [her] mouth" at the sight of her son, "Beaten and black" upon the cross, lest she too suffer the consequences of "the bleeding mouth." If Taylor's God is distant, removed from the situation, Hughes casts his as implicated in the violence. "White Master above / Grant us your love," the poem beseeches, while making clear that God will likely withhold both his love, and his help, in this situation. His son, the "Nigger Christ," offers powerful testimony to the various sins that the White God has committed upon black bodies, both male and female. If the Black Christ provides a readily available symbolic framework for rethinking lynching, then the addition of the mother adds new facets to the argument. The presence of the Black Christ's "Mammy" evokes – like Fuller, Grimké, and Clifford – the other suffering mother, Mary, especially her portrayals throughout Renaissance painting and poetry as the *Mater Dolorosa* – the sorrowful mother who weeps next to the cross upon which her son hangs. As the mother who witnesses Christ's death, their bonds of love were believed to be so strong that she actually felt his pain, suffering as he suffered.[73] Like the female activists and artists whose work has recently begun to receive recognition after decades of neglect, Taylor and Hughes place black women into a picture that usually focuses on black men. The *Mammy Dolorosa*'s appearance points toward two broad levels of suffering beyond that of the Black Christ only: lynching victims' families and the rape of black women by white men that was a feature common to the cultures of slavery and Jim Crow. In this case, the Mammy identifies with her son's agony not only through her maternal bonds but also through her own suffering at white men's hands. Taylor and Hughes created some of the most widely recognized uses of the Black Christ motif, but they obviously were not the first to draw attention to black women's roles in lynching discourse or to capitalize on Virgin Mary iconography. Their *Mammy Dolorosa* figures have a history in the creative and activist responses to Mary Turner that black women produced themselves. These women have yet to receive enough credit for what they accomplished against great odds. Hughes's poem alludes to those odds with the line "Mammy of the South / Silence your Mouth." But some women defied the command to be silent.

3 Brutal Facts and Split-Gut Words

Constructing Lynching as a National Trauma

The *Mater Dolorosa* refused to stay silent. In 1955 Mamie Till Bradley gave *Jet* magazine permission to publish photographs of her son's body, bloated and disfigured beyond recognition, so that readers could see what lynching looked like. Emmett Till left Chicago as a fourteen-year-old boy to visit relatives in Money, Mississippi. He returned a corpse. J. W. Milam and Roy Bryant, who killed him for allegedly whistling at or flirting with Bryant's wife, Carolyn, were found not guilty. Later, they confessed to William Bradford Huie, who published his interview with them in *Look*.[1] In this particular case, the popular magazine's title pointed toward some necessary soul-searching. Till's death shocked not only because of its brutality but also because of its affront to national self-image. Lynching seemed incongruous to a country that fought two global wars for democracy and proclaimed itself as the world's protector of peace and justice. Yet photographs of Till's misshapen body circulated throughout the media to stand as a grim reminder of what remained possible. Till entered the symbolic realm the moment his casket arrived in Chicago. Photographs capture Bradley as *Mater Dolorosa*, mourning her martyred boy (figure 7). The *Chicago Defender* quoted her prayer: "Lord you gave your only son to remedy a condition, but who

Figure 7. William Lanier, Mamie Bradley (mother of Emmett Till) meeting Till's casket in Chicago. (Prints and Photographs Division, Library of Congress, LC-USZ62-118182; used with permission of the National Association for the Advancement of Colored People.)

knows, but what the death of my only son might bring an end to lynching."[2] Soon after the funeral, Till took on increasing resonance as a sacrificial victim. His death served as a political awakening for a significant number of civil rights and black power activists who would lead the forces of change over the next two decades. Even many Americans who would not accept change as willingly as others perceived the lynching of a fourteen-year-old boy and the acquittal of his killers to be a sign of something clearly amiss between the rhetoric and reality of justice. In describing the overwhelming documentary and creative response to the event, Christopher Metress casts Till's death as a cultural trauma.[3] The boy's lynching appears repeatedly in literature and memoir as a disruptive, unsettling, and painful experience. Conversely, Till emerges as redeemer, the figure whose death heals those wounds, a symbol of spiritual and social transformation. The lynching of Emmett Till shocked, disgraced, galvanized, and ultimately woke up a nation.

In 1955, forty years had passed since the NAACP's Joel Spingarn had praised circulation of "The Waco Horror" for injecting "lynching into the public mind as something like a national problem."[4] Why were more Americans willing to see the maimed body of fourteen-year-old Emmett Till as evidence of widespread social ill than the maimed body of seventeen-year-old, mentally handicapped Jesse Washington? How did the perception of racial violence move from "something *like* a national problem" (my emphasis) to national outrage, dishonor, and trauma? The process was lengthy and involved multiple parties who often did not work in concert and sometimes, as historian Christopher Waldrep points out, did not agree on what the term "lynching" meant.[5] Some groups, like the Tuskegee Institute, helped initiate antilynching activism in the 1880s through their influential record keeping. Others, such as the NAACP, viewed stopping racial violence as a major component of its founding mission in 1909. Still other groups that became part of the conversation on racial violence were products of the years between world wars: the Commission on Interracial Cooperation (CIC), founded in 1919; its affiliate, the Association of Southern Women for the Prevention of Lynching (ASWPL), organized in 1930; and the International Labor Defense (ILD), connected to the Communist Party USA (CPUSA), both established in 1919. Writers and artists organized, too. The NAACP put together a Writers' League Against Lynching in 1933 and staged an influential exhibit, *An Art Commentary on Lynching*, in 1935. The ILD and other Communist-allied groups staged a major exhibit that same year, *Struggle for Negro Rights.*[6] In short, an overwhelming amount of activist and creative effort went toward changing the heart, mind, and law of a nation. The only real failure in this tripartite endeavor came with regard to law. Antilynching legislation passed the House of Representatives but failed in the Senate three times between 1922 and 1937.[7] However, between Jesse Washington's lynching in 1916 and Emmett Till's in 1955, multiple parties that did not necessarily see themselves united toward a common goal accomplished a seemingly insurmountable task. They changed hearts and minds.

They did it through deconstruction. Activists and artists detached lynching from the positive associations it had in American culture and equated it to a new, negative set of referents. The 1915 hit film *The Birth of a Nation* featured lynching as a solution to a problem: black criminality and the broader threat to civilization that such savagery supposedly embodied. The 1922 "Shame of America" advertisement reversed that dynamic. Now lynching was the savage threat to democratic society, the problem in need of legislative "remedy," a shame. The advertisement itself did not prompt a paradigm shift. But it did stand as a signpost for the direction antilynching rhetoric took during the 1920s and 1930s, as different stakeholders worked to destabilize and reorient the meaning of lynching. Mary Turner's legacy played a role in these larger events. As a disruptive force within lynching discourse, her story provides a useful way to focus a complex, wide-ranging history. Its presence helps reveal in particular the tools that broke the link in lynching's chain of signification. The tools themselves emerged from modernist rhetoric and aesthetics, as the NAACP, the CIC, and the CPUSA employed grotesque description – along with social science methodologies such as statistics, charts, and graphs – to demonstrate how lynching operated as an institutional and individual problem that all Americans faced. The well-placed graphic detail, the removal of a pregnant woman's fetus, intended linguistic violence: to shock readers into a rupture of meaning. Artists likewise found themselves drawn to strategies of fragmentation when trying to depict the horror of racial violence. Oscar Micheaux, Anne Spencer, and Jean Toomer cast lynching as a trauma that lays waste to individuals, communities, the landscape, and the possibility of art itself. Their works reveal how stories like Turner's seemed perfectly suited to modernism's fracturing of genre, form, and syntax. How else to render lynching as disruption but through disruption itself? Questions of rhetoric and aesthetics often went hand in hand with those of national identity. Activists and artists alike considered through stories like Turner's what happened to a body politic when the bodies in it get torn apart.

The representative stakes clearly ran high. Like texts examined in the previous chapter, activist writings from the NAACP, the CIC, and the CPUSA, and creative works by Micheaux, Spencer, and Toomer function as sites of memory, crucial interventions in a struggle to reshape lynching's meaning. Once again, disparate materials tell a complicated story. The figures examined here, unlike those from the previous chapter, did not always work toward similar goals, nor were they affiliated with one another. They did, however, sound a common theme: lynching as national trauma. This domestic emphasis differed from that of Fuller, Grimké, Clifford, and the Anti-Lynching Crusaders, who focused on the more traditionally feminine spheres of home and family. The strategies differed, too. The construction of a national trauma involved self-consciously manipulating traumatic language, the words of brutality and the syntax of breakdown, in order to turn the discourse of lynching inside out. Parallels existed in the Crusaders' pointed description and Grimké's semantic slippage, as these women showed how oppressive violence could silence. But the politics of respectability allowed them only so much leeway. Modernist rejection of genteel aesthetics gave artists and activists permission to use words as weapons, a different tactic from using silence as powerful witness and protective shield. One irony is that as multiple forces converged during the 1920s and 1930s to reframe lynching as a national trauma, black women found themselves cropped from a picture in which they had fought to be included. A second is that casting lynching as trauma also made it taboo. Emmett Till's death was shocking enough, even more so his mother's decisions to show his disfigured corpse and speak openly of her loss. That Till, rather than the mother-with-child, came to epitomize both the nation's capacity for evil and its potential for redemption is revealing. James Weldon Johnson famously described the fight against lynching as "a problem of saving black America's body and white America's soul."[8] Antilynching forces ultimately won the battle for America's soul, even as Turner herself, and women's stories more generally, moved to margins of public consciousness. When activists and artists built these sites of memory to construct lynching as trauma, black female bodies got dis-membered from the national domestic space.

The NAACP, the CIC, and Modern Social Science

Destabilizing a term can be tricky when it already has a pattern of shifting meaning. The word "lynching" is a particularly tough case. Whether a way to keep Tories from intruding on revolution, a method of maintaining order on a chaotic frontier, or a style of policing those whose ideas threaten the status quo, lynching enjoyed a form of community sanction throughout much of U.S. history. The phenomenon was not necessarily racial until the late nineteenth century. Statistical reporting in places like the *Chicago Tribune*, which began publishing numbers in 1882, and investigative work by writers like Ida B. Wells, who argued that violence was a tool of white social and economic control, transformed public consciousness of lynching in roughly two decades. As the data shifted — black victims surpassed whites by a two-to-one margin in 1887 — journalists interpreted that information for a reading public: lynching was a racial, southern phenomenon, not a variant of frontier justice.[9] Convincing the public to see lynching as a national issue, as something beyond a regional aberration and responsibility, would take several more decades. Appeals to core values began in the early twentieth century, when the United States defined itself as a beacon of freedom, equality, and justice for the world. In a 1914 editorial for the *New York Age*, James Weldon Johnson cited the United States, "the great example of democracy," for being "the only spot on the entire globe where would be tolerated the burning alive of human beings."[10] U.S. intervention in European affairs made the gulf between words and deeds more visible. Support for World War I came largely through talk of Hun atrocities, Prussian barbarities, and Turkish brutalities. Multiple individuals and groups began to lobby the federal government, President Wilson in particular, to take action that would distinguish the United States from its enemies. In 1917's "The Disgrace of Democracy: An Open Letter to President Woodrow Wilson," Howard University's Dean Kelly Miller wrote, "The evil is indeed national in its range and scope, and the nation must provide the remedy."[11] Wilson complied with a statement against mob violence in July 1918, but for many activists, official proclamations did not go far enough. The nation meant more than its leaders. The fight against lynching needed to be taken into the hearts, minds, and souls of the people. Among the many tools at their disposal, the NAACP and the CIC chose the methodologies of modern social science. Maps, statistics, tables, graphs, and other factual data broke down lynching into component parts and individual stories that overwhelmed readers with disturbing information about the problem's range and impact. The NAACP book *Thirty Years of Lynching in the United States, 1889–1918* (1919) and the CIC pamphlet "Mob Murder in America: A Challenge to Every American Citizen" (ca. 1928–29) used Mary Turner's story as one piece in a larger data pool designed to hit each citizen where he or she lived.

The editor of *Thirty Years of Lynching in the United States*, John Shillady, had stepped into the role of NAACP executive secretary in January 1918, around the same time Walter White joined the organization. Prior to the NAACP, Shillady had been a social worker, and his social sciences training helped him to envision the defining study for its time. Released in April 1919 the book documented all information known to that point: names, dates, locations, form of death, charges made against victims, and more. Shillady compiled the material using research that his assistants Martha Gruening and Helen Boardman gleaned from the Library of Congress, White's reports, and other resources that the NAACP had collected over the prior decade.[12] Appendixes categorize violence by state, race, gender, and charge, with one long appendix listing each known incident since 1889. A summation of facts explains the role of rape and other accusations. A chronologically arranged section, "The Story of One Hundred Lynchings," contains stories such as those from Brooks and Lowndes in order to "give concreteness and make vivid the facts," Shillady explains (11). Statistics only were inadequate. Numbers needed stories like those of Mary Turner to go with them. For his section on Brooks and Lowndes (pages 26–27), Shillady recasts White's words from the pamphlet version of "The Work of a Mob." Here, Sidney Johnson and Mary Turner die heroically although tragically, and the alleged rape of Hampton Smith's wife that played such an important role in the story's first versions no longer exists. Smith "had the reputation of ill treating his Negro employees," and Johnson was among "those whom he abused." Johnson shot and killed Smith after a beating, and died himself surrounded by a posse, firing until "his shot gave out." Other innocent persons who died during the manhunt for Johnson included Turner, killed "for loudly proclaiming her husband's innocence." Shillady's account of her lynching, consistent with White's, occupies the narrative and emotional center of the section and most of its physical space on the page. Shorter sentences bracket a longer description of the scene: "Her body was cut open and her infant fell to the ground with a little cry, to be crushed to death by the heel of one of the white men present." As painful as this account is to read, it assumes even more resonance when multiplied by one hundred. And that was Shillady's point: to redefine lynching through exponential horror. He destroyed lynching as myth by dividing it into data bits, then multiplying those pieces into something overwhelmingly visceral and real.

The effect leaves explosions on each page, felt in each reader's heart. Accounts such as Turner's support the statements that Shillady makes in the Foreword's first paragraph. "It is high time," he wrote, that the facts about lynching "became the common property, since they are the common shame, of all Americans" (5). To make the message visible, the book includes a U.S. map on the Foreword's facing page, noting each state's lynching numbers for the past ten years (figure 8). Shillady draws heavily from World War I–influenced rhetoric and President Wilson's words to underscore his point. "Until the recent outbreaks in Germany," the book begins, "the United States has for long been the only advanced nation whose government has tolerated lynching." Comparisons between lynching barbarism and "Hun atrocities" had been a staple of newspaper rhetoric throughout the war years, playing a particularly important role in editorials and other protest writing about the Brooks-Lowndes incident. Shillady employs similar language here to set up Wilson's remarks. It is not just the governor's job, or the president's, to end lynching, Wilson said, "but the men and women of every community in the United States, all who revere America and wish to keep her name without stain and reproach, . . . to make an end of this disgraceful evil." Lynching happens because people allow it to, and "It cannot live where the community does not countenance it" (5). The president's words played right into the NAACP's developing strategy to cast lynching as a national shame. Shillady demonstrates that lynching is not only a problem but also a collective problem across the country. Nearly every state has a painful story – a "face" to match the "number" – and therefore a responsibility to be part of the solution. The unspoken rhetorical approach here attacks racial violence on its own ground. If lynching shatters

Figure 8. This map appeared in the National Association for the Advancement of Colored People's publication *Thirty Years of Lynching in the United States, 1889–1918,* first published in 1919.

bodies, families, communities, and the nation into fragments, then Shillady fractures lynching into multiple pieces, holding all Americans accountable for their share.

Shillady took on a larger burden than most. The NAACP executive secretary left the organization and rejected social science as a tool for reform shortly after the book's publication. A severe beating from an Austin, Texas, mob left his body, and his faith in numbers, too badly wounded.[13] Others had the faith to continue. The CIC employed a strategy similar to *Thirty Years of Lynching* multiple times throughout the 1920s and 1930s. A series of pamphlets, each with the subtitle "A Challenge to Every American Citizen," would use the requisite maps, tables, statistics, and stories to prove that lynching was a problem national in scope. These pamphlets reveal the CIC's roots in the social sciences as well as Christian activism. Established in 1919 the organization emerged from the Atlanta Christian Council and the YMCA. Key leaders included cofounder Will Alexander; John Hope, president of Morehouse College; Jessie Daniel Ames, who later established the Association of Southern Women for the Prevention of Lynching; and Arthur Raper, whose 1933 *The Tragedy of Lynching* became a foundational sociological study.[14] The pamphlets' authorship is unclear, but they bear striking resemblances to NAACP material while maintaining key differences. An earlier one, "Black Spots on the Map: A Challenge to Every American Citizen" (ca. 1924), gives lynching numbers by state on a map like *Thirty Years of Lynching*, but goes further to break down southern states county-by-county. The "black spots" refer to those counties in each state with the most lynchings. "Mob Murder in America: A Challenge to Every American Citizen," four years later, returns to the national map and uses an additional table of numbers by state. This pamphlet also employs an exposé style similar to Shillady's in order to give those numbers a face. Here, the Brooks-Lowndes case plays a prominent role (other CIC pamphlets do not mention it). "Guilty or Innocent?" the first subhead asks, explaining that at least six people died in an incident where only one person had a connection to an alleged crime. One victim was a widow whose "only offense was the fact that she said she would report her husband's murderers if she knew who they were." What happened to this woman becomes clear in the pamphlet's next section, "Savagery Unchained," where readers learn that she was "hung to a limb by her feet, riddled with bullets, and then ripped open with knives." As with *Thirty Years of Lynching*, such a story stands out for its horror and resonates more fully when juxtaposed against multiple, equally brutal incidents. "Every state in the Union except four" had at least one lynching in the years the material covers, 1882–1927. Lynching would not stop until citizens themselves raised a public outcry against the "Savagery Unchained" that led to the poor widow's death; the problem "will cease when good people cease to condone it, either actively or by their silence," the pamphlet says.

"Mob Murder in America" and *Thirty Years of Lynching* reveal a few important differences. One is that the CIC does not refer to Mary Turner by name or even to Brooks and Lowndes counties by location. The victims and the place remain anonymous. Such was the case after 1919 when the incident became less of a media sensation and no longer had the power to evoke immediate recognition. A decade after events unfolded, readers might remember or be startled anew by the gruesome story of a lynched woman but not associate that story with a particular name. Another distinction is that the CIC situates its antilynching argument within a discourse of Christian, rather than secular, citizenship. "Every good citizen has a sacred obligation . . . to uphold the law," the CIC states. Even ideas about national values and international reputation fall under a religious rubric. In 1928 the nation might have been ten years removed from the patriotic fervor of World War I, but earlier language still had power in a new context. Some of the CIC's words come straight out of James Weldon Johnson: "Lynching occurs nowhere else, not even among the savages whom we are seeking to Christianize. Stories of American mobs burning human beings at the stake and exulting in their torture are regularly published throughout Europe, in Latin America, in the Orient, and even in Africa." Just as lynching hindered U.S. attempts to make the world safe for democracy before, it stands in the way of mission work now, the pamphlet explains. Rather than drawing on President Wilson or other state authorities for its official sanction, the CIC cites religious governing bodies: the Southern Baptist Convention and the Bishops of the Methodist Episcopal Church, each of whom publicly called lynching a threat to civilized, patriotic values. Perhaps the CIC's most powerful statement, however, is not the black-spotted map that challenges "Every American Citizen," but the link to each church. One portion reads, "A leading minister in Georgia has said that every lynching in that state is a church lynching, since there are always churches near enough to have made it impossible, had they done their duty." Such had definitely been the case with Mary Turner, killed on a Sunday shortly after noon in front of several hundred witnesses, down the road from one of Brooks County's oldest churches. The CIC turns responsibility for each piece of the lynching horror into an enforced communion of Christian citizenship.

The National Conference on Lynching, the Communist Party, and the Rhetoric of Outrage

If social scientists highlighted data, propagandists had faith that outrage alone could undermine lynching. At the NAACP's National Conference on Lynching, held May 5–6, 1919, at New York's Carnegie Hall, Field Secretary James Weldon Johnson's introductory address articulated a modernist strategy of using grotesque realism to foster collective responsibility for racial violence. Getting an audience's attention, and their donations, through exposé was not new to the NAACP. The organization used "The Waco Horror" to kick off its Anti-Lynching Campaign in 1916, made "The Work of a Mob" into a similar pamphlet in 1918, and later that year folded "The Story of One Hundred Lynchings" and Shillady's tables and lists into a book. Shillady, a social worker, compiled a study; Johnson – a lyricist, novelist, and poet – advocated a public relations campaign that would emphasize horrific story over dry data to evoke a visceral response. The CPUSA's approach to lynching was similar, even though the two groups disagreed on almost everything else. A booklet called *Lynching: A Weapon of National Oppression* by Harry Haywood and Milton Howard accumulates horrific story after horrific story both to make a case and to generate anger in readers. Haywood and Howard's work also sprung from a series of antilynching conferences, more modest in scope, which took place in 1929 and 1930. The gatherings had a twofold aim: to recruit blacks to the Communist cause and to point out facts about lynching that other groups had missed. Haywood and Howard cast racial violence as a weapon of race and class warfare, a struggle in which they argued the NAACP and others were naively complicit. The CPUSA's ammunition for fighting back, hoping to incite revolution, was revelation of what ruling-class savagery had done. For radicals like Haywood and Howard, lynching was not a national shame but evidence of how the nation had failed blacks and proof that they had legitimate excuse to demand a new, better one of their own.

At the 1919 National Conference on Lynching, James Weldon Johnson outlined a strategy for improving the nation he already lived in. The gathering brought together twenty-five hundred high-profile attendees, including seven governors (one of them Georgia's Hugh Dorsey), three ex-governors, three former attorneys general, and former president William Howard Taft.[15] Johnson's opening remarks to the group explained that antilynching activists were losing a public relations battle. Most Americans "do not endorse the lynching of Negroes" but "do not condemn it" either, he said, because conventional wisdom mistakenly linked it with rape.[16] Newspapers especially were at fault for perpetuating what he called the "Burly Black Brute" stereotype. Public opinion on lynching could only be changed by defeating fear of the Burly Black Brute with an equally powerful weapon. What emotions hold more power than fear? Disgust and shame: "The raw, naked, brutal facts of lynching must be held up before the eyes of this country until the heart of the nation becomes sick, until we get a reaction of righteous indignation that will not stop until we have swept away lynching as a national crime." Activists were on the right track with facts like those reported in

"The Work of a Mob" and "The Story of One Hundred Lynchings." Use these horrifying stories as shock treatment, Johnson said. Make people angry, make them sick.

To illustrate his point (his lecture notes indicate), Johnson told his audience about Jim McIlheron, who was tortured with burning irons, then set on fire just because he was a prosperous black man. He told them about Mary Turner, her fetus, and the two feeble cries. He told them about another pregnant woman killed later that year along with three others in Shubuta, Mississippi. After Alma Howze died, witnesses reportedly watched her baby kicking in the womb. These stories reinforced NAACP strategy to inject lynching into the public mind and underscored Shillady's point that every American should take responsibility for them. The cross-section of national leaders in Johnson's audience provided an ideal test market for ideas about collective responsibility and guilt: "I ask of you Americans, white or black, North or South, if you are not ashamed, if you do not hang your head in shame when you think your own country is the only civilized spot on the globe where a human being may be tortured with red-hot irons and burned alive at the stake." Johnson had used similar language in his 1914 *New York Age* editorial, "Lawlessness in the United States." In a post–World War I climate the words held new power. "This nation needs to humble itself before God," Johnson stated. "It needs to stop some of its loud boastings about humanity and democracy." The United States will never be a moral leader in the world with this "black sin" on its heart and this "bloody stain" on its hands. The only hope, he said in closing, is for "those who love America" to unite in working toward an end to lynching.

Johnson's words were on target. The kind of changes that he sought on a national level would not happen overnight. By all accounts, however, the National Conference on Lynching succeeded. Its initial list of "Suggested Objectives" highlighted the need for state and federal legislation, providing a detailed draft of a model law, and outlined strategies for improving local law enforcement, raising money, and publicity. By the time attendees left, they had resolved to pursue a federal antilynching law, formed committees to work toward others on the state level, expanded fundraising efforts, and developed an advertising campaign.[17] Specific results included the 1922 Dyer Bill efforts and the "Shame of America" newspaper ad. Both helped ideas about collective responsibility gain traction. Through national conversation on the topic, lynching became more fully established, to paraphrase Spingarn, in the public's mind as a problem. Only in retrospect would the outcomes of this work be fully apparent, however. One major test came a decade after the "Shame of America" campaign. By then, the rhetoric was fully in place to cast lynching as a national embarrassment, but the NAACP dropped the ball. In 1931 the story of nine black youths accused of raping two white women in Scottsboro, Alabama, became an international cause célèbre. The young men were not lynched, but they were convicted even after one of the women recanted her testimony. Activists, artists, and various public figures rushed to their defense, as did the Communist Party, through the ILD – much to the NAACP's chagrin.[18] Thinking of itself as the major player on the national stage of antilynching activism, the organization now found itself displaced by what it viewed as an inferior understudy. Yet even as the CPUSA positioned itself against the NAACP, it borrowed from the organizational material, remained relatively consistent with its strategies, and confirmed Johnson's belief that the best weapon in the war to change attitudes about lynching was the graphic detail.

For the CPUSA, putting a stop to lynching had less to do with changing the nation than with building a radically new one. To put things in perspective, a primary difference between the NAACP and the CIC was the role of lynching within a larger system. The CIC believed violence was the problem; their goal was to stop it. The NAACP saw violence as one part of a bigger problem, racial injustice. For the NAACP, the goal was systematic reform, bit by bit.[19] The CPUSA saw lynching as part of a larger but different problem from the NAACP, capitalist tyranny. Their goal was to bring that system down. If the party could awaken enough people to the reality of their exploitation and bring them to unite against their oppressors, then real change could begin. While Johnson advocated using "raw, naked, brutal facts" to evoke shame and disgust, the Left relied upon graphic details to provoke anger and rally troops. In December 1929 the ILD held its own, smaller antilynching conference in Charlotte, North Carolina, motivated by the recent killing of a local farm worker. It held another mass protest conference in May 1930, pledging to distribute a half-million leaflets and recruit five thousand blacks to the Communist cause.[20] Part of its effort included *Lynching: A Weapon of National Oppression* by two well-known figures in leftist circles, Harry Haywood and Milton Howard.[21] The short work, fifteen pages long, includes a few statistics (four thousand Negroes lynched since 1882, seventy-five of them women), but for the most part accumulates gruesome stories in a manner similar to *Thirty Years of Lynching*. Haywood and Howard work through incident after incident with a method that a later comrade, Richard Wright, would liken to using "words as weapons."[22] Mary Turner's story was part of the arsenal. Haywood and Howard used the lynched pregnant woman to hammer home their thesis. "Young and old, male and female have been tortured by fire," they say, adding for emphasis, "a pregnant colored woman was hanged by the ankles and her unborn child ripped from her abdomen." Like Johnson, the men employ torture and burning to signify the worst injustice of all. Haywood and Howard speak to a different sense of nationhood than Johnson's, however. "This ruling class savagery has a purpose," they explain, "to strike terror into the hearts of oppressed Negro people so that they dare not strike out for liberation." For Haywood and Howard, the ultimate goal was not just the eradication of lynching but the radical restructuring of society: rebuilding a new nation, specifically black and Communist, from the post-revolutionary fragments of the old.

The pamphlet positions itself against the rhetoric of the NAACP, the CIC, Kelly Miller, and others it calls "race leaders," whom it casts as naïve for focusing efforts on legal strategies. Laws such as the ill-fated Dyer Bill put faith in state officials and ruling classes that support lynching, either explicitly through their actions or implicitly through inaction. In addition to the multiple acts of violence like Turner's that Haywood and Howard describe, they also include examples of stories such as Scottsboro, where the National Guard went in to protect the young men "so that they could be legally lynched 'with due process of law.'" Haywood and Howard's study is not as much about Scottsboro (indeed, this is its only reference at a time when the incident was gaining a great deal of national and international attention), or even ultimately about racial violence as it is about achieving revolutionary goals. Rather than relying on the state apparatus and its defenders, Haywood and Howard argue that blacks should rely on themselves – with the Communist Party's support – to control their own destiny. The pamphlet blends black nationalist and Communist rhetoric to advocate for the rights of self-determination and, if necessary, secession. "This is the right of the Negro people in the Black Belt," the authors say, "to exercise governmental authority over this land on which they have toiled for years, and the right to separate from the United States government if they so desire" (15). While the NAACP and the CIC posit lynching as a national problem, Haywood and Howard argue that the nation itself is the problem – at least as that nation is currently conceived. As long as the capitalist system dominates, blacks will not have equal rights. Lynching maintains that system, keeps blacks in check, and prevents a "militant alliance" between black and white workers (15). The CPUSA was not the first to connect lynching with labor and power. Walter White attributed the Brooks-Lowndes lynching to debt peonage in "The Work of a Mob." Ida B. Wells used her friends' murder to show that mob violence was about economic competition, not rape, in *Southern Horrors*. However, Communists like Haywood and Howard were among the few voices casting lynching as a systematic problem that the state apparatus itself could not solve and in fact perpetuated. As such, *Lynching: A Weapon of National Oppression* provides an important look at racial violence as a destabilizing force in the nation – even if some would not mind hastening along the process of destabilization.

Despite differences in the two goals – forming a new nation or changing the old one for the better – the strategies for representing lynching remain relatively consistent throughout NAACP, CIC, and CPUSA material. Each group deconstructs lynching in some way. They divide violence into bits of data or excerpts of stories so that each can be multiplied exponentially. They aim to break down violence, spread it thin, and diminish its power by revealing its true name. Ironically, Mary Turner's story undergoes a similar fracturing process, and her name disappears. Between Shillady's 1919 *Thirty Years of Lynching* and Haywood and Howard's 1932 pamphlet, she becomes the anonymous lynched pregnant woman whose story no longer gets told. Unlike the Scottsboro Boys, the nameless Mary Turner ceases to be part of a national conversation. Still, disconnected from its source and from public memory, her story evokes emotion as partial narrative. Even though the NAACP, the CIC, and the CPUSA would not agree in theory, the three groups learned in practice the fragment's potential to signify horror. The accumulation of details becomes a reason to take action, whether responsibility or revolution. Creative works approached lynching differently from those whose goals were primarily documentary. A key question that Oscar Micheaux, Anne Spencer, and Jean Toomer consider is what happens when the "raw, naked, brutal facts" become art. These artists saw racial violence as a threat to both national and textual integrity. The best approach was to turn that threat against itself. Their works posit an aesthetics of fragmentation as the most effective means for expressing a trauma that, for many, lay beyond expression itself.

Oscar Micheaux's Modern Black Jeremiad

The highly original Oscar Micheaux constructed his life and work around prototypical American stories. That he staged his cinematic confrontation with lynching within a discourse of nationhood comes as no surprise. Micheaux approached filmmaking, novel writing, and business as if he, too, was an American myth: the unconventional, aggressive, self-made man. One of eleven children, he left home at seventeen and took a series of jobs that culminated in homesteading a farm near South Dakota's Rosebud Reservation. He parlayed that experience into a 1917 novel, *The Homesteader*, which he distributed himself and then turned into an ambitious eight-reel silent film of the same title.[23] Lincoln Studios, a black film company with whom he initially negotiated, usually produced only two- and three-reelers. He is best remembered for two films: *Body and Soul* (1924), which debuted a rising star, Paul Robeson, and another gutsy eight-reeler that countered D. W. Griffith's *Birth of a Nation*, *Within Our Gates* (1920).[24] The film stirred controversy from the outset. Micheaux not only challenged Griffith's version of race relations, but he also shot the film in Chicago as 1919's Red Summer violence rocked the city. For his January 1920 premiere, Micheaux barely got by the city's censorship board, which required him to cut twelve hundred feet. Later, in Omaha, he used this to his advantage, marketing *Within Our Gates* as "the Race film production that created a sensation in Chicago, [and] required two solid months to get by the censor board."[25] Micheaux also flouted the cinematic conventions of his day. His racial melodrama – with its distinct heroes and villains, simplistic notions of right and wrong, and romantic resolution – is anything but direct, simple, or tidy. He ranges over multiple subplots and characters, and he masterfully crosscuts some scenes and blatantly mishandles other edits. The film's ending, which brings hero and heroine together to profess their love, seems out of place on the heels of its climactic and visually jarring lynching scene. Most film historians see *Within Our Gates* as typical Micheaux: off-the-cuff. Whether he made films this way because of budget constraints, because he rejected mainstream standards, or because he struggled as a director remains debatable.[26] Viewed alongside creative responses to the Brooks-Lowndes case, however, *Within Our Gates'* quirks make sense. Here, too, a family's lynching threatens bodies, families, souls, and textual integrity. Like his nemesis Griffith, Micheaux stands with one foot in melodrama and another in biblical epic. But Micheaux counters *The Birth of a Nation* with jeremiad rather than creation myth, charging a nation to deliver a promise, and calling on its best black citizens to claim that dream. *Within Our Gates* reminds viewers that lynching is the nightmare-reality preventing both.

The film follows the adventures of a young woman named Sylvia Landry (played by Micheaux favorite, Evelyn Preer), whom an intertitle refers to as a "typical intelligent Negro of our time." Like the spunky heroines of black women's turn-of-the-century fiction, Sylvia is well educated, pious, refined in bearing, solidly bourgeois in tastes, and very sensitive. She seems to bear the wounds of a previous, unspecified emotional trauma. The film takes her through several subplots: from a failed romance; to the manipulations of her calculating cousin Alma; to a struggling school in Mississippi, where she works as a teacher; to Boston, where she travels to raise money for the school and meets the charming, earnest Dr. V. Vivian (played by another Micheaux staple, Charles D. Lucas). Along the way, the director's melodramatic turns see Sylvia survive a beating from her former fiancé, a mugging and car accident in Boston, and a blackmail attempt by Alma's brother, Larry "the Leech"—all in preparation for the film's climactic scenes detailing the story of its heroine's past. Dr. Vivian, while looking for Sylvia in order to confess his love, learns from the penitent Alma that her cousin has also survived a rape attempt and her family's lynching. Sylvia's adoptive father, Jasper Landry, had been falsely accused of murdering a wealthy white landowner, Philip Girdlestone, in a dispute over sharecropping wages, and townspeople, in turn, lynch Landry and his wife. Against images of the Landrys being hanged and burned, Micheaux juxtaposes another subplot. Philip's brother Armand finds Sylvia in the Landry home and tries to rape her. When she faints during the struggle, Armand sees a scar on a chest that reveals her to be his daughter, and he appears to halt his actions. The next scenes cut to Dr. Vivian proposing to Sylvia. With her secrets revealed, Sylvia is emotionally free to marry and live happily ever after. In typical melodramatic fashion, their bond celebrates the triumph of good over evil, love over death, and the healing power of art – or artifice – over real-world brutality.

The film talks back to Griffith in multiple ways. Its title comes directly from the epigraph of Griffith's *The Romance of Happy Valley* (1919), released around the time Micheaux began shooting: "Harm not the stranger / Within your gates, / Lest you yourself be hurt."[27] Much of *Within Our Gates* counters specific elements of *The Birth of a Nation*. While Griffith's film justified disfranchisement and lynching as effective methods for controlling a degenerate black population hell-bent on undermining democracy and raping white virgins, Micheaux situates upwardly mobile, middle-class blacks at the mercy of a white population that is, at best, misguided and, at worst, scheming to hold onto its power no matter what the cost. The director advertises his film as "the greatest preachment against race prejudice and the glaring injustices practiced upon our people – it will hold you spellbound – full of details that will make you grit your teeth in silent indignation."[28] *Within Our Gates* is replete with instances of individual and systematic racism. Philip Girdlestone withholds Jasper Landry's fairly earned and clearly documented wages out of sheer meanness. A white woman from the South tries to thwart Sylvia's fundraising attempts for the Piney Woods School by telling her philanthropist friend that trying to educate blacks is futile. Meanwhile, the school is in trouble, intertitles explain, because the state contributes far less money for black education than it does for whites each year. Micheaux makes his strongest political statements against lynching. Hardly James Weldon Johnson's Burly Black Brute, Jasper Landry is an honest, hard-working family man who is guilty of no crime. Philip Girdlestone's real murderer was a cracker seeking revenge for being called "poor white trash – and no better than a Negro." Landry's wife and son Emil are innocent as well. Bloodlust, not justice, dictates this mob, which lynches another black man because its members are bored. "While we's waitin', what ya say we grab this boy?" one man states, and the crowd quickly turns on Girdlestone's servant Efrem, who had been helping them search for the Landrys. The real criminals, the film points out, are white beasts like Armand who prey upon black virgins like Sylvia (and, by implication, her mother). Micheaux argues through plot and editing – lynching scenes interweave with Armand's attempted rape of Sylvia – that mob violence both distracts attention from and maintains various forms of white-on-black oppression.

While *Within Our Gates* spoke directly to *The Birth of a Nation*, Micheaux may or may not have intended to echo events in Brooks and Lowndes counties. He probably knew about the case, which made news in Chicago where he lived. Early Micheaux scholars link this film to a specific incident but misidentify the one he had in mind.[29] If the consummate marketer had based his film upon a recent headline-making event, he would have capitalized upon the story to draw audiences and to help make his anti-Griffith statement. That the lynching's psychic wounds remained fresh would not have deterred Micheaux. Provocation was his métier. His promotional materials for *The Gunsaulus Mystery* (1921) magically catapult him from South Dakota homesteader to courtroom reporter. "Was Leo M. Frank Guilty? Do you recall the strange and tragic case of Leo M. Frank, charged with the murder of little Mary Phagan; tried, convicted, and sentenced to be hanged. . . . Oscar Micheaux, well known Race author and motion picture producer, was in the court room during this most sensational of all trials and shortly afterward wrote a story of the same."[30] A similar strategy for *Within Our Gates* would have the "well known Race author" passing as (Walter) White to investigate lynchings in Quitman. The film and the case do share details. A white farmer is killed during a wage dispute, and the accused murderer hides out in the swamp. While searching for him, the mob picks up substitute victims and, after a weeklong search, a large crowd of men, women, and children lynch a husband and wife on a Sunday. A key difference lies in the child Emil's escape. *Within Our Gates* saw enough controversy because of its graphic mob scenes – a family is hanged from a scaffold and burned on a bonfire – without showing the child's death as well. Micheaux enjoyed the role of agent provocateur, but the film, as Michele Wallace points out, has a strong moral core.[31] The primary issues it considers, like others who responded to the Brooks-Lowndes incident, concern lynching's impact upon justice, spirit, nation, even art itself. *Within Our Gates* portrays lynching as a seam ripper, pulling at the threads of self, society, and film. Micheaux makes visible both the rips and the instrument itself.

The lynching of Sylvia's adoptive mother is Micheaux's most explicit vehicle for raising questions of justice. Hurriedly dragged from her home after Jasper realizes that he will be held responsible for Girdlestone's murder, the blameless Mrs. Landry exchanges her spotlessly white kitchen for a lean-to tent in a dirty swamp. Still she finds time to retrieve and read her Bible. "Meanwhile, in the depths of the forest," an intertitle announces, "a woman, though a NEGRO, was a HUMAN BEING." The scene focuses on her prayers. "HOW LONG for Justice?" she asks. The answer provided in the next intertitle is one she does not want to hear, an announcement that the Landry family will be lynched when caught. Like Fuller, Grimké, and Clifford, Micheaux finds little justice in white law. The following scenes detail the mob's attack on Mrs. Landry, stripping off her clothes, hanging her, then burning her at the stake for a crime she did not even get accused of, much less commit. She was a righteous woman and a mother – "a HUMAN BEING," the intertitle announces in capital letters – deserving of humane treatment. Like Fuller, Grimké, and Clifford, Micheaux balances his cynicism about white law with faith in divine justice. Again, intertitles make the message clear. When Philip Girdlestone's murderer gets accidentally shot by his own kin, the text flashes, "Divine Justice punishes the real killer." Micheaux continues to suggest at other points that people who do bad things get punished. Efrem gets lynched not only for being handy to the mob but also because he took such glee in the manhunt for Jasper. Larry "the Leech" gets pursued and shot by a detective after killing a fellow gambler. And "Old Ned," a money-grubbing preacher with a devilish goatee, gets a well-deserved kick in the seat of his pants from the white men whose favor he coddles. Micheaux's good characters, in turn, get rewarded, especially Sylvia. After all her misfortune, she raises fifty thousand dollars, well beyond the five hundred dollars needed for the Piney Woods School. Of course, as the film's beloved heroine, she winds up in the arms of its handsome hero, Dr. Vivian. In this film's melodramatic universe, such chaos must be balanced by the harmony of marriage, justice must be served, and after the death of her family, Sylvia deserves a chance at new life, with her aptly named suitor.

Micheaux creates Sylvia and Dr. Vivian as unambiguously heroic central figures precisely because they work so hard for racial advancement. Sylvia lies awake at night, an intertitle says, thinking about the "eternal struggles of the race and how she could uplift it." Dr. Vivian, too, is "passionately engaged in social questions" and spends most of the film poring over journalistic debates about the role of blacks in America. *The Birth of a Nation* blamed African Americans for both interracial and interregional strife, suggesting that the post–Civil War North and South was made whole, was reborn, when white people united to purge the black threat. *Within Our Gates*, conversely, argues that blacks are central to the nation in more positive ways. Both Sylvia and Dr. Vivian embody what W. E. B. Du Bois called the "Talented Tenth"– black citizens whose economic resources, work ethic, access to education, and middle-class values qualify them to help create America's "Kingdom of Culture."[32] If Micheaux's film speaks out against *The Birth of a Nation*, it also speaks to African Americans, encouraging them to maintain faith in God and country despite the injustices they have faced. Dr. Vivian's final words to Sylvia, whom he finds despairing over the deaths of her family members, remind her to "Be proud of our country." "We shall never forget," he continues, "what our people did in Cuba under Roosevelt's command," in the recent war, and in Mexico. Even his proposal is couched in terms of national pride. "You will always be a patriot and a tender wife," he says; "I love you." Dr. Vivian's words revive the despondent Sylvia, who puts her personal trauma aside to accept his proposal. The film's final scene cuts to a fade-out of the smiling, happy couple poised on the threshold of their new life together in a new era for the race.

Such an ending makes little sense in the real world of early-twentieth-century African Americans who could not brush aside lynching's trauma so easily. In Oscar Micheaux's off-kilter cinematic vision, the ending is perfect. It also forms a pattern with other creative responses to Brooks and Lowndes that attempt to reconcile brutal facts with an uplifting faith in transcendent justice. The ending functions additionally as a necessary corrective to the celebratory, yet racist, vision that closes D. W. Griffith's *Birth of a Nation*. The two couples he unites in marriage bring together North and South after the black threat has been purged. By juxtaposing scenes of a family's lynching, interracial rape, and marriage, Micheaux calls attention to disruptions in a national narrative that Griffith smoothes over. J. Ronald Greene says that Micheaux "was throwing Griffith's sentimentality back in his face" by selecting the epigraph from *The Romance of Happy Valley* as the title, and adds, "There can be no little doubt that the film was made in anger."[33] Greene has a point. The phrase "stranger within your gates" originates in Deuteronomy 5:14, which establishes the Sabbath as a day of rest for everyone: "But the seventh day is the sabbath of the Lord thy God: in it thou shalt not do any work, thou, nor thy son, nor thy daughter, nor thy manservant, nor thy maidservant, nor thine ox, nor thine ass, nor any of thy cattle, nor thy stranger that is within thy gates; that thy manservant and thy maidservant may rest as well as thou." Here, God commands his chosen people to treat all with respect. On the Sabbath, everyone catches a break, even servants, outsiders, and animals. Griffith's epigraph also has roots in Jeremiah 7, in the prophet's Temple sermon, where he excoriates the chosen for failing to live up to God's law. God has brought you to these gates to worship him, Jeremiah says, but instead, you blaspheme his name by breaking all his commandments. Among the many "abominations" Jeremiah lists are oppressing aliens, widows, and orphans, and shedding innocent blood. If the chosen continue along their wayward path, the punishment is clear: "what I did to Shiloh I will do to this house which bears my name." Micheaux's sermon in a different temple, the film house, insinuates that those who follow Griffith's path – for instance, failing to keep the Sabbath holy by lynching families on Sunday – will face another Shiloh, site of a major defeat for the Confederacy. African Americans do not escape notice, however. The original Jeremiah also singles out the chosen for lying, stealing, murder, and other forms of "wickedness" that make up *Within Our Gates*' various subplots. The prophet's sermon does not halt threats of punishment with reminders of Shiloh, telling the chosen, "I will fling you out of my sight, as I flung away all of your kinsfolk, the whole brood of Ephraim." Efrem, Micheaux's tattletale, set the wheels in motion for the Landrys to be lynched and falls victim to the mob himself. Underneath Micheaux's cinematic twists, turns, and crosscuts, the message is fairly simple. It all comes back to Griffith, or actually Jeremiah: "Harm not the stranger / Within your gates, / Lest you yourself be hurt."

By engaging Jeremiah's Temple sermon, Micheaux borrows from a quintessential American form, the jeremiad. As Sacvan Bercovitch defines the term, the jeremiad exhorts citizens to live up to national ideals.[34] Like Jeremiah's sermon, it points out the ways people fall short in the present, looks backward toward a golden age of promise, and looks forward to a future where punishment – or reward, if listeners make the right choice – is certain. *The Birth of a Nation* acts as creation myth, narrating how the country is reborn after the fratricide of Civil War, but *Within Our Gates* challenges that myth's fundamental premise. The path that Griffith lays out will end only in apocalypse if its new Adams and Eves consecrate their marriage in black people's blood. The best hope, the true patriots, Micheaux suggests, are those like Sylvia and Dr. Vivian who work for racial uplift and the good of the nation more generally. If the film's happy ending seems incongruous, running on the heels of its most traumatic scene, then perhaps the two should stick in viewers' minds. Lynching violence threatens the social fabric and the very fabric of Micheaux's film itself. Lynching and rape become the unspoken trauma pulling at this film's seams until someone names it. *Within Our Gates* never achieves coherence – not surprising in a modernist film where form follows function, to echo architect Louis Sullivan's famous dictum. Micheaux dislocates cinematic sense just like lynching ruptures meaning. The film's final message, as Sylvia and Dr. Vivian start a new life together, is that no coherent story can actually begin until the real threat to nation is made visible: not *The Birth of a Nation*'s Burly Black Brute, but the kind of violent oppression made manifest in *Within Our Gates*. Perhaps viewers are not supposed to brush aside lynching and rape at all, but to confront them directly for the trauma they represent. Only then does union, in multiple senses of the word, become remotely a possibility.

Anne Spencer's Civilized Articulation

Poet Anne Spencer's carefully crafted work could not be more different from Oscar Micheaux's quirky cinema, but each artist approached life with a similarly headstrong individualism. Spencer published a small amount of poetry for someone who lived almost a century. Instead, she devoted most of her energy to becoming what bell hooks calls a race and gender rebel, cultivating the kind of family sanctuary that hooks defines as "homeplace."[35] The Spencer property in Lynchburg, Virginia, with its lush gardens and cottage known as "Edankraal" (combining the first letters of Anne and her husband Edward's given names with the Dutch word for "home"), was a well-known, and sometimes necessary, stopover for African Americans passing through the area. Because accommodations were sparse in the Jim Crow South, the house acted as what biographer and editor J. Lee Greene calls "an oasis in a desert of public racial discrimination."[36] Regular visitors included W. E. B. Du Bois, James Weldon Johnson, Georgia Douglas Johnson, Jessie Fauset, Langston Hughes, Sterling Brown, and Paul Robeson. If Spencer's home was an oasis, she did her best to improve the desert around her. Greene says that for most of her life, she was known as "one of Lynchburg's most vocal and active social heretics." With James Weldon Johnson, she helped establish the local NAACP chapter. On her own, she spearheaded a campaign to force white teachers from a local high school because their employment kept black teachers out of work. She opened the first public library for African Americans at Dunbar High School, working there for several decades. She refused to let her children take segregated public transportation and often scandalized the local bourgeoisie by hitching rides on the backs of grocery wagons. She upset them even further by occasionally wearing pants. Many peers embraced her unconventional energies, however, and in 1975, Virginia Theological Seminary awarded her an honorary doctorate, which she proudly called her "ornery degree."[37]

Some literary scholars have found Spencer's poetry difficult to label. Her response to the Brooks-Lowndes lynchings, "White Things," provides a perfect example of that difficulty. One of the few poems that she wrote in reaction to a specific issue or event, "White Things" does not mention the incident at all and addresses mob violence more figuratively than most antilynching works. For much of her career, Spencer (like Angelina Weld Grimké) was perceived as an apolitical poet, focusing her creative attention on love, friendship, and female self-actualization, and drawing her imagery from the natural world and religious and mythical traditions. Many readers took at face value the statement included with her published material for Countee Cullen's *Caroling Dusk: An Anthology of Verse by Negro Poets* (1927): "I write about some of the things I love. But I have no civilized articulation for the things I hate." As Greene and others have demonstrated, Spencer's words mislead. The quest for agency and autonomy remain consistent themes in her work. Her first and perhaps most famous poem, "Before the Feast at Shushan" (1920), speaks of patriarchal resistance to the female struggle for liberation. Even the innocuously titled "Grapes: A Still Life" (1929) makes a statement about race, drawing connections between the fruit's rich varieties and humankind's colorful, variegated heritage.[38] Poems such as "White Things" show that Spencer's words are definitely ironic. Someone who had no civilized articulation for the things she hated managed to compose one of the decade's most provocative antilynching statements. Spencer wrote the poem shortly after reading about Walter White's "The Work of a Mob," and published it in the March 1923 *Crisis*.[39] "White Things" differs from other creative responses to the incident by taking the subject beyond its specific historical circumstances into a meditation on lynching as manifestation of white evil, and white evil as a modern blight transforming God's garden into a barren waste.

Spencer divides the poem into two stanzas. The first examines the white race's destructive impact upon nature, and the second shows how the act of lynching mocks God himself. The poem associates blacks with the natural world, equating them with "Most things" that are colorful – "the sky, the earth, and sea." Whites, by comparison, come from a different realm, "a silvered world – somewhere," that the second stanza calls "the hell that sired them." Finding the natural world favorable but too foreign for its color, the poem explains, these white things are hell-bent upon remaking that world into a reflection of their own pale images, oblivious that their remaking drains the place of its lifeblood. They strew white feathers over the "greenly grassed plains"; blanch "the golden stars," red hills, and "darkened pine"; and transform the "ruby rose" into a "poor white poppy flower." Although these "White things" hold power, the poem states, that power comes not from strength but fear. Their white feathers reflect their cowardice, and what they fear most is colorful men. Those, they have not "blanched" but "pyred" into white ashes. Then, having fully despoiled all creation in their quest to eliminate anything they believe threatens their whiteness, they turn in the poem's second stanza upon the creator himself. A "young one" pulls a skull from the ash heap and swings it at "the face of God with all his might," saying that God, too, must submit to its dominion. "Man-maker," the "ghoul" demands, "make white!" Spencer's claim not to have any civilized articulation about the things she hates returns with a powerful ironic punch at the poem's end. She portrays lynching as the ultimate mortal sin, destroying God's creation and blaspheming his name. "White Things" therefore culminates in a multilayered speech act from its ghoul and its poet. To lynch is to proclaim power, to silence and destroy, and to damn one's soul to hell. Here Spencer echoes James Weldon Johnson's ideas that the fight against lynching is a battle to save black America's body and white America's soul. Lynching's violence lays waste to the integrity of language, spirit, and society.

Spencer's poem occupies an interesting transitional point in the trajectory of antilynching protest art. "White Things" looks forward and back in multiple ways. Like Fuller, Grimké, and Clifford, she reverses the rhetorical foundations of lynching that posit mob members as honorable men who defend white ladies from savage rapists. Rather than focusing on a woman's lynching, however, she turns her attention to the mob's psyche and the implications of its actions. Like other works examined in this chapter, Spencer's poem shows how lynching intrudes upon society and spirit. When its ghoul chooses a lynching souvenir to hurl at God along with an epithet, "White Things" makes explicit the links between racist oppression and language rupture. The destructive death march of white oppression has forced this split from God, commanding him to re-make the world into its image: no longer colorful *men*, only white *things*. The fragmented body becomes the fragmented society and soul that the artist struggles, through language, to reveal and, perhaps, to make whole. In casting Spencer's work as ahead of its time, Lee Greene compares her portrayal of whiteness in this poem to Richard Wright's in *Black Boy*. Both Spencer and Wright depict an overwhelmingly destructive power, one that transcends individual control and threatens universal precepts of right and wrong. According to both authors, Greene explains, the concept of whiteness has grown so deeply rooted and out of control that it threatens all levels of society.[40] For critic Maureen Honey, Spencer's poem takes a profoundly forward-looking approach, one that combines both ecofeminism and antiracism. Indeed, as Honey notes, Spencer is one of few authors to contextualize lynching within "male domination, white supremacy, and the destruction of nature."[41] The stance is not sur-prising for a woman who created a safe place known as Edenkraal for herself and other African Americans in the middle of town that hap-pened to be called *Lynch*burg.

Despite her forward-looking approach, the woman who was later very proud of her "ornery degree" still had to deal with backward-looking editors and her own internal struggle. Spencer shares both problems with Fuller, Grimké, and Clifford. Greene explains that she ultimately may have made the "no civilized articulation" statement as a face-saving measure. She actually did compose several works of fiction and nonfic-tion prose that confronted race and social justice issues, but they were rejected. On one hand, Greene states, Spencer may have been right. Her emotions may have compromised the works' quality. On the other hand, Spencer complained later in life that editors like Alain Locke lim-ited her output of politically inflected work during the 1920s by giv-ing male poets more leeway on racial topics and relegating females to poetry about nature and love, topics considered inferior at the time. Literary critics Gloria Hull and Maureen Honey give historical support to such claim, describing the old-boy network that Locke employed to give male writers preferential treatment.[42] The publication history of "White Things" provides a case study of these gender dynamics in action. Before the poem's publication, *Crisis* editorial staff requested that Spencer delete portions referring specifically to "white men" because they seemed "untimely and *unwise* at that time for a new black writer dependent upon others for publication" (my emphasis).[43] Such an editorial decision seems curious from the same magazine that published the new writer and investigator Walter White's graphic account upon which "White Things" was based – describing the lynching of a pregnant woman killed for making "unwise remarks." Given the editorial advice Spencer received from the *Crisis*, a later poem of hers, "Letter to My Sister" (first published in Charles Johnson's 1927 *Ebony and Topaz* as "Sybil Warns Her Sister"), deserves a closer look. "It is dangerous for a woman to defy the gods; / To taunt them with the tongue's thin tip," the speaker explains, for "the gods are Juggernaut, / Passing over . . . over. . . ." In "White Things," the ghoul claims the power of speech to defy God and destroy his creation. In "Letter to My Sister," the speaker says that a woman puts herself at risk by talking back. As a modernist work, Spencer's poem reveals how lynching calls into question the power of language. Jean Toomer's work, published the same year as "White Things," explores what happens when oppressive violence causes language to fail. To paraphrase James Weldon Johnson, can body, soul, and nation be saved? Or can art intervene to provide deliverance?

Jean Toomer's Blues Song of Mo(u)rning

Jean Toomer's "Kabnis" encapsulates the paradoxes of representing lynching in the modern nation. The closing section of *Cane*, a three-part meditation on Jim Crow and the Great Migration, "Kabnis" focuses on a racially mixed, northern-educated schoolteacher in rural Georgia who wants to capture poetically the complexity that surrounds him. He fails. Ralph Kabnis's despair over his inability to write explodes into madness after he hears the story of Mame Lamkins, a pregnant woman lynched for defending her husband. She and her fetus in particular serve as metaphors for his aborted artistic vision. Kabnis becomes convinced that he cannot produce beauty in such an ugly world. The book's last scene has him railing against being the victim of America's sin, then trudging up the stairs, Sisyphus-like, carrying a bucket of dead coals. The story has autobiographical elements but is not autobiography. Toomer found his literary voice in rural Georgia. In 1921 he left his Washington, D.C., home for a temporary job as a replacement principal for a small, black industrial and agricultural school in Sparta. Struck by the rich folk spirit that persisted among the people despite lives made difficult by poverty and violence, Toomer began to record what he saw and, more important, what he heard. The music of spirituals, work songs, and blues became the basis of *Cane* both thematically and structurally. The day before he left Sparta, he sent a poem to the *Liberator*, and on the train home he began composing the book's prose sections. Within a year, *Cane* was complete. "Kabnis" came quickly, Toomer says, "in almost a day."[44] He had been struggling to write for some time – reading widely, cultivating relationships with Greenwich Village's literary avant-garde, and producing what he called multiple manuscripts, but he had trouble finding a focus before the trip south. When *Cane* appeared in 1923, American modernists praised it as something new and unique. Many later critics would view *Cane* as an inaugural text of the Harlem, or New Negro, Renaissance, an ironic designation considering that Toomer did not identify as black. Instead, he cast himself as a "New American," a mixture of several races and nationalities. Rather than a victim of America's sin, Toomer believed that he represented the transcendent promise of the nation itself.[45]

Why such disparity between Kabnis and Toomer? Part of the answer lies in *Cane* itself. The book's boldly modern approach to style, form, and subject matter can puzzle readers. The juxtapositions are hard to pin down: brutal violence against lyrical language; poetry mixed with narrative and closet drama; the Jim Crow's South set against the Great Migration's North, each with a corresponding set of images. Linking the ten poems and six narratives of book's first part, set in the fictional Sempter, Georgia, are women who cross traditional sexual boundaries, sugarcane and cotton, the smell of pine needles and smoke, the colors of dusk, and folk songs humming in the background. In part 2, comprising seven sketches and five poems, the book moves to Washington, D.C., and Chicago – worlds of asphalt, interiors, and the cacophonies of jazz –

where men never fully connect to their own emotions or to the women they love. "Kabnis," a closet drama – meant to be read rather than performed – returns to Sempter to end *Cane*. As the final section, "Kabnis" should bring the book and its themes full circle.[46] In some ways it does exactly that; in others, it avoids closure. Ralph Kabnis could be but clearly is not the controlling perspective for any of the book's sections. If *Cane* has any defining narrative presence, it belongs to the poetic voice in "Song of the Son" and "Georgia Dusk," tasked with carrying forward to future generations the "plaintive soul" of "dusky cane-lipped throngs." Would-be poet Kabnis finds that words cannot capture the complicated essence of the place he inhabits. Caught between the beauty of land and people, and the ugliness of poverty, racism, and violence, language splits apart. Kabnis descends into an existential crisis so deep he may never recover. *Cane* seems barely to cohere as well. Even the book's graphics call attention to its fragmentary nature: visuals of arcs that never meet as complete circles divide its three sections. Yet "Kabnis" and, thus, *Cane* end with images of spiritual triumph: sunrise and childbirth. Balancing on the verge of collapse, *Cane* remains a hauntingly beautiful book. Through Ralph Kabnis, Toomer dramatizes the artist's struggle to render inexpressible experience.

Lynching's violence is one of those experiences. Toomer links Kabnis's artistic failure and his resulting spiritual breakdown to Mame Lamkins's story. Toomer likely knew about the 1918 Brooks-Lowndes lynchings from his association with other Washington, D.C., writers who responded to it. He attended the Saturday night salons at Georgia Douglas Johnson's home where Carrie Williams Clifford, Angelina Weld Grimké, and others from the city's black literary elite gathered.[47] The incident's wounds may still have been reverberating when Toomer took the job in Sparta that was the model for Sempter. Multiple scholars have discussed Toomer's relationship to lynching in general and this one in particular.[48] Lynching appears as a topic at various points throughout *Cane*, most noticeably in "Blood Burning Moon," the story that closes out part 1. There, Tom Burwell, a black man, is killed after fighting with a white man over a black woman. Preceding that story is a poem, "Portrait in Georgia," that describes a woman whose braided hair coils "like a lyncher's rope" and whose body is the color of "black flesh after flame." Noticeable about these pieces is how Toomer represents lynching differently from others. "Blood Burning Moon" links racial violence to sex and power but not rape. The poem, a "portrait," frames the white woman's and the black male victim's bodies as aesthetic objects – things white men like to see. By creating beautiful works of art about ugly topics, Toomer has prompted some critics to ask whether his aims were more aesthetic or political.[49] The answer to that question may lie in "Kabnis," where aesthetics and politics converge in the figure of Mary Turner. Toomer transforms Turner into Mame Lamkins, the narrative and emotional center of "Kabnis." In Toomer's hands Turner/Lamkins becomes a metaphor of artistic struggle, of the way language breaks down and also persists despite great odds. Through the image of the lynched pregnant woman killed for speaking out, Toomer raises key questions about art and the artist in modern society. If other artists struggled to render this story, Toomer made that struggle overt. Kabnis, his artistic vision aborted, succumbs to soul death under the oppressive weight of an ugly world. Toomer, in turn, gives birth to beauty and the possibility that souls might heal. In the hands of the New American, art bears witness to and prays for salvation from the national sin of lynching violence.

Offsetting Toomer's prayer is the opening scene of "Kabnis." The schoolteacher lies awake at night, spiritually paralyzed and on the verge of madness. He feels torn by a world so clearly divided between black and white, so beautiful and ugly at the same time:

> God Almighty, dear God, dear Jesus, do not torture me with beauty. Take it away. Give me an ugly world. Ha, ugly. Stinking like unwashed niggers. Dear Jesus, do not chain me to myself and set these hills and valleys, heaving with folk-song, so close to me that I cannot reach them. There is a radiant beauty in the night that touches and . . . tortures me. Ugh. Hell. Get up, you damn fool. Look around. Whats beautiful there? Hog pens and chicken yards. Dirty red mud. Stinking outhouse. Whats beauty anyway but ugliness if it hurts you? (85, ellipsis and punctuation as in original)[50]

Kabnis cannot comprehend the overwhelming spirituality of the people's lives, which persists despite brutal realities. He is clearly an outsider in this community, a status that leaves him feeling not only alienated but also paranoid. He even envisions himself as a potential lynching victim, hanging beneath the courthouse tower for no reason beyond the white desire to "juggle justice and a nigger" (86). Images of lynching violence and motherhood that play an important role later in the story appear with particular force in the songs that act as chorus to this section.

One, a poignant yet morbid spiritual about the final resting place, Camp Ground, speaks of a "White man's land" where "Niggers, sing" and "Burn, bear black children" (83, 87). Another, a lullaby, tells of a black mother nursing until the bough breaks, and the baby and cradle fall (84). These songs filter across the night winds, described as "soft-voiced vagrant poets" (87), to permeate Kabnis's thoughts, waking and sleeping.

Life in Georgia is surreal to him, and when he goes to Halsey's home seeking grounding in reality, he finds his existential crisis compounded by Layman's litany of racial ills, culminating with the horrific tale of Mame Lamkins. It is Sunday. The spirit-packed sounds of a church service punctuate Layman's storytelling, and a shouting sister's "high-pitched and hysterical" voice grows "perfectly attuned to the nervous key of Kabnis." The mood outside shifts when Layman reaches the story's tragic denouement, the lynching of Mame Lamkins. As the choir begins an old spiritual, even the wind itself seems to hum the blues. Layman recalls in a soft-spoken voice: "She was in th family-way, Mame Lamkins was. They killed her in th street, an some white man seein the risin in her stomach as she lay there soppy in her blood like any cow, took an ripped her belly open, an the kid fell out. It was living; but a nigger baby aint supposed t live. So he jabbed his knife in it an stuck it t a tree. An then they all went away" (92, spelling consistent with original). When Layman is done, the sister gives out another, frantic shriek: "Jesus, Jesus, I've found Jesus. O Lord, glory t God, one mo sinner is acomin home." Her cry echoes Kabnis's own reaction ("Christ no!") and accompanies the crash of a rock breaking the window. Kabnis is certain that a note attached to the rock, warning "the northern nigger" to go home (92), is meant for him and that he will be the next lynching victim. The story changes Kabnis for the worse: he becomes a "scarecrow replica" of his former self (93), certain that a lynch mob – complete with baying hounds – is now on his trail, even though the rock-sent note is clearly meant for another character, Lewis (who, from Toomer's description, seems loosely based upon NAACP investigator Walter White). Halsey takes in Kabnis after the latter quits teaching, and the two spend the idle hours between jobs drinking to excess in Halsey's cellar, known as "the Hole."

One difference between Kabnis before and after hearing Mame Lamkins's story is having a metaphor for what ails him. He wants to be a poet, he tells Halsey, Lewis, and others in the Hole with him, but he has failed because he cannot find the words to convey what he sees and feels. Toomer's aberrant spelling captures Kabnis's struggle: "Th form that burned int my soul is some twisted awful thing that crept in from a dream, a godam nightmare, an wont stay still unless I feed it. An it lives on words. Not beautiful words. God Almighty no. Misshapen, split-gut, tortured, twisted words" (111). The language here is significant, as Lamkins comes to embody Kabnis's failed artistic vision, and her fetus the image of his tortured soul. He says of that soul, "I wish t God some lynchin white man ud stick his knife through it an pin it to a tree" to put it out of its misery (111). Kabnis's appropriation of Lamkins's and her fetus's images is disturbing but not surprising, given what the story encapsulates for him – the essential, overpowering ugliness of a place. The story has shifted since the beginning. At first Kabnis felt trapped between his inability to reconcile beauty and ugliness, but by the end he no longer has access to beauty, for him the mark of a successful artist. The soft-voiced, vagrant poets no longer whisper to him across the night winds; twisted awful things populate his dreamscape instead. Kabnis is trapped within a self-perpetuating cycle of ugliness and pain, which he thinks can be remedied only through death. Even Halsey's sister Carrie's attempts to heal him yield no result. In the final scene he kneels before her, while she "takes his hot cheeks in her firm cool hands [and her] palms draw the fever out" (117). Just as she raises her hands in prayer, Halsey calls Kabnis up to work, and the failed poet grabs his bucket of dead coals with a savage jerk and trudges upstairs. It seems as if Kabnis has resigned himself to a spiritual death if not a physical one. What, then, to make of the happy ending that follows, with its images of sunrise and rebirth? Why are poetry and redemption possible for Jean Toomer but not for Ralph Kabnis?

To state the obvious, the protagonist and author are two separate entities. Distinct differences exist between Toomer and his fictional counterpart, despite the story's autobiographical roots. Toomer does make connections between the two. As he would explain in a letter to his literary mentor Waldo Frank, dated April 26, 1922, "Kabnis sprang up in almost a day, it now seems to me. It is the direct result of a trip I made to Georgia this past fall. . . . I barely avoided a serious time."[51] Although Toomer never specifies what happened to him during the "serious time," one may easily speculate that a Washington, D.C., native who frequently crossed racial boundaries and held little firsthand knowledge of Jim Crow's strict rules did not fare well in the rural South. In future correspondence with Frank, Toomer would describe Kabnis, the struggling artist, as a figure for himself. In one undated letter he proclaims, "Kabnis is *Me*."[52] Where Kabnis reaches his artistic nadir in Georgia, however, Toomer finds artistic culmination. But that culmination did not happen easily or without help. Toomer's letters show that while Kabnis may have sprung up in a day, "Kabnis" did not. Toomer originally wrote the piece as a drama, but could not get it published or produced as such. Influential director and producer Kenneth Macgowan rejected "Kabnis" for *Theatre Arts Magazine* for several reasons, mainly because he did not recognize the work as an actual play, but as "a sort of novel seeking new form." Although he did admire its "vividness" and "emotional tension," Macgowan told Toomer that "Kabnis" would need serious revision, specifically some "central action," to work.[53] Harold Loeb eventually accepted the piece for *Broom*, putting Lola Ridge on the job of cutting and sharpening. Under Ridge's and Frank's guidance, "Kabnis"—originally conceived as a sprawling drama in *Cane*'s first section—emerges as a powerful final commentary on the text's composition. Although Toomer faced some difficulty bringing his text to fruition, he ultimately succeeds where Kabnis fails because the two have different aesthetic visions. Kabnis's equation of art with beauty cannot fathom a creative expression borne out of violent oppression. The shouting sister's shriek punctuates the insertion of a very ugly truth into that equation, sending Kabnis into an existential tailspin. Toomer, conversely, did what any good modernist writer working with some of the best blue pens in Greenwich Village would do: made difficulty the subject of his writing, letting a fractured form follow jarring thematic function.

"Kabnis" the story offers two alternatives to paralysis, even if Kabnis the character does not recognize them. One is distinctly political. Halsey's Hole is not just a place for drinking and carousing with wild women; it also houses Father John, a deaf, blind ex-slave whom everyone but Carrie believes is mute. Kabnis sleeps there after his outburst about poetry and believes that he hears Father John, "Mumblin, feedin that ornery thing thats livin on my insides" (114). Father John's words, which emerge full-force the next morning in Carrie's presence, do indeed fuel Kabnis's rage. "Sin," the elderly man mutters. Kabnis takes the phrase personally, linking it to his own soul-sickness. "[T]h only sin is whats done against th soul," he says. "The whole world is a conspiracy t sin, especially in America, an against me. I'm the victim of their sin. I'm what sin is" (116). While Kabnis focuses inward, on the ugliness that consumes his soul, Father John channels his rage outward, onto white America. In the ex-slave's world, sin is "fixed . . . upon the th white folks. . . . f telling Jesus – lies. O the th sin white folks 'mitted when they made th Bible lie" (116–17). As with Mame Lamkins's story, Toomer reinforces this statement's emotional impact with a narrative disruption, following Father John's words with an unidentified "BOOM!" from the floor above. Another mirroring occurs between Father John and Kabnis. The blind, deaf, supposedly mute man who lives in a cellar can see, hear, and speak what the failed poet, stuck in his own interior abyss, cannot. Through Father John's words, Toomer connects lynching to a larger system of oppression via slavery – both are sins, "whats fixed upon the white folks." But Kabnis rejects the possibilities for transformation that the blind man's outward-looking vision might provide for both his aborted artistic agenda and his spiritual crisis – if he would only use those split-gut words to speak up about sin rather than continue to let them devour his soul. "You old black fakir," Kabnis says to Father John. Carrie rebukes him for this response, "Brother Kabnis is that your best amen?" (117). She and Father John, conversely, participate in the story's final redemptive moment. Having said his piece, the ex-slave finds peace. "Jesus, come," Carrie prays when Kabnis is gone, and as the sun rises, "Light streaks through the iron-barred cellar window. Within its soft circle, the figures of Carrie and Father John" (117).

This sunrise also sends out a birth song, pointing toward Toomer's second alternative to existential and artistic paralysis. The writer found his own literary voice through music more so than political action. As Toomer explains to Frank about his time in Georgia, "It was there that I heard the folk songs rolling up the valley at twilight, heard them as spontaneous and native utterances. They filled me with gold, and tints of an eternal purple. Love? Man, they gave birth to a whole new life."[54] Toomer's words recall Kabnis's experience near the story's beginning as well as reinforce his other maternal metaphors with respect to the character. In a later autobiographical sketch, he explains that he wanted *Cane* to memorialize the musical spirit that he found down South and believed was dying out. "*Cane* was a swan-song. It was a song of an end," Toomer states.[55] As several scholars have noted, *Cane* achieves this work of mourning by acting formally and thematically as a blues-based book.[56] Compositionally, it is organized like a traditional blues, in three parts, with poetry acting as chorus to the stanzas of the longer sections. Within several stories, sketches, and closet dramas, poetry functions similarly as chorus. Others, such as "Kabnis," are punctuated with actual songs. In its southern sections, *Cane* testifies to the triumphs and failures of human spirit that Toomer found when he traveled to Jim Crow Georgia in 1921. The book records through multiple genres an abiding beauty that Kabnis could not reconcile with the crushing ugliness that he saw around him. (Fittingly, *Cane*'s northern section, in sketches like "Seventh Street," takes on a jazz-like quality.) The shout that pierces Kabnis's soul potentially connects him to a much longer song, pointing the way toward another redemptive path, but the tortured artist hears only the tune from his own "nervous key"; he matches the sister's cry to Jesus with a resounding "Christ, no." Toomer, unlike his fictional counterpart, recognized music's potential to alleviate despair, especially the existential pain born of violent oppression. The blues emerged, musician and literary critic Adam Gussow explains, as a coping mechanism – a way to name, take ownership of, and transform the powerful emotions brought about by white-on-black violence into something that could be expressed.[57] The blues became a radical assertion of humanity in this way: a ragged spiritual beauty that refuses to die despite ugly realities. *Cane*, even though written by someone who perceived himself as an outsider to southern black culture (and "Kabnis" recognizes that position) pays tribute to the place of the blues and to music more generally within that culture. *Cane* is ultimately a book about mourning and morning, an outcry that comes from a fragmented spirit and the music that holds promise for a new day.

Toomer's prayerful blues is not that different a strategy from the antilynching activist's raw, naked, brutal facts with respect to the national sin of lynching. Both offered hope for saving bodies and souls. Both did so through positioning lynching as the point of rupture, where human lives, communities, spirits, nations, and language split apart. Such a repositioning differed quite a bit, however, from lynching as the point of union where whites consolidated power through the scapegoating and purging of blacks. To wrest a word from one meaning and affix it to another takes a metaphorical act of violence or, at minimum, a lot of work. Artists like Toomer and activists like James Weldon Johnson brought to their efforts a wide range of strategies over a span of several decades. Some, like Harry Haywood and Milton Howard, saw their words as weapons. Others, like Oscar Micheaux, would no more describe themselves as activists than John Shillady would describe himself as an artist. At some point the artist and the activist usually do part company. Statistics, maps, and other kinds of facts proved lynching to be a pervasive, systematic threat – "an American shame," "a challenge to every American citizen," even "a weapon of national oppression." Film, literature, and visual art revealed lynching as existential, spiritual crisis – laying waste to bodies, landscapes, psyches, and souls. Black spots on a map cannot convey the emotional impact of lynching. For that, one needs the broken voice of a would-be poet crying in agony for someone to nail his tortured soul to a tree. The ultimate difference is this: if activists envisioned solutions through law or revolution, then artists saw the imagination as both a tool of social justice and way out unto itself. As *Cane* ably demonstrates, the act of imagining negates despair.

Nation, Representation, and Disappearing Women

What Ralph Kabnis might call the art of the split-gut word eventually came to dominate lynching representations. During the early 1920s, and increasingly throughout the next two decades, artists and writers would privilege grotesque images over the sentimental kind that Fuller, Grimké, and Clifford employed. Oscar Micheaux's *Within Our Gates* centers on the hanging and burning of a husband and wife. Anne Spencer has a young ghoul pick through a victim's bones for a skull to hurl at God. Jean Toomer's failed poet becomes lost in despair, his broken language reflecting his broken spirit. In each case, lynching becomes a traumatic event that radiates outward from the individuals directly affected to increasingly broader populations. It may even preclude the possibility of creativity itself. At the same time, these works comment powerfully upon the human spirit's ability to survive brutal oppression and upon the artist's ability to create change. By 1935 grotesque images were fully established as the primary representational mode in antilynching creative work. That year saw two significant art exhibitions in Manhattan, the NAACP's *Art Commentary on Lynching* and the Communist-backed *Struggle for Negro Rights*, and two significant publications, Erskine Caldwell's "Kneel to the Rising Sun" and Richard Wright's "Between the World and Me." Running throughout the visual and the literary is an overwhelming presence of "raw, naked, brutal" figures. Many of these depictions draw from the violence of pro-lynching news accounts, postcards, and photographs popular earlier in the century. Rather than celebrate the spectacle of tortured and mutilated bodies, antilynching art and literature used the violence to elicit the kind of negative reaction James Weldon Johnson described. If such images had a market, the underlying logic went, then the marketplace would provide. "Let 'em swoller . . . till they vomit or bust wide open," a character from Ralph Ellison's *Invisible Man* would say in a different context.[58] Johnson was ultimately right. Force-fed an abundance of such images, Americans would eventually feel sick and ashamed.

It comes as no surprise that modernist approaches – whether in documentary or creative work – ultimately came to dominate antilynching discourse. Scholars such as Grace Hale and Jacqueline Goldsby cast lynching as something that went hand-in-hand with the construction of a modern white nation. Both Hale and Goldsby point to a paradox: a very old set of practices adapted quickly at the turn of the century to new debates and technologies in order to consolidate and police racial hierarchies. A primary factor differentiating blacks from whites, Hale argues, was that images of dehumanized black bodies served as products that a white-dominated marketplace could consume. The courageous work of people like John Shillady, Will Alexander, and Jessie Daniel Ames stands as testimony that not all whites condoned lynching. However, as Hale explains, for some "the slippage between titillation, self-righteousness, and disgust remained. White southern elites blamed 'crackers,' and northern whites pointed a finger at white southern barbarity." As whites deferred blame, blacks paid the price for what Hale calls a "deadly amusement."[59] The game kept one constantly off balance, through violence that Goldsby calls "both shocking and ordinary, unexpected and predictable, fantastic and normal, horrifying and banal." Illogical as it may sound to contemporary readers, many of whom think of lynching as something aberrant, confined to a particular region or class, the phenomenon fit squarely into what Goldsby situates within the nation's "cultural logic" at the time. It was the logic of terrorism, perfectly suited to maintaining blacks as second-class citizens.[60]

Modern activists and artists turned that logic around through a different kind of violence. The "raw, naked, brutal fact," whether employed as social science methodology or product of a creative mind, meant to destabilize the positive associations lynching held in the popular imagination. Often this called for blurring the lines between activism and art, or the beautiful and the ugly – precisely where Ralph Kabnis had trouble, but Jean Toomer the modernist did not. Russ Castronovo describes how ideas of beauty and violence came into conflict at the turn of the century, forcing people like W. E. B. Du Bois and his colleagues at the *Crisis* to renegotiate their ideas of art itself. Beauty, Castronovo explains, became "a site of 'crisis' where violence is aestheticized even as aesthetic formalism is linked to social transformation." If the lynched black body had become an aesthetic object that white spectators could derive pleasure and gain a sense of community from seeing, then Du Bois believed beauty alone was not a sufficient force to overturn lynching.[61] Sometimes the split-gut word was right for the occasion. Du Bois may have been correct, given the many cultural productions that relied upon graphic facts and grotesque renderings to emerge between the years of Jesse Washington and Emmett Till's deaths. In 1916 photographs of Washington's lynching circulated as both consumer product and antilynching propaganda. In 1955 Till's killers went free, but his death became, as David Halberstam famously noted, "the first great media event of the civil rights movement."[62] Activists and artists employed the tools of modernism to transform the discourse that reconceived lynching as a national shame.

Even as Mary Turner became the metaphor of despair, through Kabnis's split-gut word, and, paradoxically, a vehicle for imaginative redemption, through Toomer's birth song, the actual woman disappeared from public memory. Only John Shillady invoked her name when adding resonance to data. For the most part, she remained at the edges of the national lynching narrative, as brutal fact, trope, and increasingly spectral figure. Soon after the May 1918 incident made headlines across the country, story elements quickly fell away. The first to disappear were lesser-known male victims, followed in turn by the white farmer and his wife, then Sidney Johnson, Mary's husband, Hayes, and finally Mary Turner herself. The last publication to mention her before contemporary artists began recovering her story was Haywood and Howard's 1932 *Lynching* booklet. In that document, she is an anonymous "pregnant colored woman . . . hanged by the ankles and her unborn child ripped from her abdomen." No motive, no location, no name. Through her disap-

Figure 9. Flag, announcing lynching, flown from the window of the National Association for the Advancement of Colored People headquarters. (Prints and Photographs Division, Library of Congress, LC-USZ62-33793; used with permission of the National Association for the Advancement of Colored People.)

pearance Turner serves as a different kind of metaphor, a representative woman's story. Women like Fuller, Grimké, Clifford, and the Anti-Lynching Crusaders made an effort to shift the gaze onto lynching as a women's issue. For them, domestic space radiated outward from home to nation, and a woman's lynching stood as evidence of something gone clearly awry within the whole spectrum. Not all activists and artists who focused on the modern body politic omitted women's bodies or their perspectives. Oscar Micheaux dared to film a woman being hanged and burned at the height of Red Summer. Anne Spencer was a committed feminist. The women of the ASWPL made a documented difference. But the mid-twentieth-century discourse of lynching was overwhelmingly gendered male. The NAACP had a sign that it used in the 1930s to hang outside its Manhattan offices, "A Man Was Lynched Yesterday"[63] (figure 9). The organization did not have an equivalent sign for a woman. The woman's designated place, to return to an earlier point, was the *Mater*

Dolorosa to the male's Black Christ. The only way to get one's voice heard, as Mamie Till Bradley discovered, was to engage in what Lauren Berlant calls "diva citizenship": "when a person stages a dramatic coup in a public sphere in which she does not have privilege."[64] Otherwise, one remained on the margins of the national lynching story, a ghost. Demanding retribution, ghosts have a habit of returning.

4 Contemporary Confrontations

Recovering the Memory of Mary Turner

A well-known exchange in the 1997 *Journal of American History* highlights the complex relationship between lynching, memory, and race. The debate centered on an article by historian Joel Williamson titled "Wounds Not Scars: Lynching, the National Conscience, and the American Historian." Williamson, who is widely recognized for his foundational work in race and southern history, describes how he "discovered" during the late 1960s that a horrific wave of racial violence had washed across the turn-of-the-century South. Williamson writes, "Nothing in my living experience as a southerner and an American, nothing in my training and practice as a historian and a professor, had prepared me for this." In an unusual move for the *Journal*, editors ran the conflicting and sometimes contentious referees' reports as a roundtable, "What We See and Can't See in the Past." Providing one of the most scathing comments was Robin D. G. Kelley, who said that if Williamson did not see lynching before, he did not look. At a minimum, Kelley explained, Williamson's statement demonstrated that he had not read the work of significant African American and Jewish historians, who treat the subject at length. David Leavering Lewis made similar remarks about Williamson's consideration of white sources. Did he somehow miss newspapers,

William Faulkner, and Lillian Smith? Editor David Thelen explained that he ran Williamson's piece because it serves a reflexive purpose. It "challenges us to think about what we see and do not see, to reflect on what in our experience we avoid, erase, or deny, as well as what we focus on." Thelen gave the last word to Jacquelyn Dowd Hall, who observed that conventional wisdom about lynching and memory is wrong. Even many historians believe that as numbers declined, lynching disappeared from national consciousness. Not true, Hall said. It moved to a liminal space between remembering and forgetting where all traumatic memories go. The nation did not undergo collective amnesia about the subject of lynching so much as it experienced selective acknowledgment. Some individuals were more able and willing to consider that painful past than others. Williamson did not see the history of racial violence prior to his research because, to paraphrase him, everything in his experience as a white southern male had trained him not to look. Meanwhile, Hall explained, the "parallel universes of women's history and African American history" saw very different stories.[1]

My experience of learning about lynching, as described in the Introduction, was somewhat different from Joel Williamson's. Maybe the difference is generational, or maybe, being female, I already occupied a parallel universe that gave me another perspective. Some of what Williamson says rings true of me, however. White southerners frequently remind themselves to "look away," as the song goes. (The tune of that song, "Dixie," was the same as my high school's fight song, so I was reminded at every sporting event.) But white southerners just as frequently get our noses rubbed in the stink of historical memory so that the rest of America does not have to look at itself. (If I had a quarter for every image of police dogs and firehoses, then I would be one rich civil rights scholar. If I gave a quarter to anyone who could identify a picture of the bed where Black Panther Fred Hampton was killed, I'd still be rich.) Sometimes, after so many rubbings, our noses get out of joint and we retreat into the defensive posturing of Old South iconography, or worse. Sometimes, like me, we get obsessed, which is another defense mechanism. Collecting references to Mary Turner became my private demon for years: it helped me avoid writing and thinking. In some ways the process was necessary; I needed to recover enough material to create a rich and complex story. In other ways I kept looking in a manner that did not seem healthy. I followed footnote trails, logged multiple tours of duty in libraries, did endless Internet searches, tracked down artists and writers using stalkerlike methods. Worse, I felt compelled to connect even the most tenuous allusions, even ones I was unsure of. A reference to a woman "strung up, slit open, and burned just about up" in Alice Walker's *The Third Life of Grange Copeland* (1970) may or may not be significant. Octavia Butler may have had Turner in mind when she wrote in *Kindred* (1979) about the hanging/beating of a pregnant woman until she miscarries on the ground, but I don't know. I was certain that Allison Saar's *Strange Fruit* (1995), a sculpture of a woman hanging upside down, depicted Turner, but she said no.[2] I knew that my work on this book was done when I heard Muhammad Ali, in an interview from the 1970s, make a reference to a lynched pregnant woman, and I did not take notes. I probably should have, because Ali's comments raise questions: where would he have heard the story, and why would he have heard it at that particular time?

My obsession did yield some results: enough material to reveal patterns that help to answer these questions. Responses to Mary Turner peaked from 1918 to 1923, as activists, artists, and writers used her story to recast lynching from solution to problem: a woman's murder showed how mobs threatened the domestic spaces of home and nation. Further removed from the event's immediacy, it started to fall out of public discourse. By 1932 the story of what happened in Brooks and Lowndes counties dissolved into the brief mention in a Communist Party USA pamphlet of something terrible that happened to a pregnant colored woman. Several elements converged to send Turner's story into the liminal space of history. First, as lynching became firmly established as a national trauma, that trauma was gendered male (despite the efforts of earlier activists), and Turner did not fit the narrative. Second, as graphic description became the dominant form of representing lynching, and grotesque stories became more commonplace, Turner's no longer held the same shock value. Third, creative and documentary sources about Turner stopped circulating or went out of print, as did a lot of African American and women's literature from the time. The stories that did circulate often did so through oral history, also the result of lynching becoming a traumatic, or taboo, subject. When Turner's story did start to reenter mainstream public discourse in the 1970s, the paths are fairly clear. The first was the 1969 Arno Press reprinting of Walter White's *Rope and Faggot*. White's "The Work of a Mob" also reappeared in a November

1970 anniversary edition of the *Crisis*. A third route was the 1975 reissue of *Cane*, with a new introduction by Darwin T. Turner and a footnote that gave the historical background for Mame Lamkins.[3] A different path was the African American oral history that resulted in the multiple contradictory versions that one sees in public memorials today. Why did Turner's story reemerge, and what is it being used to say? Again the convergence of particular forces – black feminism and postmodernism – set the stage for the recovery of a marginalized black female who could disrupt traditionally male historical narratives. Since the 1980s, public memorials, historical reenactments, and works of art and literature have pointed directly at the image of a lynched pregnant woman as a paradigmatic instance of racial violence. The figure draws its power specifically from the liminal spaces, as a story less familiar than those of iconic males and therefore more shocking, more readily available to accomplish its demanding cultural work.

Different sources employ the female figure toward three primary ends. For the National Great Blacks in Wax Museum in Baltimore, Maryland, a life-size, graphically rendered display of Hayes and Mary Turner's lynching stands at the crossroads of two key narratives, one about progress, one about deterrence. If mob violence destroyed black families in the past, drug and gang violence destroys them in the present. The museum makes that connection clear through another exhibit next to the Turners, "The Boulevard of Broken Dreams," which explains, "Now We Lynch Ourselves." Visitors, often school groups, are encouraged to follow the more positive models that race leaders in the museum's other displays set out for them. A pregnant woman's lynching serves a different kind of shock therapy for community activists who gather at the Moore's Ford Bridge near Monroe, Georgia, each July to remember those who were murdered there in 1946. A controversial reenactment that began in 2006 culminates with the removal of a visibly pregnant female victim's fetus, followed by a call for justice. Making this violent act visible intends to jog the memories of anyone who has knowledge about the case and might still be alive. Although this story does not address Turner directly, its emphasis on bearing witness, along with its conflation of the two Georgia stories, makes it relevant to the discussion. Of special importance was the 2008 reenactment, which included a naming ceremony for victim Dorothy Malcolm's baby, who some say was removed like Mary Turner's. That year the baby was christened, in absentia, "Justice." Finally, female artists and writers draw upon the figure of the pregnant woman to confront male-dominated narratives of lynching. Freida High Tesfagiorgis's pastel composition *Hidden Memories* (1985) defines Turner's lynching as a key moment of violence against women that too many have been unable or unwilling to see. As the first artist in six decades to acknowledge and name Turner's memory, Tesfagiorgis engaged in a significant act of recovery. Later works speak to the complexity involved in such recovery projects. Artist Kara Walker, in *Do You Like Creme in Your Coffee and Chocolate in Your Milk* (1997), and writer Honorée Fanonne Jeffers, in "dirty south moon" (2007), comment in very different ways on the necessity and difficulty of negotiating those liminal spaces where memories travel.

As I said early on, difficulty is a theme of this book. Whether display, reenactment, or creative work, each of the sites of memory examined in this chapter challenges audiences to look at a past that most Americans, not just a particular demographic, have been trained not to see. These contemporary lynching responses refuse to be ignored or unconsciously consumed. They not only make us look at the ghost; they make us interact with it. Given the choice, a lot of people might "look away." In some cases, that was my first reaction, and I was obsessed with seeking them out. Ultimately, I am glad I chose to stick around, even when they were hard to digest. Works of art, literature, and public memorial force confrontation with the negative emotions associated with lynching in order to transform those emotions into positive action, whether healing, mourning, calling for justice, or simple recognition that lynching happened. These works demand our attention and our reaction as thinking, feeling, ethical human beings. In this way, Great Blacks in Wax, Moore's Ford reenactments, artwork by Tesfagiorgis and Walker, and Jeffers's poetry all perform a different role in the trauma process from texts examined in chapter 3. In the 1920s and 1930s, activists and artists deconstructed lynching, destabilizing meaning until solution became problem. For contemporary cultural workers, re-membering is the task at hand: shaping an explosive, elusive, and incomprehensible past into something that can be acknowledged, honored, and mourned. The difference between now and then is the difference between putting together and blowing apart. Yet the contemporary responses examined here have an explosive power of their own. Both confrontational and constructive, they engage audiences in the process of shaping new narratives that face rather than avoid the ghost. Lisa Woolfork describes a similar process in her book on slavery reenactments, *Embodying American Slavery in Contemporary Culture*. Through what she calls "bodily epistemology," participants, observers, viewers, or readers travel back imaginatively to a scene of cultural trauma in order to invest that memory with sacred or therapeutic value. The creative and public works examined here likewise invite audiences into the liminal spaces where the memory of lynching travels. The journey is not intellectual, but visceral, making specific descriptors hard to find. As Woolfork explains, taking her cue from Janie in Zora Neale Hurston's *Their Eyes Were Watching God*: "You got to go there to know there."[4] Such is true of contemporary works that engage the memory of Mary Turner. I do my best to describe the journey.

Public Memorial: The National Great Blacks in Wax Museum

Baltimore's National Great Blacks in Wax Museum, founded in 1983, created in 1989 the first public memorial to the Turner lynching. Life-size, graphically rendered wax figures depict Hayes, Mary, their baby, and a white mob member. A colleague in African American history told me about it, and I thought she was kidding me. I could not imagine someone wanting to cast that story in wax. She urged me to go, but I put it off for years. I wanted to write an academic book about this lynching, but I did not want to see a realistic representation of it.

I finally visited Great Blacks in Wax in 2006, while traveling up the East Coast. An African American named Carl at my hotel's front desk helped me with directions. "Why do you want to go there?" he asked me point-blank. No doubt he was used to fielding questions about Inner Harbor and Camden Yards.

"I'm working on a book about something they have on exhibit," I tried to answer vaguely.

He stared at me. "I hope it's not the one I'm thinking about."

"Probably is."

"It'll make you want to turn militant."

I decided to look at his eyes rather than stare at my map.

"It did that to a lot of people. I'm writing about the responses of activists, artists, and writers."

Carl shrugged and gave me a final warning. "You better check your feelings at the door."

"It wouldn't be the first time I've had to do that," I replied, taking the map and thanking him for the directions.

The museum is located on East North Avenue in a working-class black neighborhood. The location is particularly important, as the museum takes pride in showing that "tourism can thrive in a nontraditional setting."[5] And thrive it does. According to its Web site, Great Blacks in Wax serves a steady stream of visitors, approximately three hundred thousand people, each year. Its exhibits occupy three floors. The top focuses on children's stories and figures central to Maryland history. The middle, or main, floor follows African American historical progress from slavery to freedom, ending with figures such as Martin Luther King Jr., Shirley Chisholm, and as of 2009, Barack Obama. The museum takes an international approach, linking black history in the United States to a broader African and diasporic heritage. Its displays include political leaders, entrepreneurs, folk heroes, sports legends, entertainers, scientists, artists, and children. In fact, finding a significant black presence not accounted for in this inclusive museum proves difficult. Great Blacks in Wax serves as a one-stop historical survey for schools and other tour groups. The day I went, two different middle-school-age groups were there, studying descriptions and listening to Howard "Mr. Gene" Stinnette, one of the artists who created the wax figures, narrate an accompanying audio guide. Indeed, the mission is primarily educational. Dr. Joanne Martin, who cofounded Great Blacks in Wax with her husband, Dr. Elmer Martin, explains that the museum intends to "use education, history, and example to help mainly culturally disadvantaged youth overcome feelings of alienation, defeatism, and despair." Great Blacks in Wax does this using figures that represent stories of racial progress and those that represent less uplifting, but still important counternarratives – what its mission statement calls the "little known, often neglected facts of history."

The space I wanted to see, the exhibit my black concierge said would make me militant, was in the basement. Visitors fittingly descend to the lower depths of black history. They proceed right to left around the museum's smallest public area while the song "Nearer My God to Thee" echoes softly. The Turner exhibit comes first. It is one of two wax displays in the room, and the only one in that room to focus on actual historical figures. An audio loop provides basic facts about the May 1918 lynchings, with details even ghastlier than those Walter White or any newspaper reported. The mutilated figure of Hayes Turner, in a yellow shirt and blood-stained denim overalls, hangs by a noose, castrated, with his ears and nose cut off and his face bashed in. Cats gnaw at his intestines, which lie scattered on the ground. (The audio guide states that the mob sewed the cats into Mary's stomach, taking bets on which would claw its way out first.) To the left of Hayes, Mary hangs upright above fire logs. She is naked and immolated with her legs cut off. The third figure in this horrific display, a white man, pulls the baby from her stomach. Above the glass case that houses the Turner memorial, three signs drive home the message:

- Get angry over the oppression that Black people and other people are still suffering today and put yourself in a position to resist now as your ancestors did back in the day when lynching was a national past time as popular as baseball games and circuses.
- Identify with the victims and martyrs, and never forget them. But do not get bitter or despondent over what they endured.
- They waged holy war through marches, protest demonstrations, art, organizational unity, the ministry, lectures, politics, donations to the cause, and even armed self-defense.

Standing before the exhibit, I did not turn militant. Actually I scribbled notes furiously, but later I recalled the Black Arts Movement's radicalism. Mr. Gene's depictions of the Turner lynchings are raw and potent in the way that Amiri Baraka says poetry should be raw and potent in his piece, "Black Art." As Baraka makes clear, poetry – and by implication all art – draws upon those stark realities to counter, and rise above, the world's multifaceted challenges. One could not pull off an installation like this in a mainstream museum.

Signs above the Turners make clear that once viewers have descended into lynching hell, they next will ascend through the narrative of racial uplift and resistance. Appropriately the room devotes other walls to racial violence and antilynching work. Panels list hate groups, memorialize "5,000 names of Lynching Martyrs," and replicate photographs and postcards. Throughout, wax replicas of body parts in jars along with rope and fire distinguish between the mutilation, torture, and burning that racial lynching meant and its more commonly understood notion of death by hanging. Other panels depict stories of activists, artists, and writers who fought – paraphrasing James Weldon Johnson – to save America's soul and transform lynching from an acceptable form of criminal justice to shameful act. Near the exit, a "Memorial to the Martyrs of Lynching" reminds viewers to engage productively with the past:

As you leave this memorial, do not leave in despair.

Think not of our suffering but of what we might have been had we lived.

Think what the world might have missed.

We could have been liberators, builders, sages, or prophets leading our
   people to the dawning of a new day.

Most importantly, think of the unfinished work that you – the living – still
   must do.

The room, like the museum as a whole, presents history with a message.
Part of that message involves progress. Lynching destroyed black bodies, minds, and spirits. Leaving the exhibit in despair perpetuates mental
and spiritual destruction. The best response to the mob's deadly work is
the unfinished work of the living.

The point is made clear by a second display, alongside the Turner di-
orama, which is called "The Boulevard of Broken Dreams." Here, visitors
peer into a dismal scene. Drug users and alcoholics lie scattered about
the detritus of addiction and urban blight in an alleyway where a caption
reads, "Now We Lynch Ourselves." It is an old strategy. "The Boulevard
of Broken Dreams" recalls a 1978 prison documentary, *Scared Straight!*.
The film features inmates at New Jersey's Rahway State Prison who reveal to juvenile delinquents the brutality of life on the inside. The goal is
to "scare" the young men into a "straight" life through fear tactics. The
older men tell the juveniles horrifying stories, scream, and curse at them.
(In fact, the televised version of the film became a rare instance where the
FCC allowed the word "fuck" to be said on air.) While most criminal justice professionals view *Scared Straight!* as a failure, its deterrence narrative
retains cultural significance and emotional resonance.[6] "The Boulevard
of Broken Dreams" draws upon that power to scare its viewers straight
back into Great Blacks in Wax's progress narrative. The display shows its
viewers something most find familiar, a scene of urban decay, complete
with drugs and alcohol. But it equates that scene with the other horrifying elements in the room: body parts in jars and the mutilated figures of
the Turners. It further defamiliarizes that scene by saying something unexpected: "Now We Lynch Ourselves." Like the older inmates, it berates
the younger, potential offenders by linking them not to the victims or to
the race leaders but to the mob member next to Hayes and Mary, doing
something vicious to the future generation. We no longer need this man,
the exhibit says, when we voluntarily use drugs and alcohol to kill ourselves – unless, the implicit message goes, we choose a different path.

When I walked past "The Boulevard of Broken Dreams" and back up to the main floor, a group of middle-school children walked past me down the stairs. I wanted to tell them not to go. The museum restricts the exhibit to viewers over the age of twelve, but still, the thought of those tweens standing in front of the Turners made me physically sick. But that is the museum's point. The museum even sells T-shirts that say "Today we lynch ourselves" as a reminder – not of mob violence but of black-on-black violence, self-murder, community decay, and other dangers to which various addictions can lead. The Turner lynching retains the power to shock. Great Blacks in Wax uses that image to shock a very different audience for a very different reason than Walter White had in mind in 1918. Sometimes the effects stay much the same, however. "It'll make you want to turn militant," the concierge said. Signs around the figures give viewers permission to feel angry but remind them to do something responsible rather than give in to despair. Great Blacks in Wax tries to manage emotional effects by connecting past and present. Underlying the museum's mission is the perception that too many people, young people in particular, have not made the connections themselves. To go back to Hall, conventional wisdom suggests not only that subjects like lynching have been forgotten but also that history itself does not exist as an integral part of one's public or private life. Collective amnesia may or may not be real. Most certainly, however, history as taught at Great Blacks in Wax is rare, especially in well-funded, mainstream institutions. The museum locates itself in a poor neighborhood and targets its message at youth in order to construct the past both as a source of nourishment and pride, and as a corrective and spur to action. In the same way that Johnson believed that "the raw, naked, brutal facts" could change the culture of lynching, Great Blacks in Wax links racist violence to the violence of substance abuse in order to create change. Despite what Carl said, Great Blacks in Wax probably does not want feelings checked at the door. The museum wants visitors to take a good, close look at the worst of the past – figured as the lynching of a black father, mother, and baby – and to channel the resulting emotions into what it deems appropriate behavior. The "Memorial to the Martyrs of Lynching" provides the lead. If lynching victims might have been "liberators, builders, sages, or prophets" had they not died, so too might anyone who avoids the real-life Boulevard of Broken Dreams lead "our people to the dawning of a new day."

Great Blacks in Wax offers another, quite literal avenue of critique beyond its uplift and deterrence narratives. By choosing its location within a specific neighborhood and basing its message upon a lesser-known but particularly heinous lynching of a black family, the museum sends a powerful message about looking. Visitors see history at its best and worst. They also see laid bare the United States' most basic ideals and realities – not just through the wax figures and Mr. Gene's narration but also in the surrounding area and the museum's story itself. Great Blacks in Wax has expanded from a exhibit of four pieces that the Martins lugged to schools, churches, and malls, to a small storefront shop in downtown Baltimore, to its present location taking up a sizeable portion of a city block. The museum provides a key piece of the effort to revitalize a working-class community's commercial district. Great Blacks in Wax has taken what it saw as a Boulevard of Broken Dreams and worked, through foresight and pluck, to turn that street into a destination. People seek *it* out. At least I did. In doing so, we travel to a place off the beaten track of Baltimore's tourist sites and off the beaten track of history. Visitors therefore encounter a present and a past they might not normally see. Internet reviewers of Great Blacks in Wax testify that the museum makes an impact, even as some describe the neighborhood as "scary."[7] If the museum's explicit message to schoolchildren is "Now We Lynch Ourselves," its implicit message to visitors of all ages is "We Will Be Seen." Different subjects control the verbs in those two statements. The former "we" speaks specifically to a "you" who should keep to a straight path, one that Great Blacks in Wax's model of East North Avenue improvement embodies. The latter "we" refers to the museum's community and its historic figures depicted in wax, whose stories refuse consignment to the liminal spaces of national consciousness.

Historical Reenactment: A Mass Lynching at the Moore's Ford Bridge

I knew the Moore's Ford Memorial Committee (MFMC) from conferences on racial violence; I ran across the annual lynching reenactments at the Moore's Ford Bridge by accident – in the middle of a class. My senior honors seminar on racial violence and reconciliation was

planning a field trip to meet Committee members, and we were studying their site in advance. The reenactments, which began in 2005, are
actually sponsored by another group, the Georgia Association of Black
Elected Officials. Still, the MFMC maintains a link to them. Someone in
class asked, "What's that?" and pointed to the link. I was willing to ex-
periment. We spent the next few minutes watching, and then I realized
that the story was starting to look eerily familiar. I grew antsy, wanted
to turn the computer off. It wasn't just me seeing Mary Turner everywhere. One of the students called out, "Hey, isn't that the story in your
book?" When the YouTube video was over, I said we were done for the
day. Most everyone said they needed a little time to process what they
had seen, too. On the field trip, a few students talked to participants, and
some said they would go back with me to the one taking place later that
summer. No one did.

In the original Moore's Ford Bridge incident, twelve to fifteen armed
men ambushed a car driven by a white man, Loy Harrison, who carried
two black couples, Roger and Dorothy Malcolm, and George and Mae
Murray Dorsey. Harrison had bailed Roger Malcolm out of jail, where
he had sat for eleven days after stabbing a white man, Barney Hester.
Hester would live, but that was not the point. Both Malcolm and Dorsey,
the latter a decorated war veteran, had been seen with white women.
Black voters could be a decisive factor in upcoming gubernatorial elec-
tions. The men who stopped Harrison's car near the Moore's Ford Bridge
believed that blacks needed to be reminded of their place. They ordered
Harrison out of his car, walked the Dorseys and Malcolms down to the
banks of the Apalachee River, and shot them multiple times. President
Harry Truman sent in the FBI, but the investigation met a wall of local
silence. In 1991, after a man who said he witnessed the attack came forward, prosecution seemed possible.

Reenactments today serve two purposes. Organizers seek justice in a
case that Georgia's former governor, Roy Barnes, reopened in 2000. In
2007 state and federal investigators found additional evidence in a Walton County farmhouse. Some of the men who killed the Malcolms and
Dorseys may still be alive. The reenactment covers a broad swath of
Monroe and Walton County. By replaying the incident before local residents along the city streets and county road where it happened, organizers hope to shake loose the forces of silence that have held sway for
more than sixty years. Proceedings end with a notice of reward: thirty-

five thousand dollars for information that leads to the arrest and prose-cution of the killers. Organizers also post a filmed version of events on YouTube.[8] The reenactment thus takes the Moore's Ford story into the streets and beyond, onto the Internet, toward a second end: the reclama-tion of space that is physical and memorial. People see those who stand for justice take history back from the mob. With every July 25 reenact-ment and every YouTube hit, GABEO and friends own the story of the Moore's Ford Bridge.

The reenactment that I attended, in 2008, was typical in many ways.[9] Following custom, ceremonies begin with a rally at Monroe's First Af-rican Baptist Church. This year, speakers covered the Moore's Ford in-cident timeline, called for passage of the Emmett Till Unsolved Civil Rights Crime Act (S.R. 535), and introduced family members of the Malcolms and the Dorseys who were present that day. The church was packed, with several hundred in attendance, racially mixed but mostly black. About four o'clock, GABEO's president, Rep. Tyrone Brooks (D-Atlanta), began shepherding the crowd outside, where a convoy of vehicles completed a circuit driving tour of the Moore's Ford lynching. With headlights on and a police escort, the group looked like a funeral procession, and on the highway out of town, traffic pulled over. As the cars neared stops, local whites lined up to watch. Some looked on curi-ous, bemused. Some smiled, some frowned. Each year, the first scene is the house formerly occupied by Barney Hester, on Hester Town Road. Actors portraying Malcolm and his wife Dorothy argue, Hester tries to mediate, and the story takes what will be its fatal turn. Next the group drives back into town proper, to the county jail where Malcolm was held until Harrison bailed him out. While there, attendees watch a different set of actors provide the story's Jim Crow context. Eugene Talmadge, running for governor at the time, gives a stump speech before a group of fawning white ladies. Talmadge's segregationist tirade ends at 5:30 p.m., a crucial moment. From then on, the reenactment moves in real time. Harrison, the Malcolms, and the Dorseys are on their way home from picking Roger up from jail. The convoy travels back down county roads, where it waits at the Moore's Ford Bridge. There, a mob of men springs from hiding behind trees, intercepts Harrison's automobile, orders the Malcolms and Dorseys out of the car and down a path toward the water, shoots them multiple times, and then, as the coup de grâce, cuts out the visibly pregnant Dorothy Malcolm's fetus.

Describing what actually happened at the bridge in 2008 is difficult. I had watched the YouTube video multiple times and thought I knew what to expect. But hyperreality was no preparation for the surreality of it all. My driving companions and I parked several yards away and walked to the bridge with the rest of the crowd. Yellow crime-scene tape held spectators off from where the actors would be. Old hands at the reenactment coached newcomers where to stand.

"This is the best place to be for the first scene."

"The lynching will be over there in the field."

Tyrone Brooks bellowed over a megaphone. "Please, move to one side or another. The car has to come through."

Actors playing mob members waited in the woods. They are not local. There has always been trouble finding white people to play these roles, according to reenactment coordinator Bobbie Paul. The first year, blacks in white masks played the killers. This year, Paul brought in Unitarian Universalist and Quaker friends from Atlanta – pacifists, who now lurked in the trees holding firearms loaded with blanks.

The small talk around me seemed loaded, too.

"Is this your first?"

"You know you can watch this any time you want on the Internet."

Brooks came over the microphone in a whisper. "Stay on one side of the road. Loy Harrison is bringing the Malcolms and the Dorseys. We need total quiet."

Silence. For a moment.

Then a blur. Men ran out of the woods yelling Loy Harrison's name. They pulled the actors from the cars. Spectators scrambled over one another to gawk and take pictures. Then we moved as a herd into the field. I saw and felt only the people around me, bodies pushing up against me, trying to get closer to see. Mob members barked orders, the women from the car started to cry. At the Apalachee's edge, more crowding, gunshots firing in volleys, a man's voice growling, "Cut it out." Gasps, moans, the snaps and whirs of cameras, and finally a closing prayer. When it was over, I stood there stunned for several minutes as spectators, black and white, took away bits of crime scene tape and other scraps they found on the ground as souvenirs. The woman who played Dorothy Malcolm walked past me carrying a black baby doll caked in dark red barbecue sauce.

The reenactments have not been without controversy. The Moore's

Ford Memorial Committee, an interracial group formed in 1997, has worked for justice and reconciliation in what has come to be known as the last mass lynching in America. Some of its members, including Robert Howard, a longtime area civil rights activist, and Hattie Lawson, chair of the Athens Area Human Relations Council, attend the July 25 events. Howard himself has played Roger Malcolm. Other Memorial Committee members, such as Richard Rusk, stay away. The basic area of contention centers around historical facts. Laura Wexler, in her extensive research for the book *Fire in a Canebrake*, could find no evidence of a baby's removal or that Dorothy Malcolm was even pregnant. At the 2008 reenactment, however, Tyrone Brooks says that Dan Young, the funeral director who handled the bodies, confirmed both stories for him.[10] The larger question that troubles MFMC members is whether the reenactments serve a higher cause of justice or eerily reinscribe the act of spectacle lynching. They do employ strategies similar to those used by earlier activists. Multiple groups from the NAACP to the CIC, to the Communist Party found that stories based in graphic details, including those about lynched pregnant women, can use anger and shame to motivate people into action. Conversely the reenactments do perform a gruesome lynching, down to large crowds visiting the scene taking photographs and souvenirs, including bits of crime scene tape that separated actors from audience and other detritus from the ground. One big difference between the real thing and the reenactment – aside from no one getting hurt – is that by far most of the spectators, picture takers, and souvenir gatherers at the Moore's Ford Bridge were black. The spectacle itself therefore serves a different purpose than turn-of-the-century productions that stage-managed white power at the expense of black bodies. But what?

The Moore's Ford reenactments likely serve a therapeutic function similar to what Woolfork describes in *Embodying American Slavery*. Ritual reenactments related to slavery have become fairly common, though controversial, in recent years, along with a growing market for what is called "slave tourism." Travelers explore such places as dungeons where captives were held in Ghana, participate in a *Maafa* ceremony in Brooklyn, or travel Underground Railroad routes in multiple states. The National Great Blacks in Wax Museum has such an exhibit, just as startling as its lynching scene: a slave-ship replica where visitors experience a version of the Middle Passage. The point of such "experiential involvement,"

Woolfork explains, is to connect in a real, visceral way to that which participants perceive as authentic.[11] Even though such memories, and especially their physicality, are painful or horrific, recalling negative aspects of the past is the point. Mainstream cultural institutions have too long elided those negative emotions, preferring instead what some tourism theorists refer to as the "McDisneyization" of history: sanitized, controlled, and predictable. Many travelers and spectators seek out instead "black spots" on the map, including but not limited to slave sites, as counters to such tightly managed environments. As Woolfork notes, the term "black spots" has potency when applied to reenactments of racial trauma.[12] "Black spots" on a map hearken back to NAACP and CIC rhetoric that cast lynching as a national sin. Travelers seek out such places these days not just in search of historical counternarratives and, thus, more complete pictures of the past. The point is to work through those traumas or expiate those sins. Of the Middle Passage figures at Great Blacks in Wax, Woolfork explains, the goal is "affective response (be it fear, despair, anger, anxiety, or hope)" that communicates "traumatic aspects of black history in an empathic way." For others, such as those who perform *Maafa* commemorations, the goal is a form of mourning that is distinctly spiritual, a "sacred psychodrama" akin to Holy Communion.[13]

After the 2008 reenactments my driving companions and I (all literature and cultural critics) contextualized the experience in terms of medieval mystery and passion plays. These public performances of familiar biblical stories took place yearly, usually coinciding with festivals or holidays. Stages were located at different stops around town, and actors came from different trades, with each guild responsible for a particular story. Towns often produced mystery plays in cycles, meaning the story followed an arc from creation to judgment. Passion plays often took place around Easter and focused on the death and resurrection of Christ.[14] The lynching reenactment follows the mystery play's movement through space and the passion play's theme of redemption. Like these earlier vernacular performances, spectators know how the story begins and ends. They know its source of evil. They know its martyrs. The connections between lynching and crucifixion run deep, although the Moore's Ford story has no actual cross or tree (only blood, or barbecue sauce). So, too, do the connections between salvation, redemption, and justice, which come together on the day of judgment when all God's children get their due. Each year on July 25 when hundreds gather at the First African Baptist Church in Monroe, Georgia, to commemorate America's last mass lynching, two different kinds of spectacles take place. In one, marchers take back the streets for a justice long delayed, forcing local residents to look at an incident that most would probably rather keep buried in 1946. In another, congregants follow a macabre pageant from station to station in an effort to transform into something sacred the evil that happened in their own backyards. The pictures and souvenirs they pick up take on a different meaning, not as turn-of-the-century postcards and fragments of black bodies but as holy relics. By posting their effort on YouTube, reenactors take their story national, and indeed the Moore's Ford incident, as a significant "last," has representative import. The movement from evil to redemption therefore becomes possible anywhere, anytime, with a quick Internet search, making the Moore's Ford passion play available for all to see.

So where is Mary Turner in all this? The reenactment took on the added depth of sacred rite when organizers named the Malcolms' baby. Those who believe that Dorothy Malcolm was pregnant have become increasingly vocal during the past few years, even as fact contradicts belief. As Bruce E. Baker observes in his study of racial violence in Laurens County, South Carolina, and Sherrilyn A. Ifill demonstrates in her examinations of Maryland's Eastern Shore, communities can and do conflate incidents.[15] Through the complex operations of historical memory, two stories become one. This appears to be the case concerning Dorothy Malcolm and Mary Turner. Details from an older mass lynching that made national headlines with both male and female victims have been superimposed upon a later one. As the Moore's Ford story traveled through private discourse, it took on the quality of urban legend: it became the story of what happens to women who get lynched in Georgia. For Moore's Ford reenactment organizers, however, Dorothy Malcolm's baby is not the stuff of legend, but historical reality. The name chosen, Justice, reflects what mob members took from the Malcolms and the Dorseys and what reenactors seek when they take back the streets of Monroe and Walton County.

The name, obviously, has an iconic ring – Justice Malcolm – echoing another life taken early by violence. Tyrone Brooks, in his speech that day, emphasized the name's civil rights connotations and the event's spiritual impact. This baby, Brooks explains, "was denied the right to be born, play, go to school, graduate, be a productive citizen, to be a loving husband and father. Until today this baby was denied a name because his mother was denied the right to give him a name. Until today when he is reborn in spirit in each of us. Today we march his name into history."[16] With its baby martyr Justice Malcolm reborn spiritually into each spectator at the 2008 Moore's Ford reenactment, the event's links to ritual and myth become even more apparent. One reason for gathering each July 25 is indeed to call for justice. Some of the men who killed the Malcolms and the Dorseys might still be alive, and seeing that murder acted out might really root them out. A new reason for gathering each July 25 will be to call for Justice. Participants follow the path of a story they know well to watch a scene of suffering, mourning, and now, with the naming of the Malcolms' baby, redemption. When his name is marched into history, the sin at the Moore's Ford Bridge can potentially be washed clean.

Visual Art: Freida High Tesfagiorgis and Kara Walker

What does it mean to present the "raw, naked, brutal facts," as James Weldon Johnson called them? In the cases of Moore's Ford and Great Blacks in Wax, the strategy is to elicit a visceral reaction, but toward different ends. Earlier accounts cast lynching as the problem, not the solution for a perceived problem of crime. Contemporary accounts depict lynching as present force as well as historical reality. Its legacy continues to impact, whether as trauma that repeats, sins in need of redemption, or spur to activism. A museum and a reenactment draw upon images of a violated family, specifically a mother-and-child dyad—as microcosm of violated communities and generations. Both want audiences to see, through graphic representations, how the victims died. They do not intend passive spectatorship, however. The founders of Great Blacks in Wax and the organizers at Moore's Ford want viewers to translate what they have learned from that act of looking into responsible, positive work that will benefit the descendants of families and communities that violence has harmed. The museum reminds visitors before they leave the lynching exhibit of the unfinished work that the living must do. The spirit of baby Justice is reborn at a Baptist church. In these two uses of lynched pregnant woman imagery, gender is significant to the extent that it facilitates dialogue about historical memory. Similarly, an earlier generation called upon Mary Turner's image to construct lynching as a national issue, but that was not the only avenue of conversation. Turner's lynching compelled many activists, artists, and writers primarily because it allowed them to focus on black women who had been left out of that conversation. Contemporary artists and writers have found that conditions remained much the same. Freida High Tesfagiorgis, Kara Walker, and Honorée Fanonne Jeffers—all part of a larger feminist recovery effort—have reclaimed black women's voices as central to the narrative of violence and resistance through depictions of the lynched pregnant woman.

That effort began with Tesfagiorgis's pastel work *Hidden Memories*. Like earlier representations of Turner, this one remains personally potent for the artist. The piece was composed in 1985 and published in Robert Henkes' *The Art of Black American Women*, but Tesfagiorgis no longer shows it publicly. (She politely referred me to Henkes.) Still, the piece did important cultural work by naming a process, and a story, that speaks to ways women have been marginalized.[17] At the time, the memory of Turner's lynching might be accurately described as hiding in plain sight: page 29 of *Rope and Faggot* to be exact. Kara Walker, for instance, drew upon images of lynched and beaten pregnant women without knowing Turner's name or details about her story. Honorée Jeffers spent much of her childhood in Georgia and did not hear of Turner until she was well past graduate school.[18] Turner's, like other women's histories, may have been "visible" in a book, but male-dominated narratives overshadowed or completely buried it. *Hidden Memories* acknowledges the fact of lynching violence against black women and identifies a key victim. By juxtaposing Mary Turner's name and story against the title, Tesfagiorgis suggests that such memories, while traumatic, must be recalled. Hiding, burying, erasing, or denying constitutes a double crime. First comes the violence, then the cover-up. Doing the opposite—recovering—involves two steps as well, although the process is more recursive than the idea of linear "steps" would imply. First comes the bringing to light, truth telling, bearing witness, and afterward, the making right, justice, or healing. *Hidden Memories*, an abstract piece, echoes these themes. Strong vertical lines like a forest form the field. Against this background sits the focal point: a long treelike column with a darker nooselike form inside. The rounded end of the noose causes the tree to bulge out as if pregnant. The noose-form might also be interpreted differently, as a medieval torture implement or malformed insect. Either way, the imagery evokes visceral pain. This tree is dying—blighted and scarred. Underneath its rounded "belly," circles within circles uncover the hidden-memory text of "MARY TURNER," written in upper-case letters, along with "GEORGIA" below to drive the point home. This painting announces in bold strokes and bold letters that it bears witness to a history of violence against black women. Their stories are acknowledged and named.

With *Hidden Memories* and works such as *Homage to Ida B. Wells* (1990), Tesfagiorgis established herself as a leading figure among black women artists recovering forgotten voices and stories. As a scholar, she became a leading critical voice. Significantly, one of her essays helped pave the way for the defining exhibition, *Bearing Witness: Contemporary Works by African American Artists*. Curated by Jontyle Theresa Robinson in 1996 and first housed at Spelman College, the show gathered works by Lois Mailou Jones, Elizabeth Catlett, Betye Saar, Faith Ringgold, Barbara Chase Riboud, and many more, including Tesfagiorgis. Robinson's introduction credits Tesfagiorgis's ideas about art and "Afrofemcentrism" (a term she coined in 1993 and later replaced with "black feminism") with forming the exhibition's ideological framework. *Bearing Witness*, Robinson explains, depicts the world and speaks the truth from a black woman's perspective.[19] Even when artists convey very difficult images, the end result can be empowering, for black women control the representation and, thus, do the naming. Rather than historical erasure, *Bearing Witness* constituted an important act of historical and artistic recovery: reclaiming memories, myths, images, even styles and materials. During these years, black women such as Tesfagiorgis did not stumble by accident upon stories such as Turner's. Violence against women was itself a "hidden memory," an unspoken truth. Women's stories and voices were buried, too, mere footnotes to the "real" history, literature, and art. Across multiple fields, women reclaimed those memories from their liminal spaces. "Bearing Witness" might indeed be a way to define the two decades of feminist recovery work that produced a major art retrospective, such novels as Alice Walker's *The Color Purple* (1982) and Toni Morrison's *Beloved* (1987), and histories such as Paula Giddings's *When and Where I Enter* (1984) and Darlene Clark Hine, Elsa Barkley Brown, and Rosalyn Terborg-Penn's *Black Women in America* encyclopedia series (1994).

Not everyone, however, agrees upon what recovery means or what it should look like. In the art world, one prominent controversy took shape around Kara Walker. Protests came to a head in 1997, the year she won a MacArthur "Genius" Grant, making Walker, at twenty-eight, the youngest artist to do so. She also happened to be pregnant that year. Her notebook sketches from that year, exhibited later as *Do You Like Creme in Your Coffee and Chocolate in Your Milk?* contain vivid reactions to these two key life events. Among the sketches are several pieces that employ the lynched pregnant woman and fetus motif. We exchanged a couple of brief emails about them. Although Walker did not know Turner's specific story when she began that body of work, she said that she "was struck by the perverse cruelty of the act" and "the perverse cruelty of the image," which resonated with her in multiple ways.[20] She did not say this, but it seems that through this image, Walker finds a vehicle to express her frustration over contemporary society's reactions to a powerful, contentious black woman's voice. Walker is known primarily for silhouettes such as *Gone, An Historical Romance of a Civil War as It Occurred Between the Dusky Thighs of One Young Negress and Her Heart* (1994) and *The End of Uncle Tom and the Grand Allegorical Tableau of Eva in Heaven* (1995). Installation pieces like these can cover entire rooms and feature shadowlike forms of masters, slaves, or other figures familiar from that era – often engaged in graphically violent or sexual acts. The debates over Walker's work centered on whether the artist replicated or exploded stereotypes. Artist Betye Saar led the way in speaking out and tried to organize boycotts of Walker's exhibits. In one letter-writing campaign, Saar wrote, these "images may be in your city next," and signed herself "an artist against negative black images." Later, Saar explained, "I felt the work of Kara Walker was sort of revolting and negative and a form of betrayal to the slaves, particularly women and children; that it was basically for the amusement and the investment of the white art establishment."[21] Phillippe Vergne, organizer of the recent Walker retrospective *My Complement, My Enemy, My Oppressor, My Love*, counters claims such as Saar's by describing Walker's work as art that means to shock, means to offend, means to shake viewers out of their comfort zones. Walker's approach to the historical memory of lynching may differ significantly from those of a reenactment or a wax museum, but audiences may find her creations no less confrontational. Vergne states, "Walker embraces the body – its uses, abuses, indulgences, tolerances, constraints, and exultation – to lay bare the truth that the spectacle of bodies in pain, in ecstasy, constitutes history."[22] Indeed, Walker speaks a complicated truth about race, sex, and power that many do not want to hear.

She certainly makes museum visitors look at images they are not used to seeing as art. Masters and slaves swap tongues and genitals, enormous penises float like balloons, feces falls from anuses, babies fall from vaginas. If one does not look too closely, the images can be deceptively simple, like the past itself. Some look almost childlike, even cartoonish in their innocence, but they clearly are not. The silhouettes themselves can menace. Like the nation's vexed history of race, those enlarged black shadows completely fill a museum room's white walls, taking up a lot of space in the present. In Walker's notebook sketches, pregnant women and babies appear particularly compelling. Like Jean Toomer's Mame Lamkins, they function as metaphors of a creative vision, showing the female artist and her work, figured as child, under attack. They seem especially compelling given the public flack a pregnant Walker took in the year of her MacArthur Grant. In one image, a baby falls from the mother's exploding womb. In another, a pregnant woman is strung up like a piñata, while a boy holds a stick like a bat ready to strike her. The most compelling image, reminiscent of Mary Turner, involves a white male – his tousled hair, freckles, suspenders, and boots giving him a "cracker" appearance – whose foot is about to crush the head of a naked baby curled up in fetal position. Both figures are drawn in red pencil, with text above them exclaiming "Use Red When You Want to Make It Relevant!" (figure 10). In fact, the sketch does stand out as one of the few pieces to use the color red, including the pregnant female piñata. As a silhouette artist Walker used mainly black and white up to that point. After the year 2000 she began to employ primary colors more often, but she still uses red infrequently. In works like *Stone Mountain, Georgia*, from 2001, it shows up in curtains that frame where viewers' eyes should go: following the gaze of black girl in a hoop skirt looking out at the popular monument to the Confederacy. In *Familiar*, also from 2001, red sets the background for black trees and a horse whose head forms the shape of a Ku Klux Klan hood.[23] For Kara Walker, red is the color of violence, the color of relevance, the color of witness. It first appears in her notebook sketches through the image of the lynched black woman and her fetus, whose story tells harsh truths about the wages of speaking out, at a time when Walker herself was being publicly condemned for telling her own harsh truths.

Figure 10. Kara Walker, selection from *Do You Like Creme in Your Coffee and Chocolate in Your Milk?*, 1997, watercolor, colored pencil, graphite on paper, 11⅝ × 8³⁄₁₆″, one from a set of 69 drawings. (Courtesy of Walker Art Center, Minneapolis, Minn., Justin Smith Purchase Fund, 1998, and Sikkema Jenkins & Co., New York.)

Walken, like Tesfagiorgis, does not want to talk about Mary Turner. She answered my e-mails courteously, and that was it.[24] Unlike Tesfagiorgis, Walker did not intend her notebook sketches to be fully realized pieces, but attempts to work through ideas in visual form. They were not trying to tell Turner's story in the same way as *Hidden Memories* or Great Blacks in Wax. She did not know the details or even Turner's name at the time she drew upon an image that affected her so powerfully. Yet both Tesfagiorgis and Walker join a line of creative women whom this image has vexed. To return to a question posed in chapter 2: how does a black woman respond to this horrific story of black female victimization? The politics of respectability that informed the work of Fuller, Grimké, and Clifford may no longer be the same for women like Tesfagiorgis and Walker. But the postmodern aesthetics that facilitate their recovery projects, that demands the disruption of traditional narratives and the fracturing of formal artistic conventions, may have its limits, too. Walker generated so much controversy because she offended people's sensibilities, their notions of what was considered acceptable for a creative black woman – or anyone for that matter – to express. As public venues such as Great Blacks in Wax and Moore's Ford reenactments testify, audiences crave some form of redemption from historical memories of traumatic violence, particularly when those memories come packaged in confrontational ways. Conversely, postmodern artists such as Tesfagiorgis and Walker demonstrate that redemption and healing are constructions just like any other narrative, possible but not always granted, complicated and not always complete. For Walker especially, the focus is rage over redemption. Depicted in relevant red, or larger-than-life shadows from the past, that rage may be less beautiful to some viewers, yet it is no less true.

What does one do with the feelings that emerge from a Kara Walker exhibition? The National Great Blacks in Wax Museum and Moore's Ford reenactments direct audiences toward emotional outlets. Tesfagiorgis points toward the potential for healing even as her work admits the limitations. Walker's work wounds but seems to offer no balm. Entering into Walker's space goes beyond a purely aesthetic experience, at least for some viewers – as controversies surrounding her work suggest. I visited the Walker retrospective, *My Complement, My Enemy, My Oppressor, My Love*, when it came to the Whitney Museum of American Art in 2007, expecting something provocative but not at all what I found: three small drawings of a lynched pregnant woman that formed part of Walker's 1997 notebook series. The docent, a midwesterner-turned-Manhattanite friend of mine from graduate school, accused me of seeing Walker's work as nail to my book-in-progress hammer. (It wasn't the first time I'd heard that line.) My friend told me about the artist's MacArthur Grant; said that the drawings definitely referred to the Saar episode, not Mary Turner; and walked away saying things I did not listen to about Walker's "more fully realized work." I was angry. How could he not see what was clearly there in front of him? Ultimately it does not matter if viewers come out of a Walker show knowing facts about Turner's story, because an artist's mission is grappling with something distinctly different from facts: truth. In retrospect, what made me angry is that my friend ignored a truth I wanted him to acknowledge. Walker captured something in her notebook sketches that I, as a Mary Turner scholar, had not yet seen in the archive of responses and wanted to articulate. Fully realized or not, the notebook sketches, like the silhouettes that sometimes resemble violent, sexualized balloon images, depict a rage with no particular place to go. Uncoupled from redemption, this rage is the most dangerous kind. Most people prefer that it keep to the liminal spaces where they prefer not to look. Every so often an artist comes along with the brave idea that the best way to handle a dangerous emotion is to show its true face.

Literature: Honorée Fanonne Jeffers

Like Walker, Honorée Fanonne Jeffers does not fear giving voice to her truth. For Jeffers, Mary Turner's story reflects an internal struggle, both personal and aesthetic, similar to that of other artists. Jeffers has addressed Turner's lynching in two texts: a 2005 short story, "If You Get There Before I Do," which references Turner just once, and the poem "dirty south moon," which deals more explicitly with the lynching. Although Jeffers is a relatively new voice in southern and African American writing, her literary roots run deep. The daughter of Black Arts Movement poet Lance Jeffers, the author spent part of her childhood with her maternal grandparents in Eatonton, Georgia – home to Alice Walker (whom her mother taught in junior high school) and Joel Chandler Harris (whom Jeffers takes to task in her collection *Red Clay Suite* for his patronizing use of trickster tales). Eatonton is just down the road from Flannery O'Connor's Milledgeville; less than an hour from Sparta, the model for Toomer's Sempter; and about three hours from where Turner was lynched. Jeffers's writing focuses on connections to place and past, and takes its imagery from African American and Native American folk traditions, the blues, Deep South spirituality, and Georgia history. Jeffers's "dirty south moon" is a clear product of this multifaceted heritage. Engaging in an outspoken feminist – or to use Walker's term "womanist"– recovery of Mary Turner's story, Jeffers talks back to Kabnis and through *Cane* to a variety of cultural productions. In particular, her poem confronts the iconography of southern pastorals that refuse to acknowledge lynching at all, male-centered histories of racial violence that do not include women, and the misogynist language and male-dominated narratives of racial oppression found in hip-hop.

"dirty south moon" was a piece I came across through a random Internet search. Every now and then I would type in "Mary Turner and lynching" to see what popped up. Some time around 2005 I hit upon an interview with Jeffers in which she mentioned working on a poem related to the subject. I contacted her immediately, telling her about my book, and she sent me a draft of "dirty south moon." If I was not yet ready to finish this book, I knew what text I wanted to end it. I emailed Jeffers back, asking if I could interview her, expecting the polite rebuff once again. Certainly, came the reply. It would be another couple of years before we got around to a telephone interview, but we wound up talking extensively – quite a bit of preaching to one another's choir, actually. I praised her for writing that poem, and she praised me for writing this book. In a telling comment about the place of black women's stories in historical memory, Jeffers (an author and college professor who spent much of her childhood in Georgia) did not learn about Turner until she read Philip Dray's *At the Hands of Persons Unknown* in 2002. As an earlier generation discovered, this story's power emerges from the gaps between despair and redemption, silence and voice, blindness and bearing witness.

"dirty south moon" has an immediately striking visual appearance (Appendix 8). Consisting of thirteen stanzas, and grouped into tercets that are in turn grouped into phrases and fragments rather than complete sentences, the poem is marked by multiple caesuras. Its sound strikes readers as well. Phrases repeat, but not often enough to form a regular pattern, giving the poem a staccato rather than a rhythmic beat.

The recurring lines, "the tattoo of beauty" or "beauty's tattoo," which refer to a drumbeat and a physical mark, further draw readers' attention to these formal elements of sight and sound. Jeffers first composed "dirty south moon" as a pantoum (a quatrain-based poem, where the second and fourth line of each stanza become the first and third line of the next), and while it retains very little of that original, tightly wound structure, one does find some echoes in the repetition of phrases. The poem instead gives from the beginning a sense of something missing or erased, something gone awry. It lacks as well the sense of closure that a traditional pantoum might offer, where the last line can be the same as the first, which may have been one reason that Jeffers ultimately abandoned strict adherence to that form. In *The Making of a Poem*, Mark Strand and Eavan Boland give a clear reason for drawing upon the pantoum's resources, however. With this form, the "reader takes four steps forward, then two back," offering "possibilities for the making and evoking of time past that are not to be found in straightforward narrative and not entirely in lyric either." Yet Jeffers's poem shows that some stories defy even the most flexible of structures for conjuring up the past.[25] In fact, she found it confining. In the telephone interview, she explained that she worked on the poem for several years off and on. The original pantoum, she said, was "pedestrian" and "plodding"—too much like a "message poem"—that did not allow her to express the grief that the incident made her feel. What ultimately made "dirty south moon" work was transforming it into something more fragmentary, shifting it from a poem that was more narrative to one that told a story through images.

Those images guide the reader through a three-part structure that mirrors its three-line stanzas. The poem opens with the line, "the moon is here," as if it has arrived to illuminate a film set, one cast in terms of memory with the repeated phrases "childhood tableaux" and "thrall of nostalgia beating." Some evoke a typically southern pastoral scene: "clapboard church" and "white dress on clothesline." Like moonlight and memory in a Hawthornian romance, however, this vision plays tricks. Other repeated phrases warn readers not to believe everything they see. Something is wrong in this pastoral tableau, although the trouble is evoked at first, not spoken directly. "Out *out* spot of moon," one line reads, recalling Lady Macbeth, blood, and guilt. The white dress sways on the clothesline like a hanged human form, "side to side." The poem's first part ends with a jarring image that seems nonsensical for readers who do not know what follows: "necklace of a woman's body." The poem's second part, beginning with stanza five, solves the mystery, making clear that this woman has been lynched. This is a "truth" that readers can believe, unlike the unreliable pastoral images from stanza 1: the "truth of billie's trees," referring to the "strange fruit" hanging from trees in Billie Holiday's antilynching song. The song is also "toomer's tune," referring to one source for the poem's title, *Cane*'s "Blood Burning Moon." And this truth, moreover, is harsh enough to keep the "heavens raining still."

The phrase "heavens raining still," from stanza 6, followed by another, "knife opening her from side to side," is where the poem's emotional energy begins to reach its peak and where the reader begins to realize the full horror of what happened to this woman. Early responses to Turner were novel for portraying a female victim when most antilynching art and literature at the time focused on men. In this poem Jeffers goes one step further to focus on the baby. The effect is chilling. Two stanzas offer a jumble of confused, repeated images in the poem's staccato beat:

>   a falling child starts
> stops   crying   knife unlocking its mother
> no staring at her face   her name is mary
>
> child falling out   who stops crying   stomped upon
> by men swelled pale with lies   no blink of its eyes
> no staring at mother's face   no bewilderment at first light   who

The harm is both physical and spiritual. The mother is split open with a knife, the baby falls to the ground and is stomped upon, the bond between the two is severed before it has a chance to form, and both mother and child die without baptismal prayers. Upon these deaths, "nothing holy said"; afterward there are "no new creatures flying" toward heaven. All that remains at the end of stanza 9, the end of the lengthy, emotionally wrenching death scene, is "old blues." Toomer's tune. The terrible truth of Billie's trees.

And after old blues, nothing. The poem's third and final section begins with a deafening silence: "nothing holy you can't hear nobody pray." But as the previous stanza implies, silence brings no absolution. While language may be inadequate to mediate the rupture that lynching has created, it can and must bear witness. Forgetting is an even bigger sin. The next lines command the reader, specifically figured as male, to remember stories like Mary Turner's. "[B]rother," the line reads," your sister hung here hangs," the verb tense shifting to present to indicate that the past is still a tangible, visceral presence. "Don't you refuse her don't commit old sins." Tropes of sin and salvation are particularly important here as Jeffers plays upon the figure of the Black Christ, a problematic though common figure in lynching literature throughout the twentieth century.[26] Here the idea is of blood sacrifice, "dying for Ham's supposed sins"–pointless constructions of race, pointless sins. The idea is that Turner died *like* black men, but her story, as with so many other stories of violence against black women, has been neglected in conventional lynching narratives. Jeffers draws attention to Turner's sacrifice as a spe- cifically female one through the poem's epigraph, a poem by Lucille Clifton: "she is / rounder than the moon / and far more faithful." And, like other female writers who responded to Turner's story, Jeffers capital- izes upon the iconic status of the name Mary. It is not just the Christ fig- ure that was assumed bodily into heaven and intercedes for our sins, but also the Mother Mary, the poem's maternal figure who begs "for your own salvation." To forget the Holy Mother while her body is still "hang- ing there," "twisting" with her "hands begging fire," would be a mortal sin. The final lines command the brother, and by implication all read- ers, not to forget but to acknowledge a terrible, guilt-ridden gap in his- tory that the moon's light has revealed and the poem's caesura has em- phasized: "look *look here*."

Through these words and the caesura between them, Jeffers directs the reader's gaze to an absence in historical memory and its implications: the black women who continue to remain missing from the larger lynching narratives despite continued recovery work in this area.[27] Jeffers's off- kilter memorial fittingly and touchingly inserts Mary Turner into those historical gaps. The poet wants all readers to honor Turner's story (and by implication, other black women's stories), but the one whom she tells to look specifically is the "brother." It is "your sister" who "hangs" there, she reminds him, who begs "for your own salvation." The allusions work on multiple levels. From the poem's beginning, "dirty south moon" calls attention to the pastoral images that emerge from a white patriarchal version of history, warning readers to beware of the agrarian South's dirty secrets. Truth, in this poem, emerges from nature (as distinct from the constructed landscape), music, and sisters: "the moon," "toomer's tune," and the "truth of billie's tree." But Toomer, or at least his fictional creation, does not escape notice here. Jeffers's "brother" recalls Kabnis, who sees Mame Lamkins's story not as an occasion for mourning on its own terms but as a metaphor for his own artistic breakdown and existential crisis. Just as Toomer's story provides Kabnis with possibilities for redemption that he seems too self-involved to recognize, Jeffers's poem similarly suggests that the male artist needs to open his eyes and his heart. In "dirty south moon," the sister as Mother Mary intercedes for sins and begs for salvation, but the poem also reminds readers that she has a story of her own. Another specific link to Toomer occurs through the poem's title, which signifies upon "Blood Burning Moon," the story that closes out *Cane*'s first part. In "Blood Burning Moon," a black man, Tom Burwell, is lynched for slashing the throat of a white man, Bob Stone, in a fight over a black woman, Louisa. The story's last lines are those of a tune that Louisa feels compelled to sing when she sees a full moon rising from her front door. Intuiting evil on the horizon, she does not know that Tom dies while she sings, "Red nigger moon. Sinner! / Blood burning moon. Sinner! / Come out that fact'ry door." Jeffers's moon casts light on a different truth: women not only exist as part of history but they also serve purposes beyond narrative function roles. They are not merely parts of the story, like Carrie, for the brother's own salvation, or like Mame Lamkins, as "split-gut" metaphor, or Louisa, to be the prize between competing men. They sing their own blues.

Or, more pointedly, since the poem's title also signifies upon the term "dirty south," women do not live to be men's bitches and hos. "Dirty South" refers to the hip-hop scene focused in Atlanta, Memphis, New Orleans, and other New South cities. As Riché Richardson points out, Dirty South reclaims black masculinity for southern rappers, and males more generally, that stereotypes of the region as backward, inferior, and undesirable have marginalized. Dirty South hip-hop has become a formidable force, changing power dynamics in an industry where East and West Coast rappers formerly dominated. Ironically, Richardson explains, reclaiming that masculinity often means exchanging one set of stereotypes for another. Dirty South recasts "the historically raced and gendered pathologies of black men as criminal, violent, and overly sexualized that have roots in southern history."[28] Southern rappers now flaunt what used to get a black man killed. This celebration of black masculinity usually comes at the black woman's expense. Whether needy "baby mamas," predatory "gold diggers," or sexually objectified "shawties," they do not earn much respect in Dirty South lyrics. Take, for instance, the Atlanta-based band Goodie Mob's 1995 hit "Dirty South." There, the good life involves "Sippin' on Cuervo Gold off in the club drunk as fuck / Callin' them hoes bitches and smokin' my weed up," or "Fuckin' around with hoes, bustin' nuts in they mouths." And the bad life, accordingly, recognizes a black man's place within a long history of oppression. "See life's a bitch then you figure out / Why you really got dropped in the Dirty South / See in the 3rd grade this is what you told / you was bought, you was sold."[29] Goodie Mob's cover for *Still Standing* (1998) confronts racial violence directly, featuring a large tree and a man hanging in the "O" of "mob." The record's title track focuses on black males who are shot on the streets for no reason. In "dirty south moon," the speaker reminds the brother that sisters die for no reason, too.

Jeffers's poem challenges southern rap's confrontation with history and reclamation of masculinity – not to deny, but to refocus. The distinction between refocusing and denying that perspective is crucial. As bell hooks explains in "Gangsta Culture – Sexism and Misogyny: Who Will Take the Rap?" the misogyny so prevalent in lyrics is itself the product of a larger white-dominated patriarchal culture. "And what better group to labor on this 'plantation,'" she asks, "than young black men?" (116). Rather than demonizing black men, hooks argues, black feminists should intervene at the source of the problem, not at its symptom. Jeffers's poem does this to a certain extent. Its multiple layers of allusion begin by attacking the white patriarchal culture that emerged from and later romanticized Old South plantation society. But "dirty south moon" ultimately addresses the "brother," not "the father" or "the man," providing a less sympathetic view of hip-hop lyrics than hooks.[30] This poem wants listeners to hear the songs that go unsung. "[T]oomer's tune" has another verse. "[B]illie's trees" sing terrible truths about both genders. Women have shared your blues, "dirty south moon" shouts from its gaps. They have in fact sacrificed for your blues, the speaker reminds the brother. As Jeffers said, calling women bitches and hos is equivalent "to spitting on your ancestors."

The Ethics of Looking

Do you know when you desecrate a grave? Not always. You still do the damage, Susan Sontag explains; ignorance is no excuse. Anyone surprised at human depravity, she writes in *Regarding the Pain of Others*, "has not reached moral or psychological adulthood. No one after a certain age has the right to this kind of innocence, of superficiality, to this degree of ignorance, or amnesia."[31] The subject of lynching comes up often in courses that I teach, and students from a variety of backgrounds claim surprise about this history. The system conspires against them, they say; the subject is not taught in schools. I sometimes feel like Robin Kelley responding to Joel Williamson in the pages of the *Journal of American History*, just with different cultural references. Do you not listen to hip-hop, watch television, or go to movies? Have you never heard of the Jena Six?[32] I wonder if quoting Sontag will be more effective: "Remembering *is* an ethical act" (115, emphasis in original). Whether collective amnesia did or did not exist midcentury is beside the point. Making a case that lynching remains "forgotten" today is tough. Even discussion of a liminal space remains difficult after a major wave of scholarship lasting at least two decades, media attention dating back to Clarence Thomas's 1991 Supreme Court confirmation hearings, a 2005 Senate apology for refusing to pass antilynching legislation earlier in the century, and popular culture references in everything from hip-hop lyrics to the 2008 presidential election. The election of Barack Obama has convinced some people to believe they have a "postracial" license to forget again. One chooses as an individual to look at that history or not. Looking is not a clear-cut ethical act, however. Nor does it evoke a clear-cut response. *Regarding the Pain of Others* emerged from Sontag's study of violent photographs, including those from multiple wars, the Holocaust, and lynching. She concludes that such images teach us the terrible disjuncture between what we must know but will never understand: the dreadful, terrifying moment of horrific death.

What is the difference between looking at lynching photographs, a work of lynching art, and an actual lynching? The fallout over *Without Sanctuary* put those questions into circulation. Originally shown in 2002 at a Manhattan gallery, Roth Horowitz, the exhibit was titled *Witness: Photographs of Lynchings from the Collection of James Allen*. The point, as Anthony W. Lee explains, was to connect the images with "'bearing witness,' a form of honoring and mourning associated with the attention paid to the victims of the Holocaust."[33] Unexpected crowds soon overpowered the small gallery, leading historian Grace Hale to muse, "Viewers are left with an exhibit that is too close to the spectacle created by the lynchers themselves."[34] The two positions capture the widespread public debate, and no easy answers exist. As art historian Dora Apel explains, when viewing photographs such as these, context is everything.[35] Shawn Michelle Smith agrees; such photographs were always put to conflicting uses. In some cases they circulated like relics of lynchings themselves, so that "the death of a black man [enabled] whiteness to be shared" with an audience even broader than the initial spectacle. In others, they became "rallying cries for civil rights activism."[36] The same may be said for visiting the National Great Blacks in Wax Museum or attending a re-enactment of the 1946 Moore's Ford murders. Looking at wax figures of Hayes and Mary Turner is not the same as seeing them lynched. Following the crowds to the edge of the Apalachee River to watch actors fall down at the sound of blank gunshots is not the same as watching the Malcolms and the Dorseys die. Violent images in service of progress and justice are different than violence in service of racial oppression. But where does art fit in? Reading Jeffers's poetry and looking at Walker's or Tesfagiorgis's images differs from going to Great Blacks in Wax or the Moore's Ford reenactment. What happens when one enters into these very different sites of memory? Part of the difference lies in mission, the necessity to render truth versus facts. The museum and the reenactment posit themselves as alternative spaces, where spectators may engage a more factually authentic, emotionally or spiritually productive – and therefore ethically responsible – relationship to the past than mainstream venues that ignore harsher facts of black history. Just because works of art do not attempt factual authenticity does not render them less emotionally or spiritually productive, or certainly less ethically responsible. To return to Sontag, art maps the space between knowing and understanding. It may not provide facts or clear-cut outlets for redemption, but if art records agony, it offers testimony of spiritual survival. To acknowledge beauty, even the beauty borne of pain and rage, can be a moral act as well.

Conclusion

Marking a Collective Past

Public recognition of Mary Turner's memory took longer in South Georgia. Oddly enough, a racist prank helped put the wheels in motion for a historical marker to go up in 2010. In October 2002 a Valdosta friend sent me an unexpected but not surprising e-mail. Some teenage boys at Lowndes County High painted several Barbie dolls black and noosed them to tree limbs outside the school's main entrance. Public debate over what some locals called "the Barbie lynchings" lasted two months, including newspaper coverage, a November campus speak-out, and a December town meeting.[1] Talk centered on whether the act constituted a hate crime or a harmless joke. Mary Turner did not play a role in these conversations, even though the addition of a female doll gave this particular noose incident a rare but potent symbolic touch. Campus, community, and newspaper discourse instead wound circuitously around and perilously close to May 1918 without actually touching it. In the *Chronicle of Higher Education*, former director of women's studies at Valdosta State University Viki Soady linked the episode to "lynchings in the decades following Reconstruction"; however, when I asked Soady about the campus speak-out organized to protest it, she said, "No mention was made of Mary Turner."[2] Nor did anyone else that I asked remember Turner's name coming up in the town meeting, where discussion focused on race and historical education. The Lowndes High incident provided fodder for a month in the Valdosta paper's popular "Rants and Raves" column, but lynching received mention only in conjunction with the sniper attacks then taking place around Washington, D.C.– not in relation to local history. Two readers agreed that, when found, the sniper should be hanged publicly; one said that he should "be displayed on national television, naked and without any hood over his face."[3] Editor Ron Wayne had a more serious response to one reader's suggestion that the young men who hung the dolls visit the *Without Sanctuary* exhibit, then on display at the Martin Luther King Jr. National Historic Site in Atlanta: "High school students are old enough to learn more about this sad part of U.S. history and to face its realities," Wayne stated. "Perhaps some lesson plans need to be adapted or presentations made to make the students understand that this is nothing to be mocked."[4] But the paper left out a sad part of local history, readily available at the exhibit, in the Anti-Lynching Crusaders' pamphlet, and on-line, in Leon Litwack's introduction. Where the Barbie lynchings presented an opportunity for positive dialogue, none of the public conversations seemed ready to talk about what really mattered.

The Lowndes High episode was not an isolated event. Noose incidents such as this one have occurred with increasing frequency, moving from about a dozen annually during late 1990s to about fifty or sixty each year since a 2007 Jena, Louisiana, case drew nationwide attention to them.[5] The heated local discussions that often follow in a noose incident's wake tend to focus on the same debate as Valdosta: hate crime or harmless (though tasteless) prank? The former presumes knowledge of history, a deliberate attempt to intimidate through recalling painful acts of the local, or even national, past. The latter, a prank, presumes ignorance, drawing upon symbols that circulate throughout popular culture without fully understanding their implications. Thus, in the 2007 Jena, Louisiana, case, some locals perceived the white teens who hung nooses in a tree as less culpable than the six black teens who got angry enough to fight them. The forty thousand demonstrators who converged upon the town in support of the "Jena Six" thought otherwise.[6] Many demonstrators likely believed (to return to an earlier point) that ignorance is no excuse and, at this cultural moment, may not be possible. With respect to Valdosta, the question of hate crime or harmless prank elides a larger issue. Who can say what the Lowndes High School teens noosing spray-painted Barbie dolls to a tree knew about local history? Perhaps they were just on the front end of an unfortunate fad. Either way, their action revealed a crack in a ninety-year-old wall of silence that local residents were not ready, willing, or able to confront publicly in 2002. Those residents could not claim ignorance. A handful of civil rights activists, liberal churchgoers, and academics from outside the area (a friend calls them "the usual suspects") had been talking about the incident in different public venues for years. I know; I lived there. My departing gift in 2001 was a lecture for Valdosta State University's African American Studies spring series. "The Infamous Story of Mary Turner: Neglected, But Not Forgotten" packed a new campus auditorium. Words from Wayne's *Without Sanctuary* editorial could not help but strike me: "*or presentations made*" (my emphasis). By the time local residents were talking about the Barbie incident, the 1918 lynchings were an open secret, if not an open sore. Mary Turner's name most likely did not come up in 2002 because that wound was still too raw. Instead, public debate retreated to more comfortable clichés.

Getting to a point of more productive dialogue would take another six years. In 2008 another e-mail from a "usual suspect" came through. This one did surprise me. Students, faculty, and community members had formed the Mary Turner Project, an organization dedicated to remembering the 1918 lynchings. Their primary goal was to establish a historical marker where Turner died. On May 16, 2009, between 150 and 200 people gathered at the Hahira Community Center, just down the road from that spot, for a commemoration ceremony, "Discovering the Truth to Heal from the Past." One purpose of the event was to mark the lynchings with a cross at the site where a historical marker would go one year later, on May 15, 2010 (figure 11). Project advisor Mark George, a VSU sociology professor and Valdosta native, explained that the ceremony served another purpose. It offered a curative, truth-telling moment so that the community could begin moving forward. George stated, "We must acknowledge something terrible has happened before we can understand how it affects us today. Because until we acknowledge, explore, and teach one another about our collective past we will be haunted by it."[7] George proposed the 2002 noose incident at Lowndes High School as one clear example of that haunting, saying that the organization formed in part as a response to

Figure 11. Historical Marker: "Mary Turner and the Lynching Rampage of 1918." (Photograph by Julie Buckner Armstrong.)

the Barbie episode. But the commemoration's goal was not to vilify anyone, as George explained.[8] The *Valdosta Daily Times* agreed. The point was to mark a collective past as a community, even if that past was a painful one. An editorial titled "Mary Turner: A Past Unearthed" states:

> So, this weekend's ceremony is about recognizing that past, not reliving it, not demonizing anyone. The people who committed the crimes against Mary Turner and others are all dead and buried. The perpetrators never faced punishment for their actions on this mortal plan. They lived their lives and were properly buried. Mary Turner and her unborn child never received a funeral. There has been no marker to note her passing. This weekend, with first a cross and then a historical marker in the area where she died, Mary Turner will be blessed and hopefully put to rest. But for her to be at rest, we must first understand the horror of how she passed.[9]

Neither the editorial nor the Mary Turner Project sees signage as the final goal. The Project's long-term objectives include "educating ourselves and others about the presence of racism, effects of racism, and how to become involved in eliminating racism."[10] The editorial explains that the ceremony will not fix present and future problems of race, only start a conversation. But beginning to talk is better than the alternative in a place that one student called "Where Civil Rights Never Made It."[11]

What did happen in ten years to bring civil rights to this area? The story is one of racial reconciliation discourse itself. The Mary Turner Project joins other groups across the country having this kind of conversation. Communities remember and respond to legacies of racial violence in various ways: through historical markers, cold-case prosecutions, reparations movements, and other forms of truth telling, memorializing, educating, or compensating. One element these groups have in common is changing how citizens talk about race. Talking about lynching is, by nature, difficult. Both the timing and the approach to this conversation must be right. Old models of discourse based upon notions of retributive justice do not work. Scholars such as Sherrilyn Ifill and activist collectives such as the Alliance for Truth and Racial Reconciliation have found that models rooted in restorative justice are much more productive for advancing dialogue.[12] Restorative justice takes into account different stakeholders—victims, perpetrators, bystanders—not to return to some illusory time of wholeness or peace, but to build a new kind of community that acknowledges past pain as the shared experience of all residents. The community at large tells the truth about and accepts responsibility for stories formerly omitted from official history. Organizations like the Mary Turner Project cast racial violence as a collective trauma rather than a secret, a source of unspoken anger or shame. Such a move remains consistent with the trauma process as Jeffrey Alexander and others describe it in *Cultural Trauma and Collective Identity.* Communities revise their notion of identity as they revise stories of their past to incorporate traumatic events. The result is a sense of relief, both public and private, as the emotions surrounding those events become less heightened. Communities designate sites of memory—monuments, museums, sacred spaces, and ritual routines—where those emotions can be dealt with openly and honestly.[13]

Well before communities are ready to process such complicated, conflicted emotions, "the spiral of signification," as Alexander calls it, must subside.[14] Groups must no longer feel under threat. In Brooks and Lowndes, decades had passed since the original trauma and the lynching era more generally. Still, confrontation of that wound through a historical monument was more than ten years in the making. A national group called Project Change, funded by Levi Strauss, facilitated interracial dialogues in Valdosta from 1991 to 1999. A campus group, HOPE, created in 1997, pushed the VSU community to think critically about race as a systematic problem. The People's Tribunal, formed in 1998, after police beat to death Willie James Williams, galvanized blacks and whites alike and forced many to ask questions they might not have before. A series of truth-telling moments—including my 2001 presentation, a 2006 article by Christopher Meyers in *Georgia Historical Quarterly*, and in its own uncanny way, the 2002 Lowndes High School Barbie doll incident—aired stories that many did not want told. These seeds ultimately bore fruit as the Mary Turner Project. Such efforts may be seen as both the end result of the trauma process and the beginning chapter of a new civil rights discourse. Back in the early 1960s Martin Luther King Jr. made it as far south as Albany, Georgia, before, as the song goes, Chief Pritchett "turned him 'round." But as activists and scholars alike know, the movement never stopped moving. Drawing from the successes and failures of South Africa's truth and reconciliation processes, racial reconciliation discourse in the United States remains a work in progress. However, those involved point to these conversations as effective counter to both silence and violence. As a black member of the Moore's Ford Memorial Committee replied to a white student who asked if their work had made any difference, "We haven't changed the world, but you and I are standing right here having this conversation, aren't we?" In the Valdosta area, as in many communities, such conversations have been like Langston Hughes's dream, and justice itself: long deferred.

When the Mary Turner Project made plans to erect a historical marker near Turner's death site, the group joined a growing movement. The Moore's Ford Memorial Committee formed in 1997 to remember and work for justice in the 1946 murders of four African Americans near Monroe, Georgia. One of the first groups in the country to commemorate a lynching, the group put up a marker on July 25, 1999, the fifty-third anniversary of the killings.[15] Other locales have followed in rapid succession. In 2003 Duluth, Minnesota, established the Clayton Jackson McGhie Memorial, near the site where three black men were lynched in 1920. This downtown plaza became the first large-scale public monument to an act of racial violence.[16] Florida officials marked the 1922 massacre and destruction of Rosewood with a plaque erected in 2004. The marker itself came after a successful reparations suit that survivors and descendants filed against the state.[17] Recent Georgia models for the Mary Turner Project include a 2006 sign installed in Comer to honor Lemuel Penn, murdered by Ku Klux Klan members in 1964, and a 2008 marker dedicated to Leo Frank, lynched in Marietta in 1915.[18] Several of the entities behind these efforts belong to an umbrella organization, the Alliance for Truth and Racial Reconciliation (ATRR). Established at a conference held in 2005 designed to pull together disparate groups with different goals, the Alliance shares resources, strategies, and a commitment to truth and justice.[19] As groups involved with the ATRR have learned, memorial efforts involve more than negotiating city planning meetings, official historical marker guidelines, and U.S. Department of Transportation bureaucracy. The marker or the park is a tangible outcome of a long, contentious process where public and private memories of race collide. Those establishing such sites of memory see themselves as speaking truth to power, constructing narratives that run counter to official histories and dominant modes of discourse. In a famous work, poet Adrienne Rich likens such historical recovery to "Diving into the Wreck." Those who are brave enough to undertake the search will find at bottom both "the damage that was done / and the treasures that prevail."

Where they look, Rich says, is "a book of myths / in which / our names do not appear."[20] Attempts at reconciliation such as this one endeavor to create more inclusive stories about local history. Lynching claimed public space for whites by making it hostile territory for blacks. By acknowledging and mourning what happened, the historical plaque or park reclaims that public space for all memories and all people. The marker thus rewrites what had been erased. The men who killed the May 1918 victims meant for them – and the disruption to white power they represented – to disappear. After black bodies served their symbolic purposes, mob members threw them in the river or left them for convicts to dispose of. Mary Turner, who as a poor black woman dared to raise her voice, represented the ultimate insult to white patriarchal authority. The men buried her on the spot, marking her grave with a whiskey bottle that would shatter and a cigar that would burn to ash. The same men gave Hampton Smith the tallest gravestone in the Pauline

Cemetery, a solid monument designed to be seen and to last. The obelisk lists his name, birth and death dates, and the symbols of his Masonic tribe (figure 12). Long after Smith and the incident have been forgotten, his headstone tells a story, signaling the man as someone of importance. Before the Mary Turner Project marked her lynching site, the area had become an impromptu garbage dump: not much different from the way mob members left it, littered with beer cans, cigarette butts, and anything else passing motorists tossed from their automobiles (figure 13). For two years before the historical marker went up, the most ironic and cruel joke of all presided above. Towering over the exit ramp to Highway 122 was a billboard featuring a giant fetus with the caption "Heartbeat Begins at 18 Days." Those driving north on Interstate 75 would not make the connection unless they knew the story, but that is the point. As James W. Loewen argues, "All across America, the landscape suffers from amnesia, not about everything, but about many crucial events and issues of our past."[21] Historical sites and monuments, Loewen explains, tend to focus on events that the general public perceives as positive or inspirational. The results are often trivial, marking famous people who passed close by, or racist, because white community leaders preserve the spaces, erect the monuments, and choose what counts as "historic." In Valdosta, whites have controlled official public memory since the area was settled in the early nineteenth century. In 1998 I was told that no lynchings had ever occurred in Brooks and Lowndes counties. That history had been erased from the landscape, from discourse, and from most local archives. A decade later, the story was different. Historical markers ensure that the landscape and the people who inhabit it can no longer claim to suffer from amnesia or use "not knowing" as an excuse for not talking.

The historical marker's power reverberates beyond the actual site itself. By reclaiming one memory space, it symbolically reclaims others. The Valdosta area, like most cities and towns across the United States, encodes racism in the built environment. As Loewen notes, "The recent spate of Martin Luther King avenues and monuments notwithstanding, Americans still live and work in a landscape of white supremacy."[22] The requisite Confederate soldier stands guard over the courthouse in the middle of the town square. Georgia's flag, flying before all public buildings, including VSU, no longer bears the familiar Southern Cross image, but it does use an earlier Stars and Bars Confederate symbol.

Figure 12. Hampton Smith gravesite, 2002. (Photograph by Julie Buckner Armstrong.)

Figure 13. Mary Turner gravesite, 2002. (Photograph by Julie Buckner Armstrong.)

Neighborhood segregation remains intact around railroad tracks and roads. The town and the county face a racial divide typical of cities and suburbs. According to the *Valdosta Daily Times*, Lowndes High is 70 percent white, while Valdosta High is 70 percent black.[23] Until recently, Lowndes (the school where the doll noosing incident occurred) had two proms, one black, one white. Local history may have been the last thing in the minds of students who hung Barbies in the trees at Lowndes High School. They may instead have wanted to claim their school or – like the students in Jena, Louisiana – that one tree for whites only. In neighboring Brooks County as well as Lowndes, street signs and businesses still bear the family names of reported mob members, some of whom were prominent men in the community back then. As with the graves of Hampton Smith and Mary Turner, long after the actual story is forgotten, traces of what matters and what does not remain. Segregation is no longer by law but by custom. White and black spaces are marked in people's minds if not on actual streets or tracks. Both James Loewen and Sherrilyn Ifill question the message sent when monuments to people who tried to keep blacks as second-class citizens preside over the centers of justice and education.[24] Historical sites that acknowledge the legacy of injustice act as moral counters and educational tools in the face of other such symbols.

Hence their controversial nature. Marking a space entails more than adding a new sign. It means changing historical narratives that not everyone believes should be changed in the first place, and in ways upon which not everyone can agree. From one perspective, the Mary Turner Project had it easy. The group did not have to approach local authorities to receive permission because erecting a historical marker is a state issue. A marker allowed them, in essence, to be subversive and get mainstream acceptance at the same time. As Mark George put it, the state historical marker gave the subject legitimacy; it was "more than something a bunch of fringe folks wanted to push."[25] The Georgia Historical Society has a competitive application process with clearly established guidelines: the subject must be dead for more than twenty-five years, the topic must have significance beyond the local level, and the applicant must receive clearance from the Department of Transportation.[26] Because the 1918 lynchings had been the topic of an article in the *Georgia Historical Quarterly*, the Society's journal, the incident's broader significance was unarguable. Getting DOT clearance was another relatively easy hoop to jump through (and certainly easier than jumping through a local one). The biggest point of contention was the historical marker's text, a common stumbling block for groups involved in this kind of project. Applicants have 100–115 words to tell what happened and to capture its significance in a way that is both amenable to multiple stakeholders and educational for passing motorists who might chance upon a plaque unaware. The rhetorical confines make the situation difficult enough. As the two parties debated marker text back and forth, their different ideological aims became apparent. The Georgia Historical Society, as a state institution, preferred details it perceived as "facts" rooted in objective analysis. The Mary Turner Project, hoping to expose systematic racism in its multiple forms, did not believe the Georgia Historical Society analysis went far enough.

How much can one say on a 100-word plaque? Quite a bit, it seems, when some words send a long message to different parties involved. A proposed draft from the Georgia Historical Society read,

> In May 1918, the murder of a white planter by an African-American employee incited an eight-day wave of vigilantism that ultimately claimed the

lives of at least eleven local African Americans, targeted for alleged complicity in the murder. Mary Turner, eight months pregnant, was tortured, mutilated, and then shot to death near this site on May 19, 1918, after publicly denouncing her husband's lynching on the previous day. No charges were ever brought against suspected lynchers. During the period 1880–1930 there were as many as 550 lynchings in Georgia. More common in rural areas, these illegal acts of mob violence disproportionally targeted African Americans.[27]

The Mary Turner Project offered an alternative draft containing many of the same facts and following a similar structure but with notable differences:

Near this location on May 19, 1918 Mary Turner, twenty-one years old and eight months pregnant was burned alive, mutilated, and then shot to death for publicly denouncing her husband's lynching the previous day. During the same week, at least eleven other African Americans from Brooks and Lowndes Counties were also lynched because a local white farmer, known for his abuse of field hands, was murdered by his one of his African American workers. No charges were ever brought against known and suspected members of the lynch mobs that carried out these crimes. These crimes were also part of the more than 550 lynchings that occurred across Georgia between the period of 1880 and 1930, a practice that primarily targeted African Americans.[28]

The latter version emphasizes Turner's young age (different from published sources) and the specific brutality of her death, eliminates the word "complicity" from the sentence describing other deaths, acknowledges Hampton Smith's murder as well as his labor abuses, and removes the phrase about lynching being "more common in rural areas."

The story, quite simply, is altered significantly. In the Historical Society's version, a pregnant Mary Turner died horrifically for speaking out against her husband's lynching during a wave of mob violence. The murder of a respected man ("a planter") sparked the vigilantism against African Americans connected ("targeted for alleged complicity") with his death. No one was ever punished for the lynchings, because mob members were only "suspected." From 1880 to 1930 vigilante violence against African Americans was relatively common in Georgia, particularly in rural areas such as this one. The Mary Turner Project's suggested changes have an African American worker striking back against his abusive employer (now a "farmer"), and other local blacks being lynched "because" of that action. The issue of alleged complicity gets transferred from victims to perpetrators, who are now "known and suspected members of the lynch mobs" never charged for their crimes. The viciousness of those crimes gets emphasized in the marker's first sentence, which, again, gives Mary Turner's age, describes the manner in which she died, and notes the reason. By omitting the word "rural," the second version makes another small, but important, alteration. Lynchings may have been more common in rural areas at that time, but Georgia also had more rural areas. Removing the word removes the stereotype many present readers may have that lynching was relegated to marginalized, backwoods communities. That change, in conjunction with redirecting the issue of complicity onto the perpetrators, implies what scholars know to be true: that people from all walks of life, from the poor and disenfranchised to the wealthy and well-connected, participated in lynching. That is ultimately the kind of point a marker can make – or even hint at – that makes it so controversial. What local resident wants to imagine an ancestor being part of a lynching scene, whether as perpetrator, victim, or bystander? What casual readers want to consider their individual relationship to the conflicted legacy of lynching?

Such questions might hinder the revision process of any well-meaning committee, let alone two different ones. After debating the marker text for several months, the Georgia Historical Society and the Mary Turner Project finally compromised on a version that conveyed factual details about the incident without much of what each side saw as the other's loaded language. The end result is certainly more compact than previous drafts:

Mary Turner and the Lynching Rampage of 1918

Near this site on May 19, 1918, twenty-one-year-old Mary Turner, eight months pregnant, was burned, mutilated, and shot to death by a local mob after publicly denouncing her husband's lynching the previous day. In the days immediately following the murder of a white planter by a black employee on May 16, 1918, at least eleven local African Americans including the Turners died at the hands of a lynch mob in one of the deadliest waves of vigilantism in Georgia's history. No charges were ever brought against known or suspected participants in these crimes. From 1880–1930, as many as 550 people were killed in Georgia in these illegal acts of mob violence.

This final version relies upon the structure that Project members preferred, one that foregrounds Mary Turner and the vicious method of her death rather than the white farmer. Many did see the text as a setback, however, because it elided the reference to Smith's abuse of his workers: what could be viewed as resistance was now just murder. Ultimately, when it became clear that the one-year anniversary of the commemoration might approach with no actual marker in place, the consensus developed that getting the plaque cast and installed in a timely manner meant more than pressing a reluctant Historical Society to begin radicalizing the texts in its marker system.

The 2009 commemoration ceremony and the 2010 service to erect the new marker thus culminated much effort, but the Mary Turner Project does not see its work as done. The service was but one very important piece in a large puzzle that connects the legacy of past oppression to current struggles for racial justice. As others involved in similar efforts have found, making such connections is difficult but, in the long run, beneficial. As Sherrilyn Ifill explains, "Interracial conversations about lynching inevitably reveal the deep fissures and conflicts that often lie beneath the now relatively peaceful coexistence of black and white communities."[29] Opening up the past for investigation means remembering events that are painful for different stakeholders in different ways. Ifill points out that blacks do not want to remember the pain and humiliation; whites and bystanders do not want to remember the guilt. Ifill quotes Croatian writer Slavenka Drakulic, who says, "It is easier, and much more comfortable, to live with lies than to confront the truth and with that truth the possibility of individual guilt – and collective responsibility" (135). But the bad feeling remains whether one acknowledges painful memories or not. In Valdosta the 1998 Willie James Williams controversy and the 2002 noose incident drove this point home. Williams's death at the hands of white police officers empowered local radical voices to take a much more active political stance. The People's Tribunal led marches, organized mass meetings, and advocated for racial justice well beyond the issue at hand. Mainstream Valdostans, white and black, expressed shock and dismay over the actions of the group and its leader, the Reverend Floyd Rose. Even the Unitarian Universalist Church, where I attended – normally a safe haven for "the usual suspects" (or what Mark George calls "the fringe folks") – voted not to support as a body Rev. Rose's call for church backing, viewing him as a troublemaker. The People's

Tribunal, however, did more to name the "fissures and conflicts" than start them. Similarly, in 2002, the *Valdosta Daily Times*, a mainstream if not conservative publication, took the blame among many locals for stirring up trouble by reporting the noose incident. Multiple individuals called in to "Rants and Raves" to complain that the paper was blowing the story out of proportion. As one parent said, "My child is a student at Lowndes High and didn't know anything about the so-called racial problems until the media got a hold of it." Others, however, saw the Barbie episode as part of a long history of racial tensions at the school and in the local area. Under the same message from the parent was another, quite different, one: "I graduated from Lowndes High School 20 years ago and as deeply embedded and racial as it was then, it doesn't surprise me that racial acts are occurring 20 years later."[30]

The question is whether the marker really will initiate the kind of long-term dialogue or facilitate the kind of systematic change that needs to happen. As George admits, the fringe folks chose a state agency rather than local sources to gain legitimacy. Yet support from the *Valdosta Daily Times* shows promise. Another Mary Turner Project member, long-time local activist George Rhynes, notes on his blog that local television media did not cover the Project's events. And the *Times* received significant hate mail for its coverage. However, the presence of so many local residents – not just the usual suspects or fringe folks, but "apolitical people," as George called them – at the commemoration ceremony was heartening.[31] People seem ready to talk publicly, even if full-fledged community dialogue is not yet possible. As Ifill explains, all stakeholders have a story to tell, and those stories must be told. Victims need an opportunity to confront their fears, anger, and confusion. They need as well to reclaim power that potential stories of resistance might generate. Perpetrators and beneficiaries have stories, too. "Listening to, understanding, and accepting" those, Ifill says, can be "one of the greatest challenges of any truth and reconciliation process" (136). If or when that dialogue does take place – "when memory comes," a phrase Jewish historian Saul Friedlander uses to describe the overwhelming process of recovering from trauma – local residents may find that their stories have more in common than they think.[32]

To return to Freida High Tesfagiorgis's term, the local "hidden memory" of the 1918 lynchings shows consistencies across those fissures and conflicts. Stories from descendants reveal deep sadness, fear, and a desire for healing, even when they are hard to listen to. When I first started my research, a woman I met at the Brooks County Historical Museum told me that an ancestor of hers had been the sheriff at the time. J. P. Wade was first on the scene to find Hampton Smith's body. He deputized the posse that became the mob. He was supposed to be protecting Hayes Turner when masked men that he claimed not to recognize overtook his vehicle, captured Hayes, and lynched him. Years later, she said, a black worker threw lye in the sheriff's eyes and blinded him. "Why do they hate us?" she asked me. For the longest time I considered her story within its larger connection to local silence, because she also told me that no lynchings had ever occurred locally. Thinking later about the metaphorical possibilities of blindness and the very literal things that she and Sheriff Wade did not want to see, I began to realize that she would not have told me that story if she did not want me to hear it. I was up front with her about the topic of my research. Behind her fear of and confusion about black anger was a need to confess. I had a similar response from a group of white women at the Lowndes County Historical Society a couple of years later. They said that they did not remember the lynchings that took place when they were children, but one did remember Sidney Johnson being dragged down the street past her house. She did not see it, but she knew something terrible was happening that she could only imagine. What she saw in her head was the truck that usually advertised the Ritz Theater pulling behind it a giant opossum. She was terrified of opossums, too, which she had never seen but believed to be creatures somewhat like pictures she had seen of gorillas. She believed that the truck would come for her next. One of her closing remarks was telling. "Blacks hate me," she said, "and I've always been nice to them." Again, a story of blindness, confusion, and fear, from an elderly woman who retained a childhood memory of a town's racial terror. The story's trajectory of racism – linking Johnson to a nightmarish beast – is difficult to hear. However, the speaker also expresses a wish to reach across racial lines, even as she appears to lack the tools to do so.

Stories from descendants of victims and other local blacks share a sense of pain, anger, fear, confusion, and a desire for healing – although the content is very different. Like those from descendants of perpetrators and bystanders, these stories are told in spaces that feel safe. The white women above spoke to me, a white woman representing a university, within the walls of institutions they visit regularly. For added safety, they requested that I not use their names. Many area blacks shared their stories publicly for the first time at the 2009 commemoration service. Most were willing to talk in front of a group but would not be interviewed for this book. How fresh this wound remains almost a century later was made apparent in the very struggle to speak through tears. One man, a descendant of the Turner family, said that he did not talk about this story before because it hurt him too much. Those words were the only ones he managed to get out before choking up again and sitting down. Another woman barely managed, through sobs, to tell a story about her grandparents taking a wagon to nearby Barney to help relatives get out while tensions ran high. Whites grabbed her grandmother, visibly pregnant, before one said, "No, that ain't her, that's just Aunt Polly," and let her go. Despite the pain of recalling such terrible events, the day's prevailing mood was more uplifting than somber. Those gathered at the Hahira Community Center, and later at the marker site, seemed relieved to be acknowledging the past. Some had a story that they want to be known. A large group of people, from as far south as Miami, Florida, and as far north as Ohio, attended to represent Hayes and Mary Turner's extended family and their untold story. Most of what contemporary audiences know about Mary Turner comes from Walter White. Apart from White's official version that made its way through later documentary and creative responses, a different story circulated through survivor narratives and other forms of oral history. These family members described a separate set of Turner children, born before the baby so brutally killed in an act of mob violence. Those children got out, the story goes, on a train—just like the children who escaped the violence in the 1922 Rosewood, Florida, massacre. Mary stayed behind to help them, and that is how the mob found her. She gave her life so that her children could live. Their story casts the 1918 lynchings as redemption narrative, the ultimate maternal, yet Christlike, sacrifice. As Christian motif, moreover, such a story gives everyone in the community a particular, preset role to play. Victims, perpetrators, and bystanders come together in a familiar narrative about a sacrifice that had to happen so the community could be absolved of its sin.

The area has a sizable burden that includes and extends well beyond the 1918 acts of violence. For a time, Georgia led the nation in the number of lynchings, and it did so in part because of Brooks and Lowndes counties. Together, the two (which used to be one county, Irwin) were responsible for twenty-eight recorded acts of mob violence between 1880 and 1930.[33] Fitzhugh Brundage explains that Brooks in particular had "earned the unenviable position of the most mob-prone county in both the region and the state – and possibly even in the South."[34] That reputation includes another mass lynching in 1894, which resulted in five deaths and required the state militia to quell the violence.[35] Other acts that do not get reported as lynchings contribute to the history of racial antagonism. The area's most famous resident, John Henry ("Doc") Holliday lived in Valdosta before moving on to make a name for himself out west as a gambler and a gunslinger. One of his early local adventures involved members of a black regiment stationed downtown during Reconstruction. Upon finding them swimming in the Withlacoochee, he either fired his gun above his head to scare them away, or he actually shot two of them, maybe more. Area blacks reported the incident to newspapers as "a minor massacre."[36] Beyond racially motivated killing exists a whole system of economic exploitation that had its beginnings in slavery and continued well into the twentieth century. John Dittmer explains that the U.S. Supreme Court outlawed peonage labor – the system of debt repayment through compulsory labor – in 1905. But Georgia's Supreme Court, believing that the state's laws on peonage did not conflict with the federal government's, upheld the practice until 1942. The problem was that workers were often held, violently and against their will, long after their debts had been paid. Peonage labor pervaded South Georgia, especially in the turpentine camps that populated areas in and around Brooks and Lowndes. Dittmer states that the "NAACP investigated so many violations [of peonage laws] that the Atlanta Branch revived the Underground Railroad to facilitate escape from rural areas."[37] A peonage labor dispute initiated the sequence of events in May 1918 that helped make the area infamous for being "mob-prone," and the men who helped the NAACP investigate were most likely affiliated with its new "railroad."

None of this dark history squares with the sunny image conjured by the words on Valdosta's water tower, "Southern Charm ... Not Gone with the Wind." Clearly, what I was told when first researching this story – no lynchings happened here – is not true. Is the Turner family's story? Who knows? Data about lynching and historical memory suggests that communities often conflate details. It would not be unusual for traumatized surviving family members or even unrelated descendants of victims to blend their history onto Rosewood's story, just as it seems realistic that residents of Monroe, Georgia, would mix details of the Moore's Ford lynching in with those of Valdosta. Memories of racial violence could travel through time and space roughly following the path of Highway 41. Multiple scenarios may be possible. Turner's kin may have left via an "underground railroad," not a literal train on tracks. George Spratling may not have told Walter White about it because, like Frederick Douglass in the 1845 *Narrative*, he wished to protect those still ferrying escapees. In 1922 Rosewood's victims could have heard about the flight of 1918 Brooks-Lowndes victims by train and decided to implement a similar plan. In 1946, given the phenomenon of copycat crimes, the men who killed Dorothy Malcolm at the Moore's Ford bridge might have done to her what they heard men near Valdosta had done to Mary Turner. To answer the question of whether any memory of this lynching seems credible, one must return to the distinction between truth and fact. Contemporary audiences must remember that this story's official version comes from Walter White, a brilliant but flawed investigator who was known to exaggerate and who shaped his account according to the rhetorical and historical demands of his day. Before White came on the scene, different versions circulated – some of which he consulted and some of which he did not.

Still, his story revealed a truth: the mob murder of a pregnant woman and multiple men constituted a traumatic event that radiated outward from community to country. Over the next century, this story has come to represent different truths for different audiences. Mary Turner's lynching is about black women, about national shame, about forgotten voices, about hidden trauma, about the potential for healing. What is to be true about her story in the future for local residents will be up to them to decide. What is to be true about it for those outside the region will undoubtedly differ. That truth's multiplicity will surely not be captured in any historical marker's one hundred words, as significant as that marker is for remembering Mary Turner.

Appendixes

Selected Creative and Documentary Responses to the 1918
Brooks-Lowndes Lynchings

The documents that follow represent only a small portion of the works of journalism, literature, art, and popular culture that the 1918 Brooks-Lowndes incident has generated. The purpose of this selection is to reproduce some of the texts discussed in the book that are not readily available elsewhere. (Images are located within the chapters where they are discussed.) A more complete list of creative and documentary works, along with the most recent publication or Internet access information, is included in the Bibliography.

APPENDIX ONE

"Hamp Smith Murdered; Young Wife Attacked by Negro Farm Hands,"
Quitman Free Press, 24 May 1918

Hampton Smith, a well known white farmer of the county, is dead and his wife seriously wounded and in a critical condition after being attacked by negroes at their home near Barney Thursday night.

The crime in its details is the most horrible and brutal in the history of the county. Mrs. Smith had recovered sufficiently next morning to tell Sheriff Wade that the men who killed her husband and maltreated her terribly leaving her for dead, were two negro farm hands her husband had brought from Valdosta about two weeks ago. One of them was Sidney Johnson and the other was called Julius but she did not know his last name.

Mr. Smith and his wife were shot with his own rifle which had been stolen from the house by the negroes while the husband and wife were at supper and the crime shows every evidence of having been deliberately planned. When the Smiths finished their supper they walked across a narrow porch which separates the main part of the house from the kitchen and entered their room.

Mrs. Smith said her husband at once missed his rifle, a Winchester high-powered gun and asked her where it was. As he spoke the shot which killed him was fired through the window and a thin lace window curtain. It went through his body and through the partition wall into the next room. Two other shots were fired which were imbedded in the wall.

Wild with terror Mrs. Smith dashed from the room and her tracks in the fresh earth show where she jumped from the porch. She ran around the kitchen and the murderers overtook her at the end of the kitchen. At this point there was evidence of a terrible struggle where the young woman fought as long as consciousness remained. Her clothing was torn and parts of it were found scattered on the ground. Her recollection of the struggle is indistinct. Evidence points to her being shot through the right shoulder and breast while lying on the ground, the bullet evidently entering in front and coming out the back of the shoulder. It was found afterwards buried several inches in the ground.

After shooting Mrs. Smith and leaving her for dead the negroes deliberately pillaged the house. Every drawer was turned out. Outside members of the family missed nothing except a new suit of clothes and the rifle and do not know whether there was any money in the house or not. The negroes then tried to escape with Mr. Smith's car. They took the key from his pocket and took a lamp to the garage but were unable to operate the car and finally left it.

The crime was committed about nine o'clock and the alarm was not given until after midnight. Mrs. Smith after she recovered consciousness crawled to a negro house on the place about a half mile away and told them what had happened and they gave the alarm. Sheriff Wade was reached over the telephone about one o'clock.

Mrs. Smith seemed dazed and first crawled through the field to a branch several hundred yards from the house where she said she thought she lay about two hours. She bathed her wound in the water and recovered sufficiently to get to the negro house in a field on the other side of the house.

The negroes took her in and cared for her and gave the alarm to the nearest white people. Dr. Humphries was summoned from Barney to attend her and she was afterward moved to the home of Mrs. Joyce. Dr. Humphries said next morning the wound she received was not fatal but he could not tell the ultimate effects of the terrible shock she had suffered. She was in a delicate condition which made the matter problematical.

The Smiths had been married about two years and had no children. Hampton Smith, who was about 31 years old, was the son of Dixon Smith and had been living on this farm two and a half miles northwest of Barney about a year. His wife came from a town north of Atlanta and was a Miss Simmons.

The funeral of the murdered man took place Saturday at 2:30 o'clock at Pauline church north of Quitman, and the services were conducted by Rev. W. T. Gaulden, a longtime friend of the family. An enormous crowd of people was present from all parts of the county.

The body of the murdered man was brought to the McGowan Undertaking Co. Friday afternoon by Mr. McGowan and prepared for burial. Mr. Smith had been shot twice one shot going through his shoulders from one side to other [*sic*] and one going through his breast as though he had turned half way round between the two shots.

Mr. McGowan took the body to the home of Mr. Smith's parents Mr. and Mrs. Dixon Smith at two o'clock Friday night and the funeral was from there. In addition to his parents Mr. Smith is survived by one sister Mrs. Henry Spell of Valdosta and four brothers, Thomas, Will[,] Walter, and Bob Smith who live in this county. The family is prominent and the whole county has been terribly shocked over the frightful tragedy.

APPENDIX TWO

"Her Talk Enraged Them: Mary Turner Taken to Folsom's Bridge and Hanged," *Savannah Morning News,* 20 May 1918

Quitman, Georgia, May 19. – Mary Turner, wife of Hayes Turner, was hanged this afternoon at Folsom's bridge, over Little river, near Barney.

Hays [*sic*] Turner was hanged at the Okapilco river in this county last night.

His wife, it is claimed, made statements to-day about the execution of her husband and the people in their indignant mood took exceptions to her remarks as well as her attitude and took her to the river where she was hanged.

This makes five persons lynched in this section as a result of the Smith tragedy at Barney. All of Sidney Johnson's relatives including his mother and father were landed in jail at Valdosta last night. To-night, owing to the increased feeling among the people, the jail is being strongly guarded to prevent trouble.

Besides the chase after Sidney Johnson posses are to-night looking for other negroes in this section and feeling among both whites and blacks seems to be growing more intense.

APPENDIX THREE

Joseph B. Cumming, Letter to the Editor, *Augusta Chronicle*, 21 May 1918

A new capital offense in Georgia — and one so heinous that it cannot wait on the regular and orderly process of law, but must be punished by those notable protectors of society — lynchers! The designation of this crime, calling for such swift punishment, is "Unwise Remarks." This important evolution of our criminal code and its righteous treatment are thus spoken of in the following Associated Press Dispatch . . . [Cumming quotes in detail a news account of Mary Turner's lynching]

. . . Of all the horrible occurrences that have disgraced the state of Georgia, this is the most horrible.

Look at this picture: A poor, abject Negro woman is informed of the lynching of her husband — let it be granted, himself a murderer. She cannot keep silence. She cannot express her agony in terms of Christian forgiveness. She cannot even use the high-sounding phrases of the fine old pagan philosophers. She blurts out an "unwise remark." Away with her to the nearest limb! Break her neck and manifest the calm, righteous, and judicial judgment of her executioners by "riddling her body with bullets." Were these human beings or fiends hot from hell? Was she a human being? If not, let us stop calling on her race for men to fight, as we are sure they will well do, for our country and for us. Where are the grand juries? Where are the petit juries? Where are the sheriffs? Where is public opinion? Is it dead? Or is it crowded out by a handful of the most detestable murderers and cowards? God in heaven have mercy on us! Let the governor — if he will do no more — proclaim a day of deepest humiliation and most earnest prayer, in which we may plead humbly and agonizingly with the All-Father, who dreadful thought, has said: "Vengeance is mine," not to visit his righteous vengeance upon us in the slaughter on the sea and across the sea of our dear boys, who, with Negro comrades in arms, have gone to fight for the betterment of the world.

APPENDIX FOUR

The Colored Welfare League (Augusta, Georgia), "Resolutions Adopted and Sent to Governor Dorsey Urging that He Exercise His Authority Against Such Acts of Barbarism," *Atlanta Independent*, 1 June 1918

Whereas, we as a race and a part of this great nation are passing through the momentous period in the world's history.

And whereas, we are faithfully and cheerfully doing our part on the battle front, in the training camps, in purchasing of thrift stamps and liberty bonds, in Red Cross membership, in food production and conservation and in all other ways of good citizenship.

And whereas, the public press announced May 20th that a negro woman because of alleged "unwise remarks" after the lynching of her husband, accused of murder, was herself hanged by a mob and riddled with bullets, in south Georgia, near Valdosta, last Sunday afternoon.

And whereas, we deeply feel the disregard of the courts and the law in all lynchings, and especially aggrieved in this beastly act against all womanhood the Negro woman in particular.

Therefore, we do earnestly urge an expression from you as our Chief Executive of the state, and the exercise of all your legal power against this horrible and barbarous act, which shall mean much to the soothing of millions of bruised hearts and the encouragement of a struggling, patriotic, right-loving, God-fearing people.

Colored Federated Clubs of Georgia, "Resolutions Expressive of Feelings Sent to President and Governor," *Savannah Tribune*, 8 June 1918

Whereas, the Negro Womanhood of Georgia has been shocked by the lunching [*sic*] of Mary Turner at Valdosta Sunday May 19, 1918, for an alleged unwise remark in reference to the lynching of her husband; and

Whereas, we the Negro women of the state are aroused by this unwarranted lawlessness and are discouraged and crushed by a spirit of humiliation and dread; and

Whereas, we deplore the migratory movement of the Negro from the South, yet we cannot counsel them to remain in the light of these conditions under which we live; and

Whereas, our labor is in these cotton and corn fields and rice swamps, and in this frightful hour of the great world war, our sons and husbands are giving their lives in defense of the country we all love so dearly; and

Whereas, in every forward movement in our national life the Negro has come to the front and shared in the advance and crimsoned every field of strife from Boston to "no man's land" for the principles held sacred by every true American, and

Whereas, we feel that our lives are unsafe as long as this iniquitous institution exists:

We therefore are asking that you use all the power of your great office to prevent similar occurrences and punish the perpetrators of this foul deed and urge that sure and swift justice by meted out to them.

Memorandum for Governor Dorsey from Walter F. White

Below are given some of the facts discovered during a recent visit to Brooks and Lowndes Counties, with reference to the recent lynchings in these two counties:

It was learned that the following Negroes are known to have been lynched, the first six of these having been reported in the daily press:

Will Head,
Will Thompson,
Hayes Turner,
Mary Turner,
Eugene Rice,
Sidney Johnson.

In addition to these, a Negro by the name of Chime Riley was lynched and turpentine cups (those being clay cups used to catch turpentine gum when the trees are cut to obtain gum) were tied to his body, and the body was then thrown into the Little River near Banney [sic] Georgia. My informant in regard to this case told me that he went down to the river hoping to find the body when the river was low; but assumed that the body had probably become entangled in the sand bars and therefore could not be discovered. He secured, however, one of the turpentine cups which had been tied to the body of Riley. The name of this man I could not learn, but I saw him on the spot where Mary Turner was lynched. Another Negro by the name of Simon Schuman was called out of his house near Berlin on the Moultrie Road between eight and nine o'clock at night and has not been seen since. The interior of his house as well as his furniture was completely demolished. The family of Schuman is now on what is known as the Bryce Plantation. In addition to the eight mentioned above, bodies of three unidentified Negroes whose names I have been unable to learn but which I expect to receive at an early date, were taken from the Little River just below Quitman. I was informed by a minister that eighteen Negroes have been killed. I discovered only the eleven mentioned above.

The causes of the crime and lynchings I discovered were as follows:

Hampton Smith, the white farmer who was murdered, seems to have borne the reputation of grossly mistreating the hands employed on his plantation known as the Old Joyce Place on the Adel and Quitman Road. He seems to have had the habit of beating these hands and refusing to pay them wages due them. This reputation had become so wide-spread that it was practically impossible for him to secure labor. He, therefore, had been in the habit of paying the fines of Negroes convicted in the courts, and having them work out these fines on his plantation. Sidney Johnson, the Negro who admitted killing Smith, had been convicted of gaming and had been fined $30.00, which was paid by Smith. A few days previous to the tragedy Johnson had complained of being sick and had been beaten by Smith when he refused to go to work. Johnson is said to have threatened Smith for having beaten him while he was sick. Smith was shot through the window while sitting in his home Thursday night, May 16th. He was shot twice, one shot entering the back and coming out near the heart, the other shot entering the shoulder, breaking it, passing entirely through the body and coming out through the other shoulder. His wife was also shot, the bullet passing directly through the center of her breast and just missing her heart and lungs. Her wounds are not serious. In regard to the statements made to the Governor that she was subjected to severe brutality and was raped: My information is that this is not true, although a number of conflicting statements have been given in regard to this. This can be definitely ascertained by the fact that she was in her sixth or seventh month of pregnancy at the time of the crime, and I have been informed by several reliable physicians that had this been true she would be unable to give birth to the child, and a miscarriage would have resulted. I suggest that it be ascertained whether or not she has given birth to a child since that time. I have also been infromed [*sic*] by the same physicians that the shot alone would not necessarily cause a miscarriage, but that raping or even rough handling would have caused such a condition. Later: Mrs Smith gave birth to her child.

Contrary to the press accounts of the affair, Sidney Johnson was not concealed in the swamps near Quitman, but was at his home in Valdosta from the time of the crime up to the time he was killed by the posse. He is said to have made the statement to several persons that he alone was implicated in the crime of murdering Smith, and that the other parties lynched knew nothing about it until after the crime was committed. As stated above, Will Head and Will Thompson were lynched on Friday night, May 17th. Hayes Turner was taken from the jail at Quitman by Sheriff Wade and the Clerk of the County Court, Roland Knight by name, for the purpose of being carried to Moultrie for safe-keeping. Turner was taken from these officers about three and a half miles from Quitman near a bridge on the Okapilco Creek. He was hanged with his hands hand-cuffed behind him. He hung on the tree between Saturday and Monday and was then cut down by the county convicts and buried about five feet from the tree on which he was lynched. Mary Turner, his wife, made the remark that the lynching of her husband was unjust, that he knew nothing of the crime, and that if she knew the parties who were in the mob she would have warrants sworn out against them. For this she was captured on Sunday and carried to a place a few yards from Folsom's Bridge on Little River and there lynched. The method of execution in this case, was most brutal. At the time she was lynched Mary Turner was in her eight [sic] month of pregnancy. Her ankles were tied together and she was hung to the tree head down. Gasoline was taken from the cars and poured on her clothing which was then fired. When her clothes had burned off, a sharp instrument was taken and she was cut open in the middle, her stomach being entirely opened. Her unborn child fell from her womb, gave two cries, and was then crushed by the heel of a member of the mob. Her body was then riddled with bullets from high-powered rifles until it was no longer possible to recognize it as the body of a human being. The tree on which she was lynched bears the marks of several bullets from high-powered guns. Mary Turner and her child are buried about ten feet from the tree and at the head of her grave is a whiskey bottle with a cigar stump placed in the neck. It is my information that the leaders of the mob which on Friday night, May 17th, lynched Will Head and Will Thompson were S. E. McGowan, an undertaker of Quitman and W. A. Whipple, a cotton broker and merchandise dealer of the same place. The following names were given to me as being the names of men who were members of the mob, by a man who stated that he himself was a member:

Ordley Yates, Clerk in the Post Office,
Frank Purvis, Employed by Griffin Furniture Company,
Fulton DeVane, Stock Dealer and Auditor and Agent for Standard Oil
    Company,
—— Chalmers, Farmer near Quitman,
Lee Sherrill, Farmer Near Quitman,
Brown Sherrill, Employed by W. A. Whipple,
Richard DeVane, Farmer,
Ross DeVane, Farmer, Quitman, Ga.
—— Van, Barker, Quitman, Ga.
Jim Dickson, Farmer, Quitman, Ga.
Dixon Smith, Brother of Hampton Smith,
Will Smith, Brother of Hampton Smith,
and Two other brothers of Hampton Smith.

These names were given to me in confidence by a man who admitted that he was a member of the mob, on the condition that I would not divulge his name, as to do so would cause him a great deal of embarrassment, and probably death. If I might, I would suggest that the men whose names are given above be required to prove an alibi from the night of Friday May 17th. It is my information that S. E. McGowan has publicly boasted of his part in the lynching, and he is reputed to have made the following remark, "If the Germans were as thick as the grass in the courthouse yard the same thing would be done again."

A spirit of unrest exists in both Brooks and Lowndes Counties which will undoubtedly affect the labor situation in that community. It is my information that over five hundred Negroes have left the community since the lynching. Many more, because of property which they own and crops which they have now in process of cultivation, are unable to do so at the present time, but are planning to leave as soon as they can dispose of their land and gather their crops. At this time when the production of food means so much towards the success of the Government in the war such a condition is serious.

The above facts were all verified from a number of sources.

Carrie Williams Clifford
"Little Mother (Upon the Lynching of Mary Turner)"

Oh, tremble, Little Mother,
For your dark-eyed, unborn babe,
Whom in your secret heart you've named
The well-loved name of "Gabe"

> For Gabriel is the father's name,
> And the son is sure to be
> "Just like his father!" as she wants
> The whole, wide world to see!

But tremble, Little Mother,
For your unborn baby's fate;
The father tarries long away –
Why does he stay so late?

> For dark the night and weird the wind,
> And chilled the heart with fear!
> What are those hideous sounds and cries
> Each instant drawing near?

Oh, tremble, dark-faced mother,
At the dreadful word that falls
From lips of pale-faced demons,
As the black man pleads and calls.

> For they're dragging Gabe, at a stout rope's end,
> And they say, "She is bound to tell!"
> Something she knows not a thing about,
> Or they'll "Give her the same as well!"

Oh, tremble, helpless mother!
They're beating down the door,
And you'll never feel the father's kiss,
Or the stir of the baby more.

> *Oh, the human beasts were ruthless,*
> *And there upon the ground,*
> *Two bodies – and an unborn babe –*
> *The ghastly morning found.*

APPENDIX EIGHT

Honorée Fanonne Jeffers
"dirty south moon"

she is
rounder than the moon
and far more faithful.
      Lucille Clifton

the moon is here   the moon
don't believe the sun arriving for its own sake
thrall of nostalgia beating

out *out* spot of moon   don't believe the sun
or the tattoo of beauty   childhood tableaux
thrall of nostalgia beating   white dress on clothesline

beauty's tattoo   childhood tableaux   meaning of dirt
clapboard church   white dress on clothesline
swaying in obligatory side to side

don't believe in dirt   clapboard church   believe a southern moon
believe in this   swaying from side to side
necklace of woman's body

southern moon   toomer's tune   truth of billie's tree
believe the necklace of a woman's body   that heavens
should be raining still

that billie's tree sings truth   a phrase draped
at wood's throat   heavens raining still
knife opening her from side to side

phrase draped at the wood's throat   a falling child starts
stops   crying   knife unlocking its mother
no staring at her face   her name is mary

child falling out   who stops crying   stomped upon
by men swelled pale with lies   no blink of its eyes
no staring at mother's face   no bewilderment at first light   who

child   nothing holy said   no prayers over dead trees
no new creatures flying   bewildered at first light   who
only old blues

nothing holy   you can't hear nobody pray   brother
your sister hung here   hangs   sister   you know old blues
night till morning   don't you refuse her   don't commit old sins

when that is your sister hanging there   she is
twisting   dying for ham's supposed sins
think of songs on dancing tongues

twisting
have you not begged God   a familiar   have you not sent
words dancing   sung songs spontaneous   then forgot

that sister's hands begging fire   for your own salvation
not for songs unheard or used   look
the moon   look   *look here*

NOTES

Introduction

1. "Her Talk Enraged Them"; Cumming, letter to editor.
2. White, "Memorandum for Governor Dorsey"; James Weldon Johnson, *Along This Way*, 333–34.
3. Quoted in White, *Rope and Faggot*, 33.
4. Litwack, *Trouble in Mind*, 288–89.
5. Faulkner, *Absalom, Absalom!*, 146.
6. Perkins and Stephens, *Strange Fruit*, 16.
7. Toomer, *Cane*, 92. Subsequent page number references given in the text.
8. Allen et al., *Without Sanctuary*.
9. Hall, *Revolt Against Chivalry*, 150. Apel, *Imagery of Lynching*, 9–15; Apel, *Lynching Photographs*; Shawn Michelle Smith, *Lynching Photographs*.
10. Howard, letter to Cynthia Goff; Marvin Dunn, "Justice for Willie James."
11. Giovanni, "Alabama Poem," *Selected Poems of Nikki Giovanni*, 90–91.
12. Meyers, "'Killing Them by the Wholesale'"; Dray, *At the Hands of Persons Unknown*, 245–47; Janken, *White*, 32–33, 36–40.
13. Brundage, *Lynching in the New South*, 15.
14. Nora, "Between Memory and History."
15. Fabre and O'Meally, *History and Memory in African-American Culture*, 3–10.
16. Caruth, *Unclaimed Experience*, 5–6, 64
17. Goldsby, *Spectacular Secret*, 5.
18. Alexander, "Toward a Theory of Cultural Trauma," 10–24. Subsequent page number references given in the text.
19. Kundera, *Book of Laughter and Forgetting*, 3.
20. Arnold, *"What Virtue There Is in Fire,"* 3–4.
21. Thelen, "What We Can and Can't See in the Past."
22. Goldsby, *Spectacular Secret*, 8.
23. Feimster, "Ladies and Lynching," 11–12.
24. NAACP, *Thirty Years of Lynching*, 30. A table on page 33 breaks down the number of women lynched by race and state.
25. Feimster, *Southern Horrors*; Simien, *Gender and Lynching*.
26. Elsa Barkley Brown, "Imaging Lynching," 102.
27. Meyers, "'Killing Them by the Wholesale'"; Dray, *At the Hands of Persons Unknown*, 245–47; Janken, *White*, 32–33, 36–40; Zangrando, *naacp Crusade Against Lynching*, 22–50; Battenfeld, "'Been Shapin Words T Fit M Soul'"; Edmunds, "Race Question and 'The Question of Home'"; Scruggs and VanDemarr,

Jean Toomer and the Terrors of American History; Webb, "Literature and Lynching in Jean Toomer's *Cane*"; Foley, "Jean Toomer's Sparta," and "'In the Land of Cotton.'"

28. Hirsch, "Speaking Silences"; Hull, *Color, Sex, and Poetry*, 130–42; Erika Miller, *Other Reconstruction*, 86–96; Rice, "White Islands of Safety"; Tate, *Domestic Allegories of Political Desire*, 216–20.

29. Gunning, *Race, Rape, and Lynching*, 11.

30. Harris, *Exorcising Blackness*; Ayers, *Vengeance and Justice*; Tolnay and Beck, *Festival of Violence*.

31. Waldrep, *Many Faces of Judge Lynch*; Markovitz, *Legacies of Lynching*; Hale, *Making Whiteness*; Goldsby, *Spectacular Secret*; Gunning, *Race, Rape, and Lynching*; Apel, *Imagery of Lynching*.

32. Markovitz, *Legacies of Lynching*, xvii.

33. Ifill, *On the Courthouse Lawn*; Alliance for Truth and Racial Reconciliation.

Chapter One. Birth and Nation

1. *"Birth of a Nation* Offered Last Time," 5. Subsequent textual references from the same page.

2. Dray, *At the Hands of Persons Unknown*, 198.

3. Ibid., 202.

4. Wells, *Southern Horrors*, 58.

5. NAACP, *Thirty Years*, 7, 10.

6. Waldrep, *Many Faces of Judge Lynch*, 86.

7. Meyers, "'Killing Them by the Wholesale.'"

8. "Hamp Smith Murdered"; "Hampton Smith of Barney Is Assassinated."

9. "Skulking Hun Is Blamed for Racial Break in Georgia."

10. James Weldon Johnson, Address Delivered at the National Conference on Lynching.

11. White, "I Investigate Lynchings," 79.

12. Patricia Bernstein, *First Waco Horror*; Dinnerstein, *Leo Frank Case*; Arnold, *"What Virtue There Is in Fire"*; Kantrowitz, *Ben Tillman and the Reconstruction of White Supremacy*; Feimster, *Southern Horrors*.

13. "Hamp Smith Murdered"; "Hampton Smith of Barney Is Assassinated"; "Hunt for Sidney Johnson Still On"; "Farmer Killed, Wife Wounded"; "Mob Avenges Smith's Death"; "Hundreds Visit Scene of Lynching."

14. "Hamp Smith Murdered"; "Hampton Smith of Barney Is Assassinated"; "Farmer Killed, Wife Wounded"; "Boche Agents."

15. "4 Negroes Lynched"; "Boche Agents."

16. "4 Negroes Lynched"; "Mob Avenges Smith's Death"; "Hamp Smith Murdered"; "Hundreds Visit Scene of Lynching."

17. "Two More Swing Up for Tragedy at Smith Home."
18. Brundage, "Roar on the Other Side of Silence."
19. "Hamp Smith Murdered."
20. White, "Memorandum."
21. "Hamp Smith Murdered"; "Two More Swing Up."
22. Wiegman, *American Anatomies*, 94–95.
23. "Two More Swing Up"; "Her Talk Enraged Them."
24. "Her Talk Enraged Them"; "Two More Swing Up"; "Hunt for Johnson Still On"; Meyers, "'Killing Them by the Wholesale.'"
25. "Double Lynching in Georgia"; "Four Negroes Hanged"; "Georgia Mobs Lynch Four"; "Georgia Mob Lynches Negro and His Wife." "Two More Georgia Negroes Lynched in Murder Case"; "Woman is Lynched by Mob in Georgia."
26. "Georgia Huns"; Editorial, *New York Post.*
27. "Boche Agents"; "Pro-Germans Had a Hand"; "Tragedy at Barney Laid to Hun Agents."
28. Grant, *Way It Was in the South*, 302.
29. "Devil Resigns Office."
30. "Skulking Hun"; "Crackers Try."
31. "Chatham Home Guards Go to Valdosta."
32. Ibid.; "Home Guards Return From Futile Trip"; and "Johnson Is Shot to Death by Valdosta Police Officers."
33. "Home Guards Return From Futile Trip."
34. "Johnson Is Shot to Death"; "Johnson Killed by Policemen"; "Sidney Johnson Is Killed in Valdosta."
35. "Lynching Story."
36. "Besmirching Lowndes."
37. "Aftermath of the Lynchings."
38. William H. Fleming, "Memorial of Joseph B. Cumming"; "Lucy Craft Laney," in Hine, *Black Women in America*; I have been unable to locate information on the men of Augusta's Colored Welfare League.
39. "Lynchings of May, 1918."
40. "Lying Follows Lynching."
41. "Four Murdered By Georgia 'Crackers.'"
42. "Georgia's Latest Contribution."
43. "How Lynchings May Be Stopped"; "Governor Urges Negroes."
44. "Good Advice for Negroes."
45. "Southern Journals Express Horror"; "Might Against Right."
46. "Negro Women Hold Humiliation Service."
47. NACW, Convention Program, July 1918.
48. Anti-Lynching Crusaders, "Million Women United."
49. "Georgia's Latest Contribution."
50. "'Over Here.'"

51. Editorial, *New York Post.*

52. "Lynching Most Helpful to the Prussians."

53. Janken, *White*, 35; "Is It Treason?"

54. "Is It Treason?"

55. "Georgia Horrors"; "Georgia Maintains Her Record."

56. Press Release, *San Antonio Express.*

57. NAACP, Press Release, 22 May 1918.

58. Walter White to John E. Salmon.

59. White, "Memorandum."

60. White, Undated Memorandum.

61. White, "I Investigate Lynchings," 78–80.

62. Janken, *White*, 26–28.

63. White, "I Investigate Lynchings," 77; White, *Man Called White*, 39–42; Janken, *White*, 29–55.

64. White, "I Investigate Lynchings," 77.

65. Schechter, *Ida B. Wells-Barnett and American Reform*, 156

66. White, "I Investigate Lynchings," 78–80.

67. White to John Shillady.

68. Janken, *White*, 33.

69. Meyers, "'Killing Them By the Wholesale'"; White, letter to editor, *Cheyenne State Leader*, "Negro Murderer Is in Savannah Jail"; "Simon Shuman Held for Barney Crime."

70. Dittmer, *Black Georgia in the Progressive Era*, 72–76, 81.

71. Shillady to Woodrow Wilson; Shillady to Archibald Grimké; Grimké to R. R. Moton; Kelly Miller, "Disgrace of Democracy."

72. Wilson, "President's Denunciation."

73. NAACP, Press Release, 1 August 1918.

74. Dorsey, telegram to John Shillady; Dorsey, letter to Shillady, 27 August 1918.

75. Shillady, telegram to Hugh M. Dorsey; Shillady, letter to Dorsey.

76. NAACP, Press Release, 7 September 1918; Dorsey, letter to Shillady, 30 November 1918.

77. "Waco Horror," 150.

78. Patricia Bernstein, *First Waco Horror*, 159–61, 163, 169.

79. White, "Work of a Mob." Subsequent page number references given in the text.

80. Dam, letter to Walter White.

81. James Weldon Johnson, *Along This Way*, 333–34.

82. White, Memorandum to John Shillady, Re: Interview with George U. Spratling.

83. Ibid.; White, Memorandum for Mr. Dam; White, letter to Samuel Broadnax; Grant, letter to White; and White, letter to Grant.

84. Kenyon, letter to John R. Shillady.

85. Shillady, letter to Kenyon.

86. Dam, letter to Shillady, 16 November 1918; Dam, letter to Shillady, 24 December 1918; Janken, *White*, 37–38.

87. Greene, *Time's Unfading Garden*, 130.

88. Thurston, "From Lynching Beneficiary to Lynching Opponent."

89. Janken, *White*, 11–18.

90. Downs (coastal regional medical examiner, Georgia Bureau of Investigation), e-mail to Julie Buckner Armstrong.

91. Dray, *At the Hands of Persons Unknown*, 206; Zangrando, *NAACP Crusade Against Lynching*, 33–34.

Chapter Two. Silence, Voice, and Motherhood

1. Dray, *At the Hands of Persons Unknown*, 236–37; Zangrando, *NAACP Crusade Against Lynching*, 36–38.

2. Hull, *Color, Sex, and Poetry*, 117–24; Erika M. Miller, *Other Reconstruction*, 59–61; Mitchell, "Anti-Lynching Plays," 211–12; Tate, *Domestic Allegories of Political Desire*, 210–12.

3. Perkins and Stephens, *Strange Fruit*, 9–11; Mitchell, "Anti-Lynching Plays," 216.

4. Thurer, *Myths of Motherhood*, 81–84, 112–15.

5. Kerr, "God-Given Work," 128.

6. Ibid., 147–55, 166–83; Brundage, "Meta Warrick's 1907 'Negro Tableaux.'"

7. Kerr, "God-Given Work," 251–54; Fuller, letter to Hannah Moriarta; Fuller, document for Bruce A. Getchell and Alfred C. Perry; Fuller, letter to Sylvia Dannett.

8. Jackson, "(In)Forming the Visual," 31.

9. Apel, *Imagery of Lynching*, 87.

10. Fuller, letter to Angelina Weld Grimké, 31 May 1917.

11. Kerr, "God-Given Work," 250.

12. Apel, *Imagery of Lynching*, 151–52, Jackson, "(In)Forming the Visual," 35.

13. Fuller, letter to Sylvia Dannett.

14. Kerr, "God-Given Work," 223–24.

15. Fuller, letters to Angelina Weld Grimké, 25 and 31 May 1917.

16. Kerr, "God-Given Work," 259–64; Ater, "Making History," 13.

17. Ater, "Making History," 29.

18. Hull, *Color, Sex, and Poetry*, 110–150; Herron, Introduction, *Selected Works of Angelina Weld Grimké*, 3–24.

19. Grimké, *Rachel*, printed program.

20. Ibid.; Burrill, *Aftermath*; Dunbar-Nelson, *Mine Eyes Have Seen*; Johnson, *A Sunday Morning in the South, Safe, Blue-Eyed Black Boy*.

21. Hull, *Color, Sex, and Poetry*, 124, 139–45; Herron, Introduction, *Selected Works of Angelina Weld Grimké*, 6–7.

22. Grimké, *"Rachel:* The Play of the Month."

23. Herron, Introduction, *Selected Works of Angelina Weld Grimké*, 17–18; Hull, *Color, Sex, and Poetry*, 117–24; Erika Miller, *Other Reconstruction*, 59–61; and Tate, *Domestic Allegories of Political Desire*, 210–15.

24. In Herron, *Selected Works of Angelina Weld Grimké*, 296. All subsequent page number references to Grimké's stories will be given in the text.

25. Claude McKay, "If We Must Die," *Complete Poems*, 152.

26. Tate, *Domestic Allegories of Political Desire*, 218.

27. In Herron, *Selected Works of Angelina Weld Grimké*, 417–18.

28. Mary Knoblauch, letters to Angelina Weld Grimké, 13 and 4 October 1920.

29. Page numbers refer to the handwritten manuscript version of "The Waitin'."

30. Kanwar, *Unforgetting Heart;* Braxton, "Ancestral Presence," 300.

31. Hirsch, "Speaking Silences," 459; Erika Miller, *Other Reconstruction*, 96.

32. Herron, Introduction, *Selected Works of Angelina Weld Grimké*, 19; Hull, *Color, Sex, and Poetry*, 131–33.

33. Grimké, "Tenebris," *Selected Works of Angelina Weld Grimké*, 113.

34. P. Jane Splawn, Introduction, xv–xlvi.

35. Clifford, "Votes for Children."

36. Berg, *Mothering the Race*, 16.

37. Clifford, letter to Joel Spingarn.

38. Grimké, *Rachel,* printed program.

39. Carby, *Reconstructing Womanhood*; Clifford, *Race Rhymes*, 7.

40. NACW, Convention Program.

41. Hutchinson, "Jean Toomer and the 'New Negroes' of Washington"; McHenry, *Forgotten Readers*, 251–66.

42. Daniel 8:15–19; Luke 1:26–37.

43. Wheatley, "On Being Brought from Africa to America," *Collected Works*.

44. Wells, *Southern Horrors*, 70.

45. Anti-Lynching Crusaders, "A Million Women United to Suppress Lynching."

46. Zangrando, *NAACP Crusade Against Lynching*, 57–64; Dray, *At the Hands of Persons Unknown*, 261–66.

47. Mary Talbert, letter to potential state directors.

48. Talbert, Directions for Buffalo Key Women.

49. Talbert, letter to W. E. B. Du Bois.

50. Anti-Lynching Crusaders, "A Million Women United to Suppress Lynching."

51. Anti-Lynching Crusaders, Press Release.

52. Talbert, form letter.

53. Talbert, letter to Mary White Ovington; Ovington, letter to William Talbert; NACW, *National Notes*.

54. Talbert, draft letter to the Anti-Lynching Crusaders (with Johnson's hand-written note attached); Ovington, letter to Mary Talbert.

55. Talbert, Anti-Lynching Crusaders Final Report; Talbert, letters to James Weldon Johnson, 21 October 1922 and 22 May 1923; White, letter to Mary Talbert; Talbert, letter to Grace Nail Johnson.

56. White, letter to Talbert (containing a clipping of the *Pittsburgh Courier* article).

57. Talbert, letter to state directors and executive board members (with hand-written note from Johnson on top).

58. Du Bois, Reflections on the Dyer Bill.

59. Zangrando, *NAACP Crusade Against Lynching*, 64–71; Dray, *At the Hands of Persons Unknown*, 268–72.

60. Feimster, *Southern Horrors*, 226.

61. James Weldon Johnson, Address Delivered at the National Conference on Lynching.

62. Hine, "Rape and the Inner Lives of Black Women."

63. Higginbotham, *Righteous Discontent*, 186–87, 197.

64. "Justice in Georgia," *Oregonian*, 28 December 1924, 2.

65. Grasso, *Artistry of Anger*, 42–43.

66. Carby, *Domestic Allegories of Political Desire*, 109; Schechter, *Ida B. Wells-Barnett and American Reform*, 122.

67. Brundage, "Roar on the Other Side of Silence," 280.

68. Gussow, *Seems Like Murder Here*, 164.

69. Gunning, *Race, Rape, and Lynching*, 14.

70. Harris, *Exorcising Blackness*, xii, 194.

71. Alice Walker, "In Search of Our Mothers' Gardens," 235.

72. Apel, *Imagery of Lynching*, 109–10; Whitted, "'In My Flesh I Shall See God,'" 379.

73. Thurer, *Myths of Motherhood*, 81–84, 112–15.

Chapter Three. Brutal Facts and Split-Gut Words

1. Huie, "Shocking Story of Approved Killing in Mississippi."

2. Colin, "Mother's Tears Greet Son," 29.

3. Metress, "On That Third Day He Rose"; Metress, *Lynching of Emmett Till*, 1–12; Metress, "Literary Representations of the Lynching of Emmett Till."

4. Patricia Bernstein, *First Waco Horror*, 169.

5. Waldrep, *Many Faces of Judge Lynch*, 127–50.

6. Writers' League Against Lynching, Minutes; Apel, *Imagery of Lynching*, 83–131.

7. Dyer, *At the Hands of Persons Unknown*, 258–72, 341–44, 355–58, 359–62.

8. White, *Rope and Faggot*, 33.

9. Waldrep, *Many Faces of Judge Lynch*, 103–13.

10. James Weldon Johnson, "Lawlessness in the United States," 55.

11. Kelly Miller, "Disgrace of Democracy."

12. Dray, *At the Hands of Persons Unknown*, 245; Zangrando, *NAACP Campaign Against Lynching*, 41; NAACP, *Thirty Years of Lynching*. Page number references given in text.

13. Waldrep, *Many Faces of Judge Lynch*, 138.

14. For more information about the founding of the Commission on Interracial Cooperation and its relationship to the Association of Southern Women for the Prevention of Lynching, see Hall, *Revolt Against Chivalry*.

15. Dray, *At the Hands of Persons Unknown*, 257–58; Zangrando, *NAACP Crusade Against Lynching*, 49–50.

16. James Weldon Johnson, Address Delivered at National Conference on Lynching. Subsequent textual references are from this same document. NAACP, Program, National Conference on Lynching.

17. Dray, *At the Hands of Persons Unknown*, 257–58; Zangrando, *NAACP Crusade Against Lynching*, 49–50; NAACP, Program, National Conference on Lynching.

18. Carter, *Scottsboro*; James Goodman, *Stories of Scottsboro*; Hill, *Men, Mobs, and Law*; Solomon, *Cry Was Unity*.

19. Waldrep, *Many Faces of Judge Lynch*, 139.

20. Solomon, *Cry Was Unity*, 186.

21. Page number references to the pamphlet given in the text. Haywood, *Black Bolshevik*.

22. Wright, *Black Boy*, 272.

23. Bowser, *Oscar Micheaux and His Circle*, xvii–xviii; Bowser and Spence, *Writing Himself into History*, 8–9.

24. Cripps, *Slow Fade to Black*, 184.

25. Bowser and Spence, *Writing Himself into History*, 15–16; Green, *Straight Lick*, 252n1; Gaines, "*The Birth of a Nation* and *Within Our Gates*"; and Kaplan, "Birth of an Empire."

26. Taylor, "Black Silence"; Green, *Straight Lick*; Wallace, "Oscar Micheaux's *Within Our Gates*"; Cripps, *Slow Fade to Black*, 185; Bowser and Spence, *Writing Himself into History*, 17–18, 39; Regester, "Black Films, White Censors," 164–66.

27. Greene, *Straight Lick*, 1.

28. Regester, "African-American Press and Race Movies," 44.

29. Cripps, *Slow Fade To Black*, 185.

30. Regester, "Lynched, Assaulted," 50.

31. Wallace, "Oscar Micheaux's *Within Our Gates*."

32. Du Bois, *Negro Problem*, 33; Du Bois, *Souls of Black Folk*, 5.

33. Greene, *Straight Lick*, 1.

34. Bercovitch, *American Jeremiad*.

35. hooks, "Homeplace."

36. Greene and Spencer, *Time's Unfading Garden*, 67.

37. Ibid., 98, 174.

38. Ford, "Flowering a Feminist Garden"; Honey, *Shadowed Dreams*, xxxix–xli; and Anderson, "Classifying Life," 99.

39. Rice, *Witnessing Lynching*, 236; Greene and Spencer, *Time's Unfading Garden*, 130.

40. Greene and Spencer, *Time's Unfading Garden*, 134.

41. Honey, *Shadowed Dreams*, 8.

42. Greene and Spencer, *Time's Unfading Garden*, 129; Hull, in *Color, Sex, and Poetry*, 6–11; Honey, *Shadowed Dreams*, 2.

43. Greene and Spencer, *Time's Unfading Garden*, 140.

44. Toomer, letter to Waldo Frank, in Whalan, *Letters of Jean Toomer*, 35–37.

45. Toomer, letter to Horace Liveright, in Whalan, *Letters of Jean Toomer*, 171; Toomer, "The *Cane* Years," 120–21.

46. Toomer, letter to Waldo Frank, in Whalan, *Letters of Jean Toomer*, 101.

47. Hutchinson, "Jean Toomer and the 'New Negroes' of Washington"; McHenry, *Forgotten Readers*, 251–66.

48. Battenfeld, "'Been Shapin Words T Fit M Soul'"; Edmunds, "Race Question and 'The Question of Home'"; Foley, "'In the Land of Cotton'"; Harris, *Exorcising Blackness*; Scruggs and VanDemarr, *Jean Toomer and the Terrors of History*; Webb, "Literature and Lynching in Jean Toomer's *Cane*."

49. Blake, "Spectatorial Artist and the Structure of *Cane*"; Richard Eldridge, "Unifying Images in Part One of Jean Toomer's *Cane*"; Fabre, "Dramatic and Musical Structures in 'Harvest Song' and 'Kabnis'"; Innes, "Unity of Jean Toomer's *Cane*"; Krasny, "Aesthetic Structure of Jean Toomer's *Cane*"; Watkins, "Is There a Unifying Theme in *Cane*?"; Mackey, "Sound and Sentiment, Sound and Symbol"; MacKethan, "Jean Toomer's *Cane*"; Nellie McKay, *Jean Toomer*; Foley, "'In the Land of Cotton,'" and "Jean Toomer's Sparta."

50. Toomer, *Cane*, 85. Subsequent page number references given in text.

51. Toomer, letter to Waldo Frank, in Whalan, *Letters of Jean Toomer*, 35–37.

52. Ibid., 116.

53. Kenneth Macgowan, letter to Jean Toomer, in Whalan, *Letters of Jean Toomer*, 174.

54. Toomer, letter to Waldo Frank, Whalan, *Letters of Jean Toomer*, 35–37.

55. Toomer, "The *Cane* Years," 124.

56. Fabre, "Dramatic and Musical Structures in 'Harvest Song' and 'Kabnis,'"; Mackey, "Sound and Sentiment, Sound and Symbol."

57. Gussow, *Seems Like Murder Here*.

58. Ellison, *Invisible Man*, 16.

59. Hale, *Making Whiteness*, 199–201, 226–29.

60. Goldsby, *Spectacular Secret*, 25–27.

61. Castronovo, *Beautiful Democracy*, 109–122.

62. Metress, *Lynching of Emmett Till,* 3.

63. Apel, *Imagery of Lynching,* 52.

64. Berlant, *Queen of America Goes to Washington City,* 233.

Chapter Four. *Contemporary Confrontations*

1. Williamson, "Wounds Not Scars," 1235; Kelley, 'Referee's Report"; Lewis, "Referee's Report"; Thelen, "What We See," 1219; Hall, "Later Comment."

2. Allison Saar, e-mail to Julie Buckner Armstrong.

3. White, *Rope and Faggot,* 29; Toomer, *Cane,* 92n8.

4. Woolfork, *Embodying American Slavery in Contemporary Culture,* 4–11.

5. The National Great Blacks in Wax Museum, http://www.ngbiwm.com. Subsequent textual references are to this site.

6. Cavender, "Scared Straight: Ideology and the Media."

7. I read reviews on www.yahoo.com, www.frommers.com, and www.trip advisor.com.

8. Multiple, different reenactment films have been posted. Video for the 2008 event that I attended is not available. The 2009 event, which contains commentary about organizers' motivations, can be found at http://www.youtube.com/watch?v=1GCQi2jhre4. The 2007 event, strictly a reenactment video, is located at http://www.youtube.com/watch?v=LOvCZxnSanQ.

9. GABEO, "62nd Anniversary Commemoration and 4th Reenactment."

10. Wexler, *Fire in a Canebrake,* 88.

11. *Maafa,* a Swahili term, is used to describe the suffering that resulted from African slavery and diaspora. Woolfork, *Embodying American Slavery in Contemporary Culture,* 102, 108.

12. Ibid., 99, 104.

13. Ibid., 109, 136.

14. Worthen, *Harcourt Brace Anthology of Drama,* 185–90.

15. Baker, "Under the Rope"; Ifill, *On the Courthouse Lawn.*

16. Reid, "In Quest for Justice, A Name Is Born."

17. Henkes, *Art of Black Women,* 113–15; Tesfagiorgis, e-mail to Julie Buckner Armstrong.

18. Kara Walker, e-mail to Julie Buckner Armstrong; Honorée Fanonne Jeffers, telephone interview.

19. Robinson, "Passages," 16–17; Tesfagiorgis, "Afrofemcentrism and Its Fruition," and "In Search of a Discourse."

20. Kara Walker, e-mail to Julie Buckner Armstrong.

21. Saltz, "Making the Cut"; *I'll Make Me a World,* vol. 6, "The Freedom You Will Take."

22. Vergne, "Black Saint Is the Sinner Lady," 8.

23. *Kara Walker: My Complement, My Enemy, My Oppressor, My Love*, 279, 299.

24. Walker answered my one e-mail courteously but declined further interviews.

25. Strand and Boland, *Making of a Poem*, 44. Jeffers, telephone interview.

26. Whitted, "'In My Flesh I Shall See God,'" 379; Apel, *Imagery of Lynching*, 102–4.

27. Hall, *Revolt Against Chivalry*; Gunning, *Race, Rape, and Lynching*; Feimster, *Southern Horrors*.

28. Richardson, *Black Masculinity and the U.S. South*, 202.

29. Goodie Mob, "Dirty South."

30. hooks, "Gangsta Culture," 116.

31. Sontag, *Regarding the Pain of Others*, 114. Subsequent references given in the text.

32. Markovitz, *Legacies of Lynching*.

33. Lee, Introduction, 4.

34. Qtd. in ibid., 6.

35. Apel, "Lynching Photographs and the Politics of Public Shaming," 78.

36. Shawn Michelle Smith, "Evidence of Lynching Photographs," 24–25.

Conclusion. Marking a Collective Past

1. Pope, "Lowndes Students Suspended"; Davis, "FBI May Join Probe of Mock Lynching"; Pope, "Speakout Hosted By VSU Addresses Diversity"; "Parents, Others Must Bring School Changes."

2. Soady, "Women's Studies 'Where Civil Rights Never Made It,'" B12; Soady, e-mail to Julie Buckner Armstrong.

3. "Rants and Raves," *Valdosta Daily Times*, 21 October 2002.

4. Wayne, "Photos Tell Grim Story."

5. Potok et al., "Geography of Hate."

6. Jones, "Louisiana Protest Echoes the Civil Rights Era."

7. George, "Why Now."

8. George, telephone interview.

9. "Mary Turner: A Past Unearthed."

10. George, telephone interview.

11. Soady, "Women's Studies 'Where Civil Rights Never Made It.'"

12. Ifill, *On the Courthouse Lawn*; Alliance for Truth and Racial Reconciliation; Theophus Smith, "After Violence."

13. Alexander, "Toward a Theory of Cultural Trauma," 22–24.

14. Ibid., 12.

15. Moore's Ford Memorial Committee; Wexler, *Fire in a Canebrake*, 225–34.

16. Apel, "Lynching Photographs and the Politics of Public Shaming," 70.

17. "Marking Rosewood History."

18. George, telephone interview.

19. Alliance for Truth and Racial Reconciliation.

20. Rich, "Diving into the Wreck," 67–68.

21. Loewen, *Lies across America*, 18.

22. Ibid., 18.

23. "Parents, Others Must Bring School Changes."

24. Loewen, *Lies across America*, 28; Ifill, *On the Courthouse Lawn*, 17–23.

25. George, telephone interview.

26. Georgia Historical Marker Program.

27. The Mary Turner Project handed out the proposed text at the May 16, 2009 Commemoration.

28. George, e-mail to the Mary Turner Project.

29. Ifill, *On the Courthouse Lawn*, 134. Subsequent page number references given in the text.

30. "Rants and Raves," *Valdosta Daily Times*, 13 October 2002.

31. Rhynes, "Mary Turner Program"; Mark George, telephone interview.

32. Friedlander, *When Memory Comes*.

33. Brundage, *Lynching in the New South*, 270–80.

34. Ibid., 119.

35. Brundage, "Roar on the Other Side of Violence."

36. Pendleton and Thomas, "Doc Holliday's Georgia Background."

37. Dittmer, *Black Georgia in the Progressive Era*, 72–76, 81.

BIBLIOGRAPHY

Abbreviations

AWG   Angelina Weld Grimké Papers. Manuscript Division. Moorland-
            Spingarn Research Center, Howard University, Washington, D.C.

CIC   Commission on Interracial Cooperation Papers, 1919–44.
            Microfilm. Series V, Literature 1920–44.

GNP   Georgia Newspaper Project. University of Georgia Libraries,
            Athens, Ga.

JWJ   James Weldon Johnson Papers. Beinecke Rare Book and
            Manuscript Library, Yale University. New Haven, Conn.

MWF   Meta Warrick Fuller Papers. Schomburg Center for Research in
            Black Culture, New York Public Library, New York.

NAACP   National Association for the Advancement of Colored People.
            Papers. Library of Congress. Washington, D.C.

TKG   The Tuskegee Institute News Clippings File. Series II, Lynching
            File, 1899–1966. Microfilm.

Primary Sources, Creative

Clifford, Carrie Williams. "Little Mother." *The Widening Light.* In *The Writings of Carrie Williams Clifford and Carrie Law Morgan Figgs*, edited by P. Jane Splawn, 57–58. New York: G. K. Hall, 1997.

Fuller, Meta Warrick. *Mary Turner: A Silent Protest against Mob Violence.* Museum of African American History. Boston, Mass.

Grimké, Angelina Weld. "Blackness." In *Selected Works of Angelina Weld Grimké.* 218–51.

——. "Goldie." In *Selected Works of Angelina Weld Grimké.* 282–306.

——. "The Waitin'." AWG. Box 38–12, Folder 210.

Jeffers, Honorée Fanonne. "dirty south moon." In *Red Clay Suite*, 33–34. Carbondale: Southern Illinois University Press, 2007.

——. "If You Get There Before I Do." *Story Quarterly* 41 (2005): 199–219.

Micheaux, Oscar. *Within Our Gates.* Library of Congress Smithsonian Video, 1919.

Spencer, Anne. "White Things." *Crisis.* March 1923, 204. Rpt. in Rice, *Witnessing Lynching*, 236.

Tesfagiorgis, Freida High. *Hidden Memories.* In Robert Henkes, *The Art of Black American Women: Works of Twenty-Four Artists of the Twentieth Century*, 113–15. Jefferson, N.C.: McFarland, 1993.

Toomer, Jean. *Cane.* Ed. Darwin Turner. New York: Norton, 1988.

Walker, Kara. *Do You Like Creme in Your Coffee and Chocolate in Your Milk?* In *Kara Walker: My Complement, My Enemy, My Oppressor, My Love.* Minneapolis: Walker Art Center, 2007. Plates 214, 227, and 257.

Primary Sources, Documentary

"Aftermath of the Lynchings." *Daily Observer.* 25 May 1918, 2. GNP.

Anti-Lynching Crusaders. "A Million Women United to Suppress Lynching." Grace Nail Johnson Correspondence, JWJ, Series II, Box 26, Folder 6.

"Besmirching Lowndes." *Savannah Morning News.* 25 May 1918, 6. GNP.

"*Birth of a Nation* Offered Last Time in Augusta Today." *Augusta Chronicle.* 18 May 1918, 5. GNP.

"Boche Agents Are Responsible for Crime at Barney." *Macon News.* 21 May 1918, 1–2. GNP.

"Chatham Home Guards Go to Valdosta to Avert Trouble." *Savannah Morning News.* 23 May 1918, 2. GNP.

Colored Welfare League. Resolutions to Governor Hugh M. Dorsey. *Atlanta Independent.* 25 May 1918, n.p. TKG, 1918.

Commission on Interracial Cooperation. "Mob Murder in America: A Challenge to Every American Citizen." 1929. CIC, Reel 29.

"Crackers Try to Foist Fiendish Work on Huns." *Pittsburgh Courier.* 1 June 1918, n.p. NAACP, Group 1, Box C-355.

Cumming, Joseph B. Letter to editor. *Augusta Chronicle.* 21 May 1918, 6. GNP.

Dam, C. P. Letter to John Shillady. 16 November 1918. NAACP, Group 1, Box C-355.

——. Letter to John Shillady. 24 December 1918. NAACP, Group 1, Box C-355.

——. Letter to Walter White. 13 September 1918. NAACP, Group 1, Box C-353.

Dorsey, Hugh M. Letter to John Shillady. 27 August 1918. NAACP, Group 1, Box C-353.

——. Letter to John Shillady. 30 November 1918. NAACP, Group 1, Box C-353.

——. Telegram to John Shillady. 21 August 1918. NAACP, Group 1, Box C-353.

"Double Lynching in Georgia." *New York Post.* 18 May 1918, n.p. NAACP, Group 1, Box C-355.

Editorial. *New York Post.* 20 May 1918, n.p. NAACP, Group 1, Box C-355.

"Farmer Killed, Wife Wounded." *Savannah Morning News.* 18 May 1918, 1. GNP.

"Four Murdered By Georgia 'Crackers.'" *Chicago Defender.* 25 May 1918, n.p. NAACP, Group 1, Box C-355.

"Four Negroes Hanged." *Brooklyn Citizen.* 20 May 1918, n.p. NAACP, Group 1, Box C-355.

"4 Negroes Lynched for Murders of Smith and Attack on Wife." *Moultrie Observer.* 21 May 1918, 1. GNP.

George, Mark. "Why Now." *Remembering Mary Turner.* http://www.maryturner .org. Accessed June 30, 2010.

"The Georgia Horrors." *New York Sun.* 9 August 1918, n.p. TKG, 1918.

"Georgia Huns Lynch Negro Woman Three Men." *Baltimore Daily Herald.* 20 May 1918, n.p. NAACP, Group 1, Box C-355.

"Georgia Maintains Her Record." *Houston Observer.* 28 October 1918, n.p. TKG, 1918.

"Georgia Mob Lynches Negro and His Wife." *New York Tribune.* 20 May 1918, n.p. NAACP, Group 1, Box C-355.

"Georgia's Latest Contribution to Civilization and World Democracy." Unnamed editorial in NAACP files. 21 May 1918, n.p. NAACP, Group 1, Box C-355.

"Good Advice for Negroes." *Atlanta Constitution.* 24 May 1918, 6. GNP.

"Governor Urges Negroes to Fight Cause of Lynching." *Atlanta Constitution.* 24 May 1918, 1. GNP.

Grant, Athens. Letter to Walter White. 20 November 1918. NAACP, Group 1, Box C-355.

"Hamp Smith Murdered; Young Wife Attacked by Negro Farm Hands." *Quitman Free Press.* 24 May 1918, 6. GNP.

"Hampton Smith of Barney Is Assassinated, Negro Blamed." *Daily Observer.* 17 May 1918, 1. GNP.

"Hayes and Mary Turner." National Great Blacks in Wax Museum. Baltimore, Md.

Haywood, Harry, and Milton Howard. "Lynching: A Weapon of National Oppression." New York: Labor Research Association, 1932.

"Her Talk Enraged Them." *Savannah Morning News.* 20 May 1918, 2. GNP.

"Home Guards Return from Futile Trip to Valdosta." *Savannah Morning News.* 24 May 1918, 1. GNP.

"How Lynchings May Be Stopped." *Savannah Morning News.* 24 May 1918, 1. GNP.

"Hundreds Visit Scene of Lynching." *Atlanta Constitution.* 19 May 1918, 4AA. GNP.

"Hunt for Sidney Johnson Still On." *Daily Observer.* 21 May 1918, 1. GNP.

"Is It Treason?" *Advocate.* 27 May 1918, n.p. TKG, 1918.

Johnson, James Weldon. Address Delivered at National Conference on Lynching. 5 May 1919. NAACP, Group 1, Box C-334.

———. *Along This Way.* New York: Viking, 1933.

"Johnson Is Shot to Death by Police Officers." *Savannah Morning News.* 23 May 1918, 1. GNP.

"Johnson Killed by Policemen." *Quitman Free Press.* 24 May 1918, 1. GNP.

Kenyon, William S. Letter to John Shillady. 9 November 1918. NAACP, Group 1, Box C-355.

"Lying Follows Lynching." *Baltimore Daily Herald.* 22 May 1918, n.p. NAACP, Group 1, Box C-355.

"Lynching Most Helpful to the Prussians." *Commercial Appeal.* 21 May 1918, n.p. NAACP, Group 1, Box C-355.

"The Lynchings of May, 1918 in Brooks and Lowndes Counties, Georgia." *Baltimore Herald.* 27 May 1918, n.p. NAACP, Group 1, Box C-353.

"The Lynching Story." *Quitman Free Press.* 24 May 1918, 1. GNP.

"Mary Turner: A Past Unearthed." *Valdosta Daily Times.* 13 May 2009.

"Massacre at Moore's Ford." http://www.youtube.com/watch?v=LOvCZxnSanQ. Accessed June 30, 2010.

"Might Against Right." *Atlanta Independent.* 1 June 1918, n.p. GNP.

"Mob Avenges Smith's Death." *Savannah Morning News.* 19 May 1918, 1. GNP.

"Mobs Lynch Four; Seek Two Others." *New York Sun.* 20 May 1918, n.p. NAACP, Group 1, Box C-355.

NAACP (National Association for the Advancement of Colored People). Press Release. 1 August 1918. NAACP, Group 1, Box C-353.

——. Press Release. 7 September 1918. NAACP, Group 1, Box C-353.

——. Press Release. 22 May 1918. NAACP, Group 1, Box C-353.

——. *Thirty Years of Lynching in the United States, 1889–1918.* 1919; Repr., New York: Arno Press, 1969.

"Negro Murderer Is in Savannah Jail." *Quitman Free Press.* 19 July 1918, 1. GNP.

"Negro Women Hold Humiliation Service." *Savannah Tribune.* 6 June 1918, n.p. TKG, 1918.

"'Over Here' and 'Over There.'" *Houston Observer.* 26 May 1918, n.p. TKG, 1918.

Press Release. *San Antonio Express.* 5 August 1918. NAACP, Group 1, Box C-337.

"Pro-Germans Had a Hand: Enemy Agents Said to Have Worked Among Negroes to Bring on Race Troubles." *Savannah Morning News.* 21 May 1918, 1. GNP.

"Rants and Raves." *Valdosta Daily Times.* 21 October 2001.

Remembering Mary Turner. http://www.maryturner.org. Accessed June 30, 2010.

Rhynes, George B. "Mary Turner Program, Not News Worthy in Valdosta, Georgia, May 16, 2009, Why?" *Mary Turner Lynching Ignored.* http://maryturnergbr .blogspot.com/2009/05/mary-turners-lynching-1918.html. Accessed November 15, 2010.

Shillady, John. Letter to Hugh M. Dorsey. 11 September 1918. NAACP, Group 1, Box C-353.

——. Letter to William S. Kenyon. 13 November 1918. NAACP, Group 1, Box C-355.

——. Letter to Woodrow Wilson. 25 July 1918. NAACP, Group 1, Box C-353.

——. Telegram to Hugh M. Dorsey. 26 August 1918. NAACP, Group 1, Box C-353.

"Sidney Johnson Is Killed in Valdosta." *Moultrie Observer.* 24 May 1918, 1. GNP.

"Simon Shuman Held for Barney Crime." *Daily Observer.* 25 June 1918, 1. GNP.

"Skulking Hun Is Blamed for Racial Break in Georgia." *Memphis News-Scimitar.* 21 May 1918, n.p. NAACP, Group 1, Box C-355.

"Southern Journals Express Horror and Indignation over Cowardly Lynching of Female." *New York Age.* 1 June 1918, n.p. NAACP, Group 1, Box C-355.

"Tragedy at Barney Laid to Hun Agents." *Atlanta Constitution.* 21 May 1918, 7. GNP.

"Two More Georgia Negroes Lynched in Murder Case." *New York Herald.* 20 May 1918, n.p. NAACP, Group 1, Box C-355.

"Two More Swing Up for Tragedy at Smith Home: One a Woman." *Daily Observer.* 20 May 1918, 1. GNP.

White, Walter F. *A Man Called White.* New York: Viking, 1948.

——. "I Investigate Lynchings." *American Mercury.* 22 December 1928, 77–84.

——. Letter to Athens Grant. 9 December 1918. NAACP, Group 1, Box C-355.

——. Letter to the Editor. *Cheyenne State Leader.* 20 February 1919. NAACP, Group 1, Box C-355.

——. Letter to John E. Salmon. 24 May 1918. NAACP, Group 1, Box G-43.

——. Letter to John Shillady. 9 July 1918. NAACP, Group 1, Box G-43.

——. Letter to Samuel Broadnax. 10 December 1918. NAACP, Group 1, Box C-355.

——. "Memorandum for Governor Dorsey." NAACP, Group 1, Box C-353.

——. Memorandum to John Shillady, Re: Interview with George U. Spratling. 12 November 1918. NAACP, Group 1, Box C-355.

——. Memorandum for Mr. Dam, Re: Georgia Lynchings. 19 November 1918. NAACP, Group 1, Box C-355.

——. *Rope and Faggot: A Biography of Judge Lynch.* 1929; Repr., Notre Dame, Ind.: University of Notre Dame, 2001. 33.

——. Undated Memorandum, Re: Brooks-Lowndes Counties Lynchings of May, 1918. NAACP, Group 1, Box C-353.

——. "The Work of a Mob." *Crisis.* September 1918, 221–23.

"Woman Is Lynched by Mob in Georgia." *New York World.* 20 May 1918, n.p. NAACP, Group 1, Box C-355.

Secondary Sources

Alexander, Jeffrey C. "Toward a Theory of Cultural Trauma." In *Cultural Trauma and Collective Identity,* edited by Jeffrey C. Alexander et al., 1–30. Berkeley: University of California Press, 2004.

——, et al., eds. *Cultural Trauma and Collective Identity*. Berkeley: University of California Press, 2004.

Allen, James, et al. *Without Sanctuary: Lynching Photography in America*. Santa Fe, N.Mex.: Twin Palms, 2000.

Alliance for Truth and Racial Reconciliation. http://www.atrr.org/index.htm.

Anderson, Karen Leona. "Classifying Life: Metaphor, Popular Biology, and Social Categorization in Emily Dickinson, Anne Spencer, Marianne Moore, and Lornine Niedecker." PhD Diss., Cornell University, May 2008.

Anti-Lynching Crusaders. Press Release: "One Million American Women Crusade Against Lynching." Grace Nail Johnson Correspondence, JWJ, Box 26, Folder 7.

Apel, Dora. *Imagery of Lynching: Black Men, White Women and the Mob*. New Brunswick, N.J.: Rutgers University Press, 2004.

——. "Lynching Photographs and the Politics of Public Shaming." In *Lynching Photographs*, 42–78.

Arnold, Edwin. *"What Virtue There Is in Fire": Cultural Memory and the Lynching of Sam Hose*. Athens: University of Georgia Press, 2009.

Ater, Renee. "Making History: Meta Warrick Fuller's 'Ethiopia.'" *American Art* 17.3 (2003): 12–31.

Ayers, Edward L. *Vengeance and Justice: Crime and Punishment in the 19th-Century American South*. New York: Oxford University Press, 1984.

Baker, Bruce E. "Under the Rope: Lynching and Memory in Laurens County, South Carolina." In *Where These Memories Grow*, edited by W. Fitzhugh Brundage, 319–45. Chapel Hill: University of North Carolina Press, 2000.

Baraka, Amiri. "Black Art." In *Transbluesency: The Selected Poetry of Amiri Baraka/ LeRoi Jones (1961–1995)*, edited by Paul Vangelisti, 142–43. New York: Marsilio, 1995.

Battenfeld, Mary. "'Been Shapin Words T Fit M Soul': *Cane*, Language, and Social Change." *Callaloo* 25 (2002): 1238–49.

Bercovitch, Sacvan. *The American Jeremiad*. Madison: University of Wisconsin Press, 1978.

Berg, Allison. *Mothering the Race: Women's Narratives of Reproduction, 1890–1930*. Urbana: University of Illinois Press, 2002.

Berlant, Lauren Gail. *The Queen of America Goes to Washington City: Essays on Sex and Citizenship*. Durham, N.C.: Duke University Press, 1997.

Bernstein, Matthew. *Screening a Lynching: The Leo Frank Case on Film and Television*. Athens: University of Georgia Press, 2008.

Bernstein, Patricia. *The First Waco Horror: The Lynching of Jesse Washington and the Rise of the NAACP*. College Station: University of Texas A&M Press, 2005.

Birth of a Nation. Dir. D. W. Griffith. Alpha Video, 1915.

Blake, Susan. "The Spectatorial Artist and the Structure of *Cane*." *CLA Journal* 17 (1974): 516–34. Rpt. in O'Daniel, 195–212.

Bowser, Pearl, et al., eds. *Oscar Micheaux and His Circle: African American Filmmaking and Race Cinema of the Silent Era.* Bloomington: Indiana University Press, 2001.

Bowser, Pearl, and Louise Spence. *Writing Himself into History: Oscar Micheaux, His Silent Films, and His Audiences.* New Brunswick, N.J.: Rutgers University Press, 2000.

Braxton, Joanne. "Ancestral Presence: The Outraged Mother Figure in Contemporary Afra-American Writing." In *Wild Women in the Whirlwind: Afra-American Culture and the Contemporary Literary Renaissance*, edited by Joanne M. Braxton and Andrée Nicolea McLaughlin, 299–315. New Brunswick, N.J.: Rutgers University Press, 1990.

Brown, Elsa Barkley. "Imaging Lynching: African American Women, Communities of Struggle, and Collective Memory." In *African American Women Speak Out on Anita Hill-Clarence Thomas*, edited by Geneva Smitherman, 100–124. Detroit: Wayne State University Press, 1995.

Brown, Mary Jane. *Eradicating This Evil: Women in the Anti-Lynching Movement, 1892–1940.* New York: Garland, 2000.

Brundage, W. Fitzhugh. *Lynching in the New South: Georgia and Virginia, 1880–1930.* Urbana: University of Illinois Press, 1993.

——. "Meta Warrick's 1907 'Negro Tableaux' and (Re)Presenting African American Historical Memory." *Journal of American History* 89 (March 2003): 1368–400.

——. "The Roar on the Other Side of Silence." In *Under Sentence of Death: Lynching in the South*, edited by W. Fitzhugh Brundage, 217–90. Chapel Hill: University of North Carolina Press, 1997.

Burrill, Mary Powell. *Aftermath.* In Perkins and Stephens, *Strange Fruit: Plays on Lynching by American Women*, 79–81.

Butler, Octavia. *Kindred.* Boston: Beacon Press, 1979.

Caldwell, Erskine. "Kneel to the Rising Sun." *Scribner's.* January–June 1935, 71–80. Rpt. in Rice, *Witnessing Lynching*, 284–303.

Carby, Hazel. *Reconstructing Womanhood: The Emergence of the Afro-American Woman Novelist.* New York: Oxford University Press, 1987.

Carter, Dan T. *Scottsboro: A Tragedy of the American South.* Rev. ed. Baton Rouge: Louisiana State University Press, 2007.

Caruth, Cathy. *Unclaimed Experience: Trauma, Narrative, and History.* Baltimore, Md.: Johns Hopkins University Press, 1996.

Castronovo, Russ. *Beautiful Democracy: Aesthetics and Anarchy in a Global Era.* Chicago: University of Chicago Press, 2007.

Cavender, Gray. "Scared Straight: Ideology and the Media." *Journal of Criminal Justice* 9 (1981): 431–39.

Clifford, Carrie Williams. Letter to Joel Spingarn. 25 January 1913. Joel Spingarn Papers, Box 95–3. Moorland-Spingarn Research Center, Howard University.

——. "Votes for Children." *Crisis*. August 1915, 185.

Colin, Mattie Smith. "Mother's Tears Greet Son Who Died a Martyr." *Chicago Defender*. In Metress, *Lynching of Emmett Till*, 29–30.

Cripps, Thomas. *Slow Fade to Black: The Negro in American Film, 1900–1942*. New York: Oxford University Press, 1993.

Cullen, Countee, ed. *Caroling Dusk: An Anthology of Verse By Negro Poets*. New York: Harper and Brothers, 1927.

Davis, Jingle. "FBI May Join Probe of Mock Lynching: Valdosta Students Suspended for Act Using Black Doll." *Atlanta Journal Constitution*. 9 October 2002.

"Devil Resigns Office in Favor of Kaiser." *Atlanta Constitution*. 16 May 1918, 2. GNP.

Dinnerstein, Leonard. *The Leo Frank Case*. 1966; Repr., Athens: University of Georgia Press, 2008.

Dittmer, John. *Black Georgia in the Progressive Era, 1900–1920*. Urbana: University of Illinois Press, 1980.

Dixon, Thomas. *The Clansman: An Historical Romance of the Ku Klux Klan*. Rev. ed. Lexington: University of Kentucky Press, 1970.

Dorsey, Hugh M. "A Statement from Governor Hugh M. Dorsey as to the Negro in Georgia." Atlanta, 1921.

Downs, Jamie. E-mail to Julie Buckner Armstrong. 10 September 2008.

Dray, Philip. *At the Hands of Persons Unknown: The Lynching of Black America*. New York: Modern Library, 2003.

Du Bois, W. E. B. *The Negro Problem: A Series of Articles by Representative Negroes of To-day*. New York, 1903.

——. Reflections on the Dyer Bill. JWJ, Box 6, Folder 137.

——. *The Souls of Black Folk*. 1903. Repr., New York: Oxford University Press, 2009.

Dunbar-Nelson, Alice. *Mine Eyes Have Seen*. *Crisis*. April 1918, 271–74.

Dunn, Marvin. "Justice for Willie James." *Tampa Tribune*. 18 November 2007, Opinion Section, 1+.

Edmunds, Susan. "The Race Question and 'The Question of Home'": Revisiting the Lynching Plot in Jean Toomer's *Cane*." *American Literature* 75 (2003): 141–68.

Eldridge, Richard. "The Unifying Images in Part One of Jean Toomer's *Cane*." In O'Daniel, *Jean Toomer*, 213–36.

Ellison, Ralph. *Invisible Man*. 1952; Repr., New York: Vintage, 1995.

Fabre, Geneviève. "Dramatic and Musical Structures in 'Harvest Song' and 'Kabnis': Toomer's *Cane* and the Harlem Renaissance." In *Jean Toomer and the Harlem Renaissance*, edited by Geneviève Fabre and Michel Feith, 109–27. New Brunswick, N.J.: Rutgers University Press, 2001.

——, and Robert O'Meally, eds. *History and Memory in African American Culture*. New York: Oxford University Press. 1994.

Faulkner, William. *Absalom, Absalom!* 1936; Repr., New York: Modern Library, 1995.

Feimster, Crystal. "Ladies and Lynching: The Gendered Discourse on Mob Violence in the New South, 1880–1930." PhD diss., Princeton University, 2000.

——. *Southern Horrors: Women and the Politics of Rape and Lynching.* Cambridge, Mass.: Harvard University Press, 2009.

Fleming, William H. "Memorial of Joseph B. Cumming." In *Report of the Thirty-Ninth Annual Session of the Georgia Bar Association*, edited by Harry S. Strozier, 230–43. Macon, Ga.: J. W. Buree, 1922.

Foley, Barbara. "'In the Land of Cotton': Economics and Violence in Jean Toomer's *Cane*." *African American Review* 32 (1998): 181–98.

——. "Jean Toomer's Sparta." *American Literature* 67 (1995): 747–75.

Ford, Charita. "Flowering a Feminist Garden: The Writings and Poetry of Anne Spencer." *SAGE* 5.1 (Summer 1988): 7–14.

Friedlander, Saul. *When Memory Comes.* Madison: University of Wisconsin Press, 2003.

Fuller, Meta Warrick. Document for Bruce A. Getchell and Alfred C. Perry. 29 January 1967. MWF, Box 16.

——. Letter to Angelina Weld Grimké. 25 May 1917. AWG, Box 38–1, Folder 6.

——. Letter to Angelina Weld Grimké. 31 May 1917. AWG, Box 38–1, Folder 6.

——. Letter to Hannah Moriarta. 21 January 1931. Harmon Foundation Papers, Box 45. Library of Congress. Washington, D.C.

——. Letter to Sylvia Dannett. 16 September 1964. MWF, Box 17.

GABEO (Georgia Association of Black Elected Officials). Sixty-second Anniversary Commemoration and Fourth Reenactment of the Lynchings at the Moore's Ford Bridge. July 25, 2008. http://www.gabeo.org/nm/publish.news_91.shtml.

Gaines, Jane M. "*The Birth of a Nation* and *Within Our Gates*: Two Tales of the American South." In *Dixie Debates: Perspectives on Southern Culture*, edited by Richard H. King and Helen Taylor, 177–92. New York: New York University Press, 1996.

George, Mark. E-mail to the Mary Turner Project. 23 August 2009.

——. Telephone interview. 2 September 2009.

Georgia Historical Marker Program. http://www.georgiahistory.com/files/0000/0027/Marker_Application_Materials.pdf.

Giddings, Paula. *When and Where I Enter: The Impact of Black Women on Race and Sex in America.* 2nd ed. New York: Harper, 1996.

Gilmore, Glenda. *Gender and Jim Crow: Women and the Politics of White Supremacy in North Carolina, 1896–1920.* Chapel Hill: University of North Carolina Press, 1996.

Giovanni, Nikki. "Alabama Poem." In *The Selected Poems of Nikki Giovanni*, 90–91. New York: William Morrow, 1996.

Goldsby, Jacqueline. *A Spectacular Secret: Lynching in American Life and Culture*. Chicago: University of Chicago Press, 2006.

Goodie Mob. "Dirty South." *Soul Food*. Arista, 1995.

———. *Still Standing*. Arista, 1998.

Goodman, James. *Stories of Scottsboro*. New York: Vintage Books, 1995.

Grant, Donald L. *The Way It Was in the South: The Black Experience in Georgia*. Athens: University of Georgia Press, 2001.

Grasso, Linda. *The Artistry of Anger: Black and White Women's Literature in America, 1820–1860*. Chapel Hill: University of North Carolina Press, 2002.

Green, J. Ronald. *Straight Lick: The Cinema of Oscar Micheaux*. Bloomington: Indiana University Press, 2000.

Greene, J. Lee, and Anne Spencer. *Time's Unfading Garden: Anne Spencer's Life and Poetry*. Baton Rouge: Louisiana State University Press, 1977.

Grimké, Angelina Weld. *Rachel*. Printed program. AWG. Box 38–13, Folder 226.

———. "*Rachel*: The Play of the Month." In *Selected Works of Angelina Weld Grimké*, 414.

———. *Selected Works of Angelina Weld Grimké*. Ed. Carolivia Herron. New York: Oxford University Press, 1991.

———. "Tenebris." In *Selected Works of Angelina Weld Grimké*, 1913.

Grimké, Archibald. Letter to R. R. Moton. 12 July 1918. Archibald Grimké Papers, Box 39–27, Folder 549. Manuscript Division. Moorland-Spingarn Research Center, Howard University, Washington, D.C.

Gunning, Sandra. *Race, Rape, and Lynching: The Red Record of American Literature, 1890–1912*. New York: Oxford University Press, 1996.

Gussow, Adam. *Seems Like Murder Here: Southern Violence and the Blues Tradition*. Chicago: University of Chicago Press, 2002.

Hale, Grace. *Making Whiteness: The Culture of Segregation in the South, 1890–1940*. New York: Pantheon, 1998.

Hall, Jacqueline Dowd. "A Later Comment." In Thelen, "What We See," 1268–70.

———. *Revolt Against Chivalry: Jessie Daniel Ames and the Women's Campaign Against Lynching*. New York: Columbia University Press, 1979.

Harris, Trudier. *Exorcising Blackness: Historical and Literary Lynching and Burning Rituals*. Bloomington: University of Indiana Press, 1984.

Haywood, Harry. *Black Bolshevik: Autobiography of an Afro-American Communist*. Chicago: Liberator Press, 1978.

Henkes, Robert. *The Art of Black American Women: Works of Twenty-Four Artists of the Twentieth Century*. Jefferson, N.C.: McFarland, 1993.

Higginbotham, Evelyn Brooks. *Righteous Discontent: The Women's Movement in the Black Baptist Church, 1880–1920*. Cambridge, Mass.: Harvard University Press, 1993.

Hill, Rebecca N. *Men, Mobs, and Law: Anti-Lynching and Labor Defense in U.S. Radical History*. Durham, N.C.: Duke University Press, 2008.

Hine, Darlene Clark. "Rape and the Inner Lives of Black Women in the Middle West: Preliminary Thoughts on the Culture of Dissemblance." *Signs: Journal of Women in Culture and Society* 14 (1989): 912–20.

——, et al. *Black Women in America: An Historical Encyclopedia.* 2 Vols. Bloomington: Indiana University Press, 1994.

Hirsch, David A. Hedrich. "Speaking Silences in Angelina Weld Grimké's 'The Closing Door' and 'Blackness.'" *African American Review* 26 (1992): 459–74.

Honey, Maureen, ed. *Shadowed Dreams: Women's Poetry of the Harlem Renaissance.* New Brunswick, N.J.: Rutgers University Press, 1989.

hooks, bell. "Choosing the Margin as a Space of Radical Openness." In hooks, *Yearning,* 145–54.

——. *Feminist Theory: From Margin to Center.* Boston: South End Press, 1984.

——. "Gansta Culture – Sexism and Misogyny: Who Will Take the Rap?" In *Outlaw Culture: Resisting Representations,* 115–24. New York: Routledge, 1994.

——. "Homeplace: A Site of Resistance." In hooks, *Yearning,* 41–50.

——. *Yearning: Race, Gender, and Cultural Politics.* Boston: South End Press, 1990.

Howard, Willie James. Letter to Cynthia Goff. 1 January 1944. NAACP, Group 1, Box C-357.

Huie, William Bradford. "The Shocking Story of Approved Killing in Mississippi." In Metress, *Lynching of Emmett* Till, 200–208.

Hull, Gloria. *Color, Sex, and Poetry: Three Women Writers of the Harlem Renaissance.* New Brunswick, N.J.: Rutgers University Press, 1989.

Hurston, Zora Neale. *Their Eyes Were Watching God.* 1939; Repr., New York: Harper Perennial, 2006.

Hutchinson, George B. "Jean Toomer and the 'New Negroes' of Washington." *American Literature* 63 (1991): 683–92.

Ifill, Sherrilyn. *On the Courthouse Lawn: Confronting the Legacy of Lynching in the Twenty-first Century.* Boston: Beacon Press, 2007.

I'll Make Me A World. 6 vols. PBS Video, 1999.

Innes, Catherine. "The Unity of Jean Toomer's *Cane.*" In O'Daniel, *Jean Toomer,* 153–70.

Jackson, Phyllis. "(In)Forming the Visual: (Re)Presenting Women of African Descent." *International Review of African American Art* 14.3 (1997): 31–37.

Janken, Kenneth Robert. *White: The Biography of Walter White, Mr. NAACP.* New York: Free Press, 2003.

Jeffers, Honorée Fanonne. Telephone interview. 27 May 2007.

Johnson, Charles, ed. *Ebony and Topaz.* New York: Books for Libraries Press, 1971.

Johnson, Georgia Douglas. *Blue-Eyed Black Boy.* In Perkins and Stephens, *Strange Fruit: Plays on Lynching by American Women,* 116–20.

——. *Safe.* In Perkins and Stephens, *Strange Fruit: Plays on Lynching by American Women,* 110–15.

——. *A Sunday Morning in the South.* In Perkins and Stephens, *Strange Fruit: Plays on Lynching by American Women,* 103–9.

Johnson, James Weldon. "Lawlessness in the United States." *New York Age.* 12 November 1914. In *The Selected Writings of James Weldon Johnson,* edited by Sondra Kathryn Wilson, 1:55–56. New York: Oxford University Press, 1995.

Jones, Michael G. "Louisiana Protest Echoes the Civil Rights Era." *New York Times.* 21 September 2007.

Kantrowitz, Stephen. *Ben Tillman and the Reconstruction of White Supremacy.* Chapel Hill: University of North Carolina Press, 2000.

Kanwar, Asha, ed. *The Unforgetting Heart: An Anthology of Short Stories by African American Women.* San Francisco: Aunt Lute, 1995.

Kaplan, Amy. "The Birth of an Empire." *PMLA* 114 (1999): 1068–79.

Kara Walker: My Complement, My Enemy, My Oppressor, My Love. Org. Philippe Vergne. Minneapolis: Walker Art Museum, 2007. 7–27.

Kelley, Robin D. G. "Referee's Report." In Thelen, "What We See," 1258–61.

Kerr, Judith Nina. "God-Given Work: The Life and Times of Sculptor Meta Warrick Fuller, 1877–1968." PhD diss., University of Massachusetts, 1986.

Knoblauch, Mary. Letter to Angelina Weld Grimké. 4 October 1920. AWG, Box 38–1, Folder 10.

——. Letter to Angelina Weld Grimké. 13 October 1920. AWG, Box 38–1, Folder 10.

Krasny, Michael. "The Aesthetic Structure of Jean Toomer's *Cane.*" *Negro American Literature Forum* 9.2 (1975): 42–43.

Kundera, Milan. *The Book of Laughter and Forgetting.* New York: Harper Perennial, 1999.

Lee, Anthony W. Introduction. *Lynching Photographs.* 1–9.

Lewis, David Levering. "Referee's Report." In Thelen, "What We See," 1261–64.

Litwack, Leon. *Trouble in Mind: Black Southerners in the Age of Jim Crow.* New York: Knopf, 1998.

Loewen, James W. *Lies across America: What Our Historic Sites Get Wrong.* New York: New Press, 1999.

Lorde, Audre. "A Litany for Survival." In *The Collected Poems of Audre Lorde,* 255–56. New York: W. W. Norton, 2000.

Lynching Photographs. Ed. Anthony W. Lee. Berkeley: University of California Press, 2008.

MacKethan, Lucinda. "Jean Toomer's *Cane*: A Pastoral Problem." *Mississippi Quarterly* 35 (1975): 423–34.

Mackey, Nathaniel. "Sound and Sentiment, Sound and Symbol." *Callaloo* 10 (1987): 33–37.

Madison, James. *A Lynching in the Heartland: Race and Memory in America.* New York: Palgrave, 2001.

"Marking Rosewood History." *The Real Rosewood.* http://rosewoodflorida.com.

Markovitz, Jonathan. *Legacies of Lynching: Racial Violence and Memory.* Minneapolis: University of Minnesota Press, 2004.

McGovern, James R. *Anatomy of a Lynching: The Killing of Claude Neal.* Baton Rouge: Louisiana State University Press, 1982.

McHenry, Elizabeth. *Forgotten Readers: Recovering the Lost History of African-American Literary Societies.* Durham, N.C.: Duke University Press, 2002.

McKay, Claude. "If We Must Die." In *Complete Poems,* edited by William J. Maxwell, 152. Urbana: University of Illinois Press, 2004.

McKay, Nellie Y. *Jean Toomer, Artist: A Study of His Literary Life and Work, 1894–1936.* Chapel Hill: University of North Carolina Press, 1984.

McKeever, Benjamin F. "*Cane* as Blues." In O'Daniel, *Jean Toomer,* 453–58.

Metress, Christopher. "Literary Representations of the Lynching of Emmett Till: An Annotated Bibliography." In Pollack and Metress, *Emmett Till,* 223–50.

——. *The Lynching of Emmett Till: A Documentary Narrative.* Charlottesville: University of Virginia Press, 2002.

——. "On That Third Day He Rose: Sacramental Memory and the Lynching of Emmett Till." In Pollack and Metress, *Emmett Till,* 16–30.

Meyers, Christopher C. "'Killing Them by the Wholesale': A Lynching Rampage in South Georgia." *Georgia Historical Quarterly* 90 (2006): 214–35.

Miller, Erika M. *The Other Reconstruction: Where Violence and Motherhood Meet in the Writings of Wells-Barnett, Grimké, and Larsen.* New York: Garland, 2000.

Miller, Kelly. "The Disgrace of Democracy: Open Letter to President Woodrow Wilson." Washington, D.C.: Howard University, 1917.

Mitchell, Koritha A. "Anti-Lynching Plays: Angelina Weld Grimké, Alice Dunbar-Nelson, and Evolution of African American Drama." *Post-Bellum, Pre-Harlem: African-American Literature and Culture, 1877–1919,* edited by Barbara McCaskill and Caroline Gebhard, 210–30. New York: New York University Press, 2006.

Moore's Ford Memorial Committee. http://www.mooresford.org.

Morrison, Toni. *Beloved.* New York: Random House, 1987.

NAACP (National Association for the Advancement of Colored People). Program, National Conference on Lynching. NAACP, Group 1, Box C-339.

NACW (National Association of Colored Women). Convention Program. July 1918. Records of the National Association of Colored Women's Clubs, 1895–1992. Ed. Lillian Serece Williams et al. Bethesda, Md.: University Publications of America. Microfilm, Reel 20.

——. *National Notes* 26.2 (November 1923). NACW Papers, Microfilm, Reel 23.

Nora, Pierre. "Between Memory and History: *Les Lieux de Mémoire.*" *Representations* 26 (Spring 1989): 7–25.

O'Daniel, Therman B., ed. *Jean Toomer: A Critical Evaluation.* Washington, D.C.: Howard University Press, 1988.

Ovington, Mary White. Letter to Mary Talbert. 9 October 1923. NAACP, Group II, Box L-30.

———. Letter to William Talbert. 16 November 1923. NAACP, Group II, Box L-30.

"Parents, Others Must Bring School Changes." *Valdosta Daily Times*. 24 November 2002.

Pendleton, Albert S., Jr., and Susan McKey Thomas. "Doc Holliday's Georgia Background." *Journal of Arizona History* 14 (1973): 191–92.

Perkins, Kathy A., and Judith L. Stephens. *Strange Fruit: Plays on Lynching by American Women*. Bloomington: Indiana University Press, 1998.

Pollack, Harriett, and Christopher Metress, eds. *Emmett Till in Literary Memory and Imagination*. Baton Rouge: Louisiana State University Press, 2008.

Pope, Jessica. "Lowndes Students Suspended." *Valdosta Daily Times*. 7 October 2002.

———. "Speakout Hosted By VSU Addresses Diversity." *Valdosta Daily Times*. 19 November 2002.

Potok, Mark, et al. "The Geography of Hate." *New York Times*. 25 November 2007.

Regester, Charlene. "The African-American Press and Race Movies, 1909–1929." In Bowser et al., *Oscar Micheaux and His Circle*, 34–51.

———. "Black Films, White Censors: Oscar Micheaux Confronts Censorship in New York, Virginia, and Chicago." In *Movie Censorship and American Culture*, edited by Francis G. Couvares, 159–86. Washington, D.C.: Smithsonian Institution Press, 1996.

———. "Lynched, Assaulted, and Intimidated: Oscar Micheaux's Most Controversial Films." *Popular Culture Review* 5.2 (1994): 47–55.

Reid, S. A. "In Quest for Justice, A Name Is Born." *Atlanta Journal-Constitution*. 24 July 2008.

Rice, Anne P. "Disappearing Bodies and Sites of Memory." Literary Responses to Lynching. Modern Language Association Conference. Philadelphia. 29 December 2004.

———. "White Islands of Safety and Engulfing Blackness: Remapping Segregation in Angelina Weld Grimké's 'Blackness' and 'Goldie.'" *African American Review* 42 (2008): 75–90.

———. *Witnessing Lynching: American Writers Respond*. New Brunswick, N.J.: Rutgers University Press, 2003.

Rich, Adrienne. "Diving Into the Wreck." In *Adrienne Rich's Poetry*, edited by Barbara Charlesworth Gelpi and Albert Gelpi, 65–68. New York: W. W. Norton, 1975.

Richardson, Riché. *Black Masculinity and the U.S. South: From Uncle Tom to Gansta*. Athens: University of Georgia Press, 2007.

Robinson, Jontyle Theresa. "Passages: A Curatorial Viewpoint." In *Bearing Witness: Contemporary Works by African American Women Artists*, 13–37. New York: Spelman College and Rizzoli International Publishing, 1996.

Saar, Allison. E-mail to Julie Buckner Armstrong. 10 June 2006.

Saltz, Jerry. "Making the Cut." *Village Voice.* 24 November 1998.

Schechter, Patricia A. *Ida B. Wells-Barnett and American Reform, 1880–1930.* Chapel Hill: University of North Carolina Press, 2000.

Scruggs, Charles, and Lee VanDemarr, *Jean Toomer and the Terrors of American History.* Philadelphia: University of Pennsylvania Press, 1998.

Shillady, John. Letter to Archibald Grimké. 28 June 1918. Archibald Grimké Papers, Box 39–27, Folder 548. Manuscript Division. Moorland-Spingarn Research Center, Howard University, Washington, D.C.

Simien, Evelyn, ed. *Gender and Lynching: The Politics of Memory.* New York: Palgrave Macmillan, 2011.

Smith, Shawn Michelle. "The Evidence of Lynching Photographs." In *Lynching Photographs*, 10–41.

Smith, Theophus. "After Violence: Towards a Normative Practice of 'Truth and Reconciliation.'" http://www.religion.emory.edu/faculty/smith/lawrel.html. Accessed June 30, 2010.

Soady, Viki. E-mail to Julie Buckner Armstrong. 29 August 2005.

——. "Women's Studies 'Where Civil Rights Never Made It.'" *Chronicle of Higher Education.* 22 November 2002, B12+.

Solomon, Mark. *The Cry Was Unity: Communists and African Americans, 1917–1936.* Jackson: University of Mississippi Press, 1998.

Sontag, Susan. *Regarding the Pain of Others.* New York: Farrar, Straus, and Giroux, 2007.

Strand, Mark, and Eavan Boland. *The Making of a Poem: A Norton Anthology of Poetic Forms.* New York: W. W. Norton, 2000.

Talbert, Mary B. Anti-Lynching Crusaders Final Report. NAACP Papers, Group I, Box C-207.

——. Directions for Buffalo Key Women. Grace Nail Johnson Correspondence. JWJ, Box 26, Folder 6.

——. Draft Letter to the Anti-Lynching Crusaders. 11 January 1923. NAACP Papers, General Office Files, Group II, Box L-30.

——. Form Letter. 11 October 1922. Grace Nail Johnson Correspondence. JWJ, Box 26, Folder 7.

——. Letter to Grace Nail Johnson. 2 October 1922. Grace Nail Johnson Correspondence, JWJ, Box 26, Folder 1.

——. Letter to James Weldon Johnson. 21 October 1922. NAACP Papers, Group I, Box C-207.

——. Letter to James Weldon Johnson. 22 May 1923. NAACP Papers, Group I, Box C-207.

——. Letter to Potential State Directors. 14 July 1922. Grace Nail Johnson Correspondence. JWJ, Box 26, Folder 7.

——. Letter to State Directors and Executive Board Members. Undated. Grace Nail Johnson Correspondence. JWJ, Box 26, Folder 7.

——. Letter to W. E. B. Du Bois, Re: Agreement Between the Anti-Lynching Crusaders and the NAACP. 31 August 1922. W. E. B. Du Bois Papers, Reel 10, Frames 961–76. University of Massachusetts. Amherst, Mass.

Talbert, William. Letter to Mary White Ovington. 8 November 1923. NAACP, Group II, Box L-30.

Tate, Claudia. *Domestic Allegories of Political Desire: The Black Heroine's Text at the Turn of the Century.* New York: Oxford University Press, 1992.

Taylor, Clyde R. "Black Silence and the Politics of Representation." Bowser et al., *Oscar Micheaux and His Circle*, 3–10.

Tesfagiorgis, Freida High. "Afrofemcentrism and Its Fruition in the Art of Elizabeth Catlett and Faith Ringgold." *Sage: A Scholarly Journal on Black Women* 4.1 (Spring 1987): 25–29.

——. E-mail to Julie Buckner Armstrong. 23 March 2005.

——. "In Search of a Discourse and Critiques That Center the Art of Black Women Artists." In *Theorizing Black Feminisms: The Visionary Pragmatism of Black Women*, edited by Stanlie M. James and Abena P. A. Busia, 228–66. New York: Routledge, 1993.

Thelen, David, ed. "What We See and Can't See in the Past." *Journal of American History* 83.4 (March 1997): 1217–67.

Thurer, Shari. *Myths of Motherhood: How Culture Reinvents the Good Mother.* New York: Penguin, 1995.

Thurston, Robert. "From Lynching Beneficiary to Lynching Opponent: Governor Hugh Manson Dorsey and Murder in Georgia, 1913–1921." Lynching and Racial Violence in America: Histories and Legacies. Emory University, 4 October 2002.

Tolnay, Stewart E., and E. M. Beck. *A Festival of Violence: An Analysis of Southern Lynchings, 1882–1930.* Urbana: University of Illinois Press, 1995.

Toomer, Jean. "The *Cane* Years." In *The Wayward and the Seeking: A Collection of Writings by Jean Toomer*, edited by Darwin T. Turner, 116–27. Washington, D.C.: Howard University Press, 1980.

Tyson, Timothy. *Blood Done Sign My Name.* New York: Three Rivers Press, 2004.

Vergne, Philippe. "The Black Saint Is the Sinner Lady." In *Kara Walker*, 7–27.

"The Waco Horror." In Rice, *Witnessing Lynching*, 141–50.

Waldrep, Christopher. *The Many Faces of Judge Lynch: Extralegal Violence and Punishment in America.* New York: Palgrave Macmillan, 2002.

Wallace, Michele. "Oscar Micheaux's *Within Our Gates*: The Possibilities for Alternative Visions." In Bowser et al., *Oscar Micheaux and His Circle*, 53–66.

Walker, Alice. *The Color Purple.* 1982; Repr., New York: Harvest Books, 1996.

——. "In Search of Our Mothers' Gardens." In *In Search of Our Mothers' Gardens: Womanist Prose.* New York: Harcourt, Brace, Jovanovich, 1983.

——. *The Third Life of Grange Copeland.* New York: Washington Square Press, 1970.

Walker, Kara. E-mail to Julie Buckner Armstrong. 8 October 2008.

Watkins, Patricia. "Is There a Unifying Theme in *Cane?*" *CLA Journal* 15 (1972): 303–5.

Wayne, Ron. "Photos Tell Grim Story." *Valdosta Daily Times.* 12 October 2002.

Webb, Jeff. "Literature and Lynching in Jean Toomer's *Cane.*" *ELH* 67 (2000): 205–28.

Wells, Ida B. *Southern Horrors and Other Writings: The Anti-Lynching Campaign of Ida B. Wells, 1892–1900.* Ed. Jacqueline Jones Royster. New York: Bedford Books, 1997.

Wexler, Laura. *Fire in a Canebreak.* New York: Scribner's, 2003.

Whalan, Mark, ed. *The Letters of Jean Toomer, 1919–1924.* Knoxville: University of Tennessee Press, 2006.

Wheatley, Phillis. "On Being Brought from Africa to America." In *Collected Works of Phillis Wheatly*, edited by John Shields, 18. New York: Oxford University Press, 1988.

White, Walter. Letter to Mary Talbert. 24 October 1922. NAACP Papers, Group I, Box C-207.

Whitfield, Stephen J. *A Death in the Delta: The Story of Emmett Till.* Baltimore: Johns Hopkins University Press, 1991.

Whitted, Qiana. "'In My Flesh I Shall See God': Ritual Violence and Racial Redemption in 'The Black Christ.'" *African American Review* 38 (2004): 379–94.

Wiegman, Robin. *American Anatomies: Theorizing Race and Gender.* Durham, N.C.: Duke University Press, 1995.

Williamson, Joel. "Wounds Not Scars: Lynching, the National Conscience, and the American Historian." *Journal of American History* 83.4 (1997): 1221–53.

Wilson, Woodrow. "The President's Denunciation of Lynchings and the Mob Spirit." In *The Messages and Papers of Woodrow Wilson*, 1:506–8. New York: Review of Reviews, 1924.

Woolfork, Lisa. *Embodying American Slavery in Contemporary Culture.* Urbana: University of Illinois Press, 2009.

Worthen, W. B., ed. *The Harcourt Brace Anthology of Drama.* 3rd edition. New York: Wadsworth, 1999.

Wright, Richard. "Between the World and Me." *Partisan Review.* July–August 1935, 18–19. Rpt. in Rice, *Witnessing Lynching*, 304–6.

——. *Black Boy.* 1945; Repr., New York: Harper Perennial, 2008.

Writers' League Against Lynching. Minutes of the First Meeting. 4 December 1933. NAACP, Group 1, Box C-208.

Zangrando, Robert L. *The NAACP Crusade Against Lynching, 1909–1950.* Philadelphia: Temple University Press, 1980.

INDEX

CPSIA information can be obtained at www.ICGtesting.com
Printed in the USA
LVOW091449070312

272040LV00006B/22/P